Biopharmaceutical Supply Chains

Distribution, Regulatory, Systems
and Structural Changes Ahead

ROBERT HANDFIELD, Ph.D.

CRC Press
Taylor & Francis Group
Boca Raton   London   New York

CRC Press is an imprint of the
Taylor & Francis Group, an **Informa** business

CRC Press
Taylor & Francis Group
6000 Broken Sound Parkway NW, Suite 300
Boca Raton, FL 33487-2742

Version Date: 20120418

International Standard Book Number: 978-1-4398-9970-0 (Hardback)

Library of Congress Cataloging-in-Publication Data

Handfield, Robert B.
    Biopharmaceutical supply chains : distribution, regulatory, systems and structural changes ahead / Robert Handfield.
        p. cm.
    Includes bibliographical references and index.
    ISBN 978-1-4398-9970-0 (hbk. : alk. paper)
    1. Pharmaceutical industry--Materials management. 2. Business logistics. I. Title.

HD9665.5.H358 2012
338.4'79151--dc23   2012013741

Visit the Taylor & Francis Web site at
http://www.taylorandfrancis.com

and the CRC Press Web site at
http://www.crcpress.com

Contents

Preface

No work of this sort is completed by the author, who but serves as a vehicle for bringing together diverse thoughts, points of view, and ideas into a single forum. In putting together this book, there are surely too many people to thank. Those who stand out in my mind include the people at Cardinal Health with whom I worked, among them Mike Kaufman, Frank Segrave, Steve Lawrence, Linda Wiant, Tom Donohue, and Brian Ellis. Porter Bertelson was instrumental in introducing me to the innovative West Coast pharmacists who were the early adopters and thought leaders for automated dispensing and replenishment. A number of others in the biologics and pharmaceutical industries helped me to understand the dynamics of industry relationships, including, among many others, Jim Bacon at Talecris, Vicky Sanchez at J&J, Ken Thomas at Eli Lilly, Rod Smith at Astra, Lux Bennett at Abbott Labs, Scot Buesow at Genentech, Michael Gillaine at GSK, Tara Stevens at Sanofi, and Charlie Bennett at Wyeth. Analyst interviews provided a great third-party point of view, including discussions with Eric Coldwell at Robin Baird, and John Kreger at William Blair. The pharmaceutical benefits managers also identified what is proving to be one of the major forces in the supply chain, so thanks go to Dan Cordes at ExpressScripts, Bill Barre at MedImpact, and Janet Miller at Caremark. I also developed some fascinating insights at a number of conferences, including the 2011 Tracelink Nexus conference where a lot of the discussions on GS1 and serialization took place, the IDN Summit in September 2011 in Phoenix where I learned a lot about the regulatory fireball that is headed this way, and the Fee-for-Service conferences that took place during 2005–2008 in a number of different venues.

All of the people involved here helped, but there are countless others. Thanks so much. I hope that this book helps to bring together thinking in this field that will help us manage the challenging times that lie ahead.

Rob Handfield

1

Biopharmaceutical Distribution: Early Structural Developments and the Changes Ahead

INTRODUCTION

The biopharmaceutical industry is in the throes of disruptive change. The nature of this change can be traced in some measure to the evolution of the industry and the resulting pattern of third-party distribution, global regulation, government healthcare policy, healthcare funding, as well as how the general population views the biopharmaceutical industry. This book was written in an effort to trace the history of the bizarre structures that underlie biopharmaceutical distribution in the United States, and to hopefully understand what bodes for the future of the industry.

I will also seek to provide some rationale regarding the boundaries I have drawn in putting together this book. First, the book focuses on biopharmaceutical distribution—which refers to the point at which manufacturers release a finished product to the time that it is administered (whether by the individual to themselves or by a physician) and to the complicated set of distribution channels that exists between these two points. Implicit in this boundary are the numerous decision points and third parties that play a role, including manufacturers, payers, physicians, hospitals, pharmacies, transportation companies, healthcare education providers, third-party marketing organizations, government regulators, and numerous other enterprises all seeking to influence the demand and sale of drugs. We should also note that the term *biopharmaceutical* is used in this context to encompass biologics, pharmaceuticals, and vaccines. With the merging toward a single network of therapy, we no longer differentiate between solely *biopharma* or *pharma* interests. In the standard vernacular, biopharma pertains to larger molecules only (i.e., biological), which includes vaccines and biologicals (e.g., blood products), and pharma focuses on pills (e.g., solid single-dose tablet formulations). Brand-name companies are seeking to adapt to expiring patents by producing generic medicines including follow-on biologic drugs or "large-molecule" pharmaceuticals made from living matter. More companies are using solutions that span both small- and large-molecule solutions. Many companies with a large-molecule historical focus (e.g., GSK, Pfizer, AstraZeneca, Merck, Roche) are being drawn more into the small molecule space, which has been dominated by start-up firms that grew quickly (e.g., Genzymes, BiogenIdec, Genentech). By including all of these elements into a single distribution model, this not only simplifies the dialogue but also reflects the merging of biological and pharmaceutical distribution that will emerge in the new era of healthcare reform and pay-for-performance. Payers are often seeking pay-for-performance, which means that metrics showing how effective the drugs are must be demonstrated before insurance providers will agree to fund the tens of thousands of dollars often required for a single individual to take the treatment over a year.

Second, the book focuses on the U.S. biopharmaceutical distribution network. Why? Quite simply, the United States is the largest market for pharmaceuticals in the world. The brand-name pharmaceutical industry generated approximately $165B in sales in 2011, but growth is estimated only at 1% despite an aging population to $185B in 2016. The biotechnology sector is also growing and comprises about 20% of the pharmaceuticals market but is growing. Both of these components represent about one-third of the world's global market, which exceeds $800B.[*] IMS Health reports that the size of the global market for pharmaceuticals is expected to grow nearly $300 billion over the next five years, reaching $1.1 trillion in 2014. The 5–8% compound annual growth rate during this period reflects the impact of leading products losing patent protection in developed markets as well as strong overall growth in the world's emerging countries.[†]

Third, the nature of biopharmaceutical distribution is becoming exponentially more complex. Part of this challenge is due to the rise in

---

[*] IbisWorld, 32541a, Brand Name Pharmaceutical Manufacturing in the US, 2011.
[†] http://www.imshealth.com/portal/site/imshealth/menuitem.a46c6d4df3db4b3d88f611019418c22a/?vgnextoid=4b8c410b6c718210VgnVCM100000ed152ca2RCRD&vgnextchannel=b5e57900b55a5110VgnVCM10000071812ca2RCRD&vgnextfmt=default

demand for generics, which are sold at a lower cost than brand-name drugs. Large pharmaceutical companies such as Pfizer, GSK, and Merck are acquiring licensing or developing biological-based biopharma products into their research and development (R&D) pipelines. These biologics are expected to make up almost half of the market by 2016. They are also appealing as they do not have the same intense generic pressures. The U.S. Food and Drug Administration (FDA) has also approved a 12-year patent on generic biologics, which clears the way for manufacturers to focus on generic biologics that will play an important role in the future.[*] Although biologics are appealing, the distribution channels associated with them are much more difficult to manage, and many require temperature controlled environments. Traditional channels such as hospitals and pharmacies may change, as we see self-infusion or other channels begin to develop.

Understanding U.S. distribution is fundamental to building capabilities in emerging countries as biopharma companies seek to grow their revenue. Although much of the growth in biopharmaceutical revenues will occur in emerging countries, there is generally a very poor understanding of the different factors that can impact distribution and sales in these countries. By understanding the complexities of the U.S. market, biopharmaceutical companies can begin to establish a framework for strategic planning, relationship development, channel and contract management, and third-party partnership that will be needed to be successful in global emerging markets.

In a sense, the U.S. market is becoming more like the remainder of the world, in that it is an easy target for cost containment. Drugs comprise only about 10% of national healthcare costs, but many former blockbusters are going generic. In the immediate to near future, the U.S. pharmaceutical and medicine manufacturing industry is expected to undergo a gradual transformation process due to slowing revenue growth, declining R&D productivity, increasing competitive pressures, and rising safety concerns. The pressure for change will escalate as the major players face the consequences of patent expirations of some of the most profitable drugs in history, with a number of key drugs due to lose patent protection in the next two years. Approximately $65B in sales will go off patent by 2014. The time for change is now. But to understand the future, we need to begin by understanding the past.

---

[*] Ibid.

STRUCTURAL EVOLUTION OF
BIOPHARMACEUTICAL DISTRIBUTION

The pharmaceutical industry, as we know it today, emerged in the 1920s and 1930s,[*] although the principles of using chemical and biological compounds to treat human suffering have been around since ancient times. Heavy R&D investments along with major scientific breakthroughs throughout the twentieth century have led to a formidable array of drug compounds to treat a significant range of human ailments. The industry operates under strict regulation by the FDA.

The FDA appeared as part of the 1906 Pure Food and Drug Act. Otherwise known as the Wiley Act, it was named for Harvey Wiley, a chemist, physician, and professor at Purdue University who lobbied strongly for its passage. The bill appeared in large part due to lack of sanitary and safety controls in the food and drug industry. In the early years, many pharmacists created their own mixtures in the neighborhood pharmacy. Since then, ever-increasing regulations have appeared in response to industry disasters such as elixir sulfanilamide deaths and thalidomide birth defects. Today, the FDA must approve all drugs for commercial sale on the basis that a drug is clinically proven safe and effective for specific medical conditions. The FDA also provides regulation on commercial activities such as labeling, promotion, sampling, and safety monitoring.

A globalizing firm has to manage a number of regulatory bodies around the world, not just those of the home country. Firms may find themselves interacting with up to 50 or 60 agencies worldwide. The FDA is the toughest drug-regulating agency in the world. This poses some difficulties and opportunities for American firms. If a drug passes the FDA approval process, the firm that produces it can probably expect approval anywhere in the world. The FDA won't accept another country's approval and is continually the most scrutinizing in the world. Pharmaceutical manufacturers must have their drug approved by the sovereign regulatory body of any country they wish to sell in—which can sometimes affect globalizing firms' decisions. For instance, some companies will not come into the United States because the standards are too strict. However, that doesn't mean they can't earn a profit in another less stringent country. Since 1996,

---

[*] Standard & Poor's Industry Survey for Pharmaceuticals, June 26, 2003.

the FDA has approved fewer and fewer products. It is getting more and more difficult to develop a product with a high market value. Put another way, the simpler diseases have been conquered.

The Move Away from Distribution

Beginning in the early 1980s, two important events occurred that dramatically changed biopharmaceutical distribution. First, hospitals began pushing inventory management back to the wholesalers in an effort to reduce investments in inventory and receivables.* Second, pharmaceutical manufacturers started to do the same thing. In the 1990s pharmaceutical manufacturers made a decision to focus on their core competencies—R&D and marketing—and outsourced logistics activities to wholesalers. As a result, hospitals, pharmacies, and manufacturers did not want to be in the drug distribution business, yet no one was willing to pay for these services. Wholesaler compensation moved toward a system that was entirely reliant on inventory appreciation—forward buying in expectation that manufacturers would raise prices that could be passed on to customers.

Manufacturers selected wholesalers based on which wholesaler was willing to buy the greatest share of that year's production, not on which offered the greatest value in terms of cost and service. In anticipation of price increases, wholesalers would increase their inventory holdings of pharmaceutical products and reap the rewards when price increases were announced by manufacturers. At the same time, hospital pharmacies sharply increased their purchases from wholesalers, often dealing with only one wholesaler under a "prime vendor contract."† In time, three major companies emerged as the primary market leaders for pharmaceutical distribution in the United States: Cardinal Health, McKesson, and AmerisourceBergen. These organizations developed lean systems of distribution that allowed them to deliver drugs in a safe and efficient manner but that also created further complications in tracking product and pricing in the channel.

Traditionally, patients—the final consumer—received biopharma products from two sources: hospitals or retail pharmacies. These outlets functioned similarly, carrying a fairly large amount of inventory that was then

---

* "Understanding evolutionary processes in non-manufacturing industries: Empirical insights from shakeout in pharmaceutical wholesaling," *Journal of Evolutionary Economics*, 1998, p. 263.
† Ibid.

dispensed upon a demand trigger: a prescription or script. Even as retailers, hospitals, and manufacturers reduced safety stocks, the previously mentioned forward buying as well as secondary channels ensured that there was an abundance of product in the biopharmaceutical supply chain (BPS). The channel also remained intact due to the relationships among pharma sales representatives, doctors, and retailers. Pharmaceutical representatives provided education on the latest drugs and provided samples. Doctors tended to prescribe these drugs based on pharmaceutical education and experience—their own and their peers. The prescriptions could then be filled only at a licensed pharmacy, often chosen based on geography or the doctor's recommendation.

Recent changes have greatly impacted the channel. One of the biggest changes was a push on taking inventory out of the channel due to the Sarbanes–Oxley Act of 2002.* Companies now need to recognize inventory holdings in their U.S. Securities and Exchange Commission (SEC) reporting and are struggling to do so as inventory visibility is low. For example, a large pharmaceutical company placed a huge order with a wholesaler to flow through the holiday season and then cut 80% of it when it realized it had to be reported, thereby shifting the burden of inventory ownership to the wholesaler during this period.

This came to a head in 2002–2003 when Bristol-Myers Squibb was prosecuted on the grounds of falsely overstating profits. Chris Christie, the United States attorney for New Jersey (and currently governor of NJ), was instrumental in leading this charge. The biggest challenge here was for companies to move away from a technique called *channel stuffing* to a state of true disclosure of inventory holdings and sales. Thus, the practice of *forward selling* (i.e., the practice of selling wholesalers up to a year's worth of inventory and then counting these sales in the current quarter) distorted earnings and sales growth figures was challenged by the SEC. This led to a completely new fee for service distribution model led by the wholesaler, Cardinal Health.

Pharmaceutical distribution is now highly complex and fragmented. Prescriptions are filled at more than 140,000 outlets in the United States, but only 6% of sales are sold direct by manufacturers. And although consolidation has lowered the number of firms, the BPS continues to increase in complexity. Ongoing macroeconomic and regulatory events are constantly changing the shape of the competitive and operational

---

* http://www.soxlaw.com

environment in which supply chain managers make their strategic and tactical decisions. For example, within the United States, recent changes in Medicare and Medicaid reimbursement have changed compensation for many supply chain participants. These regulators are demanding that wholesalers and manufacturers increase transparency and reveal costs for purchase and prices sold to customers. A number of market channels have emerged, including mail order, direct shipping, and website pharmacies. These channels threaten to disintermediate traditional market channels.

These changes have left the BPS in a state of flux. Unfortunately, decision models that have been useful to guide managers in other industries are not easily applied to BPS problems. This is primarily due to the number of consumption points, role and number of intermediaries, and the long lead times and highly unpredictable nature of biopharmaceutical markets.

THE BIOPHARMACEUTICAL SUPPLY CHAIN (BPS)

Because of the FDA's regulations, the prescription drug market has developed a unique market supply chain in the United States (Figure 1.1). In this model, the physician plays an undeniably important role in the success or failure of the commercial operation of the prescription drug. In many ways, the physician is the primary customer when it comes to sales and marketing. Although emerging technologies and practices such as TV, website, and print ads are increasing the direct-to-consumer (DTC) model (Figure 1.1), the physician remains the primary target for most sales and marketing campaigns. It is useful to review the key players in the channel that participate in bringing biopharmaceutical products to the marketplace. A high-level picture of this channel is shown in Figure 1.2. In the remainder of the chapter, each of these channel entities is discussed in more detail.

Branded and Generic Manufacturers

The BPS begins with drug manufacturers. Generics are causing the biggest ripple in distribution of drugs throughout the BPS. Overall, margins for generics are greater than branded drugs. Currently, generic manufacturers are trying to circumvent the Big Three wholesalers (McKesson, Cardinal, and AmerisourceBergen), even though wholesalers are more

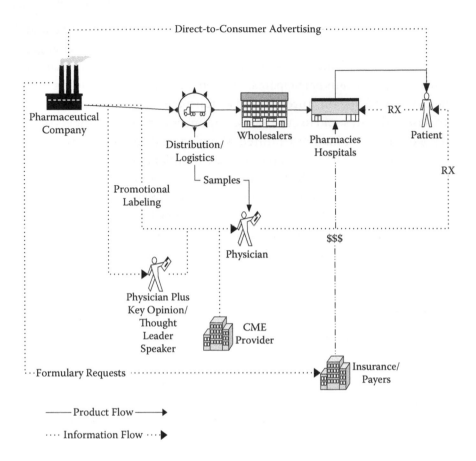

FIGURE 1.1
The role of physicians in the channel.

efficient at distributing pills regardless of price. The stable revenue profit structure of manufacturing and distributing generics is inviting competition. Manufacturers, retailers, or pharmacy benefits managers (PBMs) at one time could retake control over BPS distribution channels from the Big Three, especially after the introduction of fee-for-service (FFS). This would likely increase the growing percentage of drugs being shipped directly to consumers. As we will see, however, this did not materialize.

Large manufacturers include generic and branded manufacturers. In the case of branded product, once a product has been approved, branded manufacturers generally purchase bulk chemicals or biological products and manufacture the product, which is then formed or filled into a package and distributed to centralized sales distribution offices or warehouses. For generics, the process is the same, although the design of the channel may

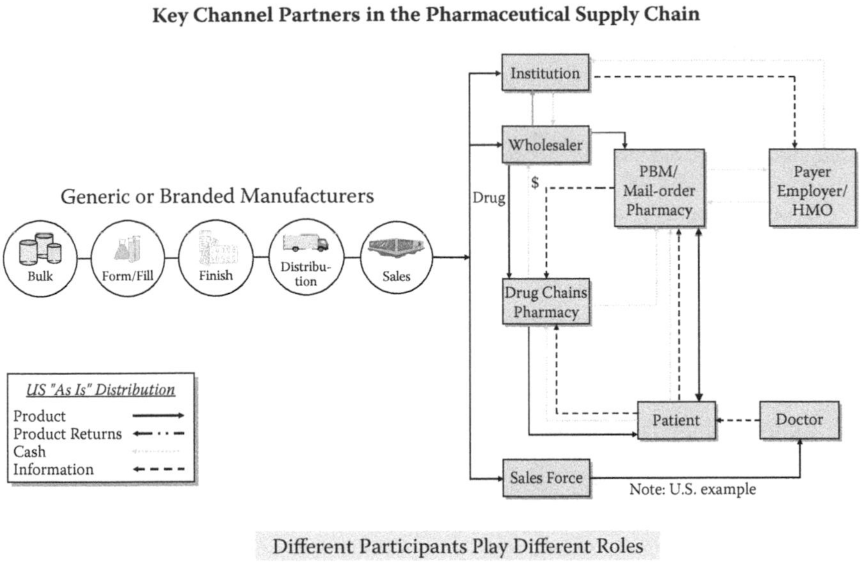

Key Channel Partners in the Pharmaceutical Supply Chain

FIGURE 1.2
Key channel partners in pharma supply chain.

be substantially different. For example, an increasing number of generics manufacturers are locating and forming partnerships with Indian and Chinese manufacturers. Because generics are off patent, pricing is substantially lower, as are margins. As one generics manufacturer commented:

> Walgreens has done reverse auctions on generic products—how much more commoditized can you get? They will tell us that "Your service is great but you have to be the lowest price." Walgreens set the trend and now many more pharmacies are using reverse auctions. The threat to generics is coming from overseas. India has more DMFs [Drug Master Files] than any other country. They are beating the United States in manufacturing, but China is not far behind. There will be a lot of low-cost generic products on the market. These countries pay low wages, have workers with a great education, their environmental controls are not the same—and there are a lot fewer restrictions.

Further, the share of generic drugs is likely to increase sharply in the next two to three years. Since wholesalers are more likely to carry branded products, it is likely that there will be a reduction in revenue for wholesale distribution. This is driven largely by the PBMs, who will purchase directly from generics manufacturers rather than wholesalers. One PBM executive interviewed noted:

From the data I have seen and IMS data—a lot of branded product will come off patent, and the trend will continue. We are also seeing a new type of single source generic coming into the market—with some exclusivity for some period of time. That hurts us—we have guaranteed generics discounts we make to our customers that are based on the assumption of lower cost. If a single source generic comes to market, however, it is difficult to get to a discount generic market price. For example, GSK could single source and not allow others to manufacture the generic. In terms of the average wholesaler price, we would get only 25% off instead of 80%—but would still have to reimburse our market at 80% discounted price.

The top branded pharmaceutical manufacturers are shown in Figure 1.3. The major sales channels for manufacturers are shown in Figure 1.4

Corporation	Total Dollars (billions)	Market Share
1. Pfizer	$26.6	16.2%
2. Merck and Co	$24.0	14.6%
3. Johnson & Johnson	$19.2	11.7%
4. GlaxoSmithKlein PLC	$18.0	11.0%
5. AstraZeneca	$13.75	8.48%

Source: IBISWorld, 2011.

FIGURE 1.3
Top five branded pharma manufacturers.

Approximate percent of Rx product sales through various channels, as reported by manufacturers:	Average (%)
All distributors	91.0%
Healthcare distributors	84.9
Specialty distributors	6.1
Chain drug warehouses (not shipped through distributors)	3.7
Direct to hospitals	0.2
Direct to clinics/doctors	0.2
Specialty pharmacies	1.8
Direct to patients	0.0
Mail-order	2.5
Other	0.8

Source: Center for Healthcare Supply Chain Research.

FIGURE 1.4
Manufacturer sales by customer and channel.

Wholesalers

Wholesalers are a critical component of pharmaceutical distribution. In short, wholesalers are responsible for all activities required to take ownership of drugs or biologics from the point of sales/transfer from the manufacturer and delivery to the end customer. As shown in Figure 1.2, that customer may be a hospital, a pharmacy, or, in some cases, the patient. Although many manufacturers or laypeople believe wholesaling is a non-value-added function involving point to point transportation, it is in fact much more than that.

Perhaps the most radical shift we have seen in the last five years is the movement toward FFS wholesaler agreements. In 2002–2003, litigation by the State of New Jersey against Bristol-Myers Squibb drove federal regulators to push for increasing transparency of inventory positions between manufacturers and wholesalers. This push resulted in the transformation supply chain contracts from a "cost-minus" pricing model (wherein wholesalers would purchase advance positions on products that were going to go up in price from manufacturers) to a position where they now asked that wholesalers pay a fair price for the cost of distribution to retailers, hospitals, and other third parties. In effect, manufacturers would now be required to pay a "fee" for wholesalers' services—something that is common in many distribution networks but that constituted a completely novel approach for the pharmaceutical industry.

The initial response to FFS was a combination of outrage, pushback, cynicism, and eventually compliance. Manufacturers felt that the benefits of FFS were accruing largely to distributors, as inventory previously held by wholesalers was reduced and effectively pushed back onto manufacturers. The first round of FFS agreements was signed in 2005, with a second round in 2006. Yet in 2011 we are seeing a renewed shift in inventory, as the impact of pandemics, supply chain disruptions, and unpredictability in demand are forcing wholesalers and manufacturers to rethink their inventory strategies. We are also beginning to witness a *reduction* in inventory in manufacturers and *improvements* in end-customer distribution and on-time performance and cost. In fact, research for this book begins to support the hypothesis that FFS agreements may in fact be *driving the pharmaceutical supply chain to become more efficient*, through lowering of distribution costs, inventory savings, Six Sigma continuous improvement, leveraging of information technology, better forecasting, and improved customer service.

Some of the many types of services that are performed by wholesalers on behalf of their manufacturing customers include the following:

- Forecasting demand
- Inventory management systems
- Ordering systems
- Purchase order systems (POS) that bill only for shipped items
- Carrying 20 or more days of inventory for pharmacies at no cost for high moving drugs
- Delivery 5X per day, 24/7, 365 days a year
- Warehouse and transportation structure enabling shipments to multiple locations
- Business continuity requirements (multiple warehouses distributed nationally to decrease probability of delivery disruptions or inventory loss)
- Credit, billing, collections—particularly collecting receivables and taking on credit risk
- Returns and recalls
- Providing pedigree

Under the buy–sell (traditional) model, wholesalers bought pharmaceutical products from manufacturers and resold the products to retailers that included pharmacies, healthcare providers, and PBMs. Profits were earned in the margin between acquisition and resale price. Years of intense competition among pharmaceutical wholesalers, low inflation, price competition from Canadian outlets, the challenge of generics to branded products, and governmental pressure on pharmaceutical firms to restrain price increases have all contributed to sharply lower wholesaler margins in the twenty-first century. Increasingly, industry observers refer to the traditional "buy-and-hold" model as being broken or at least incapable of generating profit levels adequate to wholesalers.

Mergers of distributors have whittled down the number of major wholesale firms to three, and these three currently distribute roughly 90% of wholesale pharmaceutical products. But this dominance is tenuous and could easily be disrupted by significant legal or technological changes.

In Chapter 2, we will cover in more detail the FFS model that has emerged and that relies on contracts with manufacturers that unbundle wholesaler services and charge individually for those services. In addition to inventory management, FFS distribution contracts with manufacturers provide for transparent, customized service.

Drug Chain Pharmacies

The retail pharmacy market has greatly consolidated such that the top five pharmacy chains now control approximately 85% of the retail space and therefore approximately 20% of all drugs sold. Choices and prices have been reduced by PBMs to contain costs for their clients and to ensure their own profitability. In addition, the increased proficiency of third-party logistics (3PL) providers and greater acceptance of Internet-based sales have added another method for pharma products to reach patients.

Drug chain pharmacies consist of both large retail chains such as CVS, RiteAid, and Walgreens as well as small independent pharmacies. Increasingly, the proportion of small pharmacies is shrinking as more and more are being purchased by the larger chains. The top pharmaceutical chains are shown in Figure 1.5. The top pharmaceutical retailers by revenue are shown in Table 1.1.

As shown in Figure 1.5, pharmacies have been under increasing pressure from a variety of sources, including mail service, food stores (that have integrated pharmacies), and nursing homes. As such, the pressure to drive margins has increased such that many chain pharmacies make very little money on filling branded scripts but rely on customers to purchase other products at the "front of the store" while filling their prescriptions. Consolidation has occurred at a rapid pace. In 1998, the top 10 companies were 25% of the market, and today they are more than 50% of the market.

Pharmacies also carry very little inventory. Thus, many saw manufacturers attempt to bypass wholesalers as a direct threat to their business model. Most pharmacies rely on the Big Three to replenish stores based on orders every day from every manufacturer. A full tractor trailer pulls up every morning at a pharmacy at 4 a.m. with goods presorted for put-away zones. The efficiency of the wholesalers is huge, allowing pharmacies to operate at 26–27 inventory turns per year. As many go to generics, inventory turns are not as important, but these now represent almost 60% of all prescriptions, so availability is critical. There is some collaboration with wholesalers and manufacturers to ensure availability of product. When manufacturers were forced to go to FFS, most pharmacies sided with wholesalers, stating that they were vehemently opposed to direct shipping

	2008			2007			Change in Number of Outlets (%)	Sales Growth (%)
	Outlets (#)	Dollars ($mil)	Market Share (%)	Outlets (#)	Dollars ($mil)	Market Share (%)		
Chain and mass merchandiser with pharmacy	30,996	$101,178	34.9%	29,598	$98,062	34.1%	4.7%	3.2%
Independent pharmacy	17,565	38,086	13.1	17,863	38,744	13.5	-1.7	-1.7
Food stores with pharmacy	9,866	20,917	7.2	9,865	21,975	7.6	0.0	-4.8
Mail service[a]	256	45,972	15.8	258	45,087	15.7	-0.8	2.0
Hospitals	10,635	31,956	11.0	10,502	31,422	10.9	1.3	1.7
Clinics	82,163	33,791	11.6	78,616	33,424	11.6	4.5	1.1
Nursing homes/home health	5,028	16,671	5.7	4,929	16,251	5.6	2.0	2.6
Healthcare plans	1,267	1,305	0.4	1,288	1,514	0.5	-1.6	-13.8
Miscellaneous	8,169	998	0.3	7,964	1,013	0.4	2.6	-1.5
Total	165,945	291,477	100.0	160,883	287,598	100.0	3.1	1.3

Source: IMS National Sales Perspectives.

Note: Includes prescription and pharmacy-dispensed diagnostic products; hospital data are the number of departments; mass merchandiser estimate is from the NACDS Economic Department.

a Mail is not projected.

FIGURE 1.5
Manufacturer sales by customer categories 2007–2008.

TABLE 1.1

Top Chain Retail Pharmacy Companies, by Pharmacy Sales, 2010

Rank	Company	Pharmacy Sales (in millions)	Total Sales (in millions)
1	Walgreen Co.	43,823	67,420
2	CVS Caremark Corporation	38,994	57,345
3	Rite Aid Corporation	17,086	25,200
4	Wal-Mart Stores, Inc.[a]	15,616	260,261
5	The Kroger Co.	7,886	78,080
6	Safeway, Inc.	3,695	41,050
7	The Stop & Shop Supermarket Corporation	3,465	68,881
8	Target Corporation	3,033	67,390
9	Sears Holdings Corporation	2,495	15,593
10	SUPERVALU INC.	2,313	28,911
11	Sam's Club	1,781	49,459
12	Publix Super Markets, Inc.	1,558	25,135
13	Costco Wholesale dba Costco Pharmacies	1,449	76,255
14	Medicine Shoppe International	1,436	1,595
15	H.E. Butt Grocery Co.	1,223	15,100
16	Giant Eagle, Inc.	980	8,600
17	Albertson's LLC	888	3,700
18	Meijer, Inc.	659	14,653
19	Wegmans Food Markets, Inc.	624	4,953
20	Fred's, Inc.	589	1,842
21	Fred Meyer	584	8,715
22	Kinney Drugs	557	743
23	Winn-Dixie	507	7,248
24	Shopko Stores Operating Co., LLC	506	2,300
25	Hy-Vee	476	6,484

Source: CSGIS Directory of Drug Store and HBC Chains, http://www.chainstoreguide.com/ accessed June 15, 2011.

Note: Results reflect end of fiscal year 2010.

[a] U.S. stores division only reflects discount stores, supercenters, and neighborhood markets.

from manufacturers, which had no core competencies in this area. Direct distribution posed a number of risks, including increased cost of goods pricing, more transaction processing costs (think of the number of purchase orders from all the different pharmaceutical manufacturers instead of a consolidated purchase order from a single wholesaler), reduced service levels, delays on operational and technology programs, and less visibility and tracking of shipments.

One of the major problems facing independent pharmacies are Medicare plans that are slow to make payments and that reimburse pharmacists at less than the cost of some prescriptions they fill for seniors. The larger chains can tolerate slimmer margins and hope to make up the difference with a volume increase due to Medicare Part B and are also able to offset margin pressure with sale of other items. But independent pharmacists are likely to become a dying breed in this environment.

Hospitals and Group Purchasing Organizations

Hospitals are usually independent entities that serve local communities and may or may not be affiliated with other hospitals. Increasingly, hospitals are forming partnerships to take advantage of purchasing power, to streamline their billing and services, and to enable reduced costs. Hospital buying behavior has changed significantly. Beginning in the early 1980s, hospitals began pushing inventory management back to the wholesalers in an effort to reduce investments in inventory and receivables. By the early 1990s, hospital pharmacies had sharply increased their purchases from wholesalers at the expense of manufacturer direct sales, often dealing with only one wholesaler under a "prime vendor contract."*

Hospitals face many challenges. Many are faced with patients who cannot pay. In fact, up to 10% of their patients who are treated cannot afford to pay for services renders. While U.S. healthcare costs escalate, the ability of the Obama administration's healthcare law to drive profitable growth is uncertain at best. And then there is the oncoming trend around personalized medicine. The overarching concept of personalized medicine is that information about a patient's protein, gene, or metabolite profile can be used to tailor medical care to that individual's needs. A key attribute of personalized medicine is the development of so-called companion diagnostics, whereby specific molecular assays that measure levels of proteins or genes or specific mutations are used to stratify disease status, select from among different medications and tailor dosages, provide a specific therapy for an individual's condition, or initiate a preventative measure that is particularly suited to that patient at the time of administration.

---

* "Understanding evolutionary processes in non-manufacturing industries: Empirical insights from the shakeout in pharmaceutical wholesaling," *Journal of Evolutionary Economics*, 1998, pp. 262–265.

However, the key to this will be the need for electronic patient records. Hospitals are notorious for serving a disproportionate amount of uninsured patients and also lag considerably in electronic records. One of the areas that will be particularly impacted is oncology, where there are companion diagnostic tests linked to specific diagnostics for diseases such as breast cancer and chronic myelogenous leukemia. In such areas, tissue-derived molecular information will be combined with an individual's personal medical history, family history, and imaging and laboratory tests to derive a personalized therapy. To enable this capability, hospitals will need to be able to collect and assess information about each individual patient—family history, social circumstances, environment, and behaviors to select his or her preventive and therapeutic care.

This is a vision of the future that remains difficult to imagine, given the low levels of supply chain capabilities that exist in most hospital systems today. Consider that in the United States less than 40% of office-based physicians reported using full or partial electronic medical records and only 20% reported using a system described as minimally functional including the following features: orders for prescriptions, tests, lab results, and clinical notes.*

Group purchasing organizations (GPOs) represent one partner to hospitals that emerged many years ago. These entities combine the purchase power of multiple hospitals to negotiated reduced pricing from manufacturers of pharmaceutical and biological products. Most hospitals rely on large group purchasing organizations, which act as middlemen between manufacturers and hospitals. However, some hospitals are bypassing GPOs and working directly with wholesalers, which provide sophisticated replenishment systems to minimize pharmacy inventories in hospitals. (This is discussed in Chapter 6.) For the most part, GPOs are not highly sophisticated organizations but are simply tasked with leveraging volumes from wholesalers and passing on the discounted rate, plus their markup profit to the hospitals.

Understandably, GPOs are actively involved in pushing for lower costs from manufacturers and wholesalers. GPOs are increasingly pushing for increased access to wholesaler data. They are positioning themselves to

---

* "National Center for Health Statistics: Preliminary Estimates of Electronic Medical Record Use by Office-Based Physicians: United States, 2008," http://www.cdc.gov/nchs/data/hestat/emr_ehr/emr_ehr.htm Retrieved December 2009.

be the data-mart for hospitals in the future. Contract negotiations are increasingly pushing for competitive pricing and release of sales data and including stipulations regarding release of sales data on a real-time basis to allow GPOs to negotiate even more competitive pricing.

Another issue on the horizon for GPOs is safe harbor. I attended a recent conference in Washington, DC, discussing the safe harbor issues whereby Medicare legislation states that no party can make a profit as a third party in distributing drugs to patients. In general, GPOs do not perceive any type of threat from current discussions around safe harbor restrictions in Washington, DC. They also recognize that they need to address new forms of value-added services in the channel or risk being eliminated.

Health Maintenance Organizations and Pharmacy Benefits Managers

Health maintenance organizations (HMOs) are basically insurers that work with institutions to administer health plans. HMOs will typically work with pharmacy benefits management organizations to administer and manage costs associated with pharmaceutical and biological products.

The Obama healthcare bill could further complicate the role of payers. The bill would help create winners and losers. For integrated, "fixed-fee" healthcare providers, like Kaiser Permanente and Geisinger Health System, which insure only 5% of the U.S. population today, market share could grow to be as much as 20% of the population by 2014.

The rise of personalized medicine will also render this process even more complex. Pay-for-performance is a trend that has achieved traction in Europe and which is entering into the debate in Washington. The higher costs of biologics with the promise of better results and a general lack of outcomes data seem likely to stir the pay-for-performance debate. Biologics make up only 1% of claims but represent 15% of prescription costs. Some biologic treatments are expected to cost hundreds of thousands of dollars over the life of a patient. Clearly, if payers wish to provide affordable healthcare, the cost of biologics needs to be addressed. To date, generic biologics lowered cost in Europe only 25–30% due to regulatory pressure, if they became available at all.

Some of the relevant facts concerning pay-for-performance include the following:

- Agencies in the United Kingdom, the European Union, Australia, and the United States already exist to analyze cost–benefit of drugs; there are no standards yet, but the United Kingdom demands pay-for-performance.
- A health data network is in place in Denmark and is expected to be in 2013 for the United Kingdom and in 2014 for the United States; by 2020 there will be data for assessing the performance of many drugs.
- As part of the stimulus bill, $1.1 billion was directed at comparing drugs, medical devices, surgery, and other ways of treating specific conditions—all for "fact-based" cost savings. As a newer therapeutic class, biologics are more susceptible to the "outcomes" debate than traditional pharmaceuticals.

The problem in pay-for-performance, of course, is that there are no definitive standards. Some possible metrics may be physiological in nature (e.g., using metabolics or biomarkers and using normal or nano-systems). These must also be linked to disease endpoints, involving improved imaging for tumor progression and bone loss, and associated with cardiovascular fitness outcomes. The premise behind this trend is that the focus is on delivering healthcare outcomes, not disease treatments. This is certainly beneficial for patients but will require major changes in the present model, with payers less likely to need healthcare subsidies. The impact on manufacturers and wholesalers is less clear.

Part of the value proposition here is that return on investment (ROI) is contingent on low insured turnover, customized products and services (e.g., wellness programs), and education to help patients understand why treatment is not needed based on test results. The ROI analysis does not include payer values of supporting safer treatments and will most surely require new actuarial models to account for risk classes. There are also massive impacts in terms of how to drive drug development that is targeted on specific segments of the disease cycle, genotypic population, and even geo-specific populations. Drugs will be increasingly linked to a companion biomarker or diagnostic, which should ensure that drugs yield a therapeutic effect in the majority of patients with fewer side effects. Some of the questions that arise in this model include the following:

- At what level do large employers or coalitions of small to mid-size employers get involved in tracking the use and expense of drugs and biologics under the medical benefits and under the pharmacy benefits?

- To what extent have expensive drugs and biologics for cancer care hit the radar screen of employers, large and small?
- In Request for Proposals (RFPs) for insurers as vendors of health insurance benefits for employees, to what extent do employers outline their requirements for the benefit design, for the availability of case management, in disease management, specialty pharmacy, pre-certification, and so forth?
- How do large employers track the performance of payers/insurers with specificity of approvals or denials for treatments prescribed by experts for cancer; are employees as patients receiving the benefits that they deserve?
- How specific do employers get in terms of discussing coverage policies regarding drugs and biologics with insurance companies?
- What is the large employer preference for management of its drug benefits plans—insurers or PBMs—and why?

In short, these changes will radically reshape the nature of the whole industry. Today, the FDA relies heavily on the opinion of key physicians located at major research centers such as Duke, John Hopkins, and the University of California–Los Angeles (UCLA) to determine whether a drug is put "on formulary" for approval by Medicare and insurance providers. As such, there are always a lot of politics involved.

A key player in the evolving healthcare model is the PBM, who will generally work with a specific institution in administering its drug prescription program. Some large corporate institutions (e.g., General Motors) have established their own plans to administer drugs to employees as opposed to working through a PBM. PBMs are key players in the distribution of prescription drugs. Their decision to place a drug on a company's formulary has a major impact on sales of that drug.

A major hurdle that pharmaceutical industry managers must face in the channel is the approval process administered by PBMs. The PBM has a template that is used to identify where a manufactured drug fits into the standard formularies. This formulary includes generics (tier 1), preferred or lower-cost brands (tier 2), and nonapproved or less approved drugs (tier 3). It would be unlikely for a PBM to deny coverage for a requested drug, but sales of certain drugs can be significantly influenced based on the reimbursement model inherent in the approval process. Increasingly, PBMs are moving toward step therapies—requiring a person to try one drug before going on to another, more expensive one. (For example, the patient might be advised to try using ibuprofen before celecoxib.)

The process of setting a standard formulary also involves working with institutional health plans and employer groups—which may also influence how to set co-payments. Co-payments may be established based on dollars or percentages. For example, a tier-1 drug may require a $10 co-payment, $20 for preferred, or $50 for nonpreferred. In every situation, there is a high incentive for consumers to purchase a generic product if available or work with the prescriber (physician) to first apply another therapy.

When introducing a new product, pharmaceutical manufacturers must consider the PBM when setting price, rebates to wholesalers and pharmacies, physician education, and other elements.

BRINGING THE SUPPLY CHAIN TOGETHER

All of these parties—manufacturers, wholesalers, PBMs, hospitals, pharmacies, and other third parties—must somehow come together in the face of increasing challenges and difficulties in the marketplace. New healthcare legislation, electronic medical records, the rise of personalized medicine, pay-for-performance, and increasing traceability in the supply chain are only some of the major challenges on the horizon. In an effort to try to bring these elements together, we explore the pharmaceutical distribution landscape in greater detail in the chapters that follow.

In Chapter 2, we examine some of the broad forces that are impacting the industry, including compensation, channel forces, product specific forces, and other emerging elements.

In Chapter 3, we cover the key regulatory forces shaping the nature of the industry and speculate about the future trend that healthcare and FDA legislation will take in the future.

In Chapter 4, the specific case of hospital delivery and "the race to the bedside" to control the channel all the way to the patient in the hospital is discussed. The impact of new distribution technology on hospital efficiency and care is projected based on technology trends.

In Chapter 5, the special case of oncology drugs and their distribution is examined in more detail. Some of the specific challenges with this industry are explored in greater detail.

Finally, in Chapter 6 I cover some of the major challenges and opportunities that lie in the future and postulate what are some important actions for the industry as a whole to take.

These chapters involved many, many interviews with executives in biopharmaceutical manufacturing, wholesaling, insurance, hospital administrators and physicians, and other related industries. They reflect the key facts that lie in front of us. How these will fall out remains to be seen.

2

Key Forces and Myths of Distribution in the BPS Supply Chain

KEY FORCES OVERVIEW

To better understand the changes occurring in the biopharmaceutical supply chain (BPS), I have spent the last eight years working alongside a number of key industry participants. I have spent a good amount of time working with one of the largest pharmaceutical wholesalers in the United States. During this time I interviewed hundreds of executives working for hospitals, biopharmaceutical manufacturing companies (including both clinical and commercial managers), group purchasing organizations (GPOs), and insurance companies. In addition, data were analyzed from an extensive literature review (over 750 practitioner press articles), and detailed interviews with industry thought leaders took place over this time.

The goal of this activity was to identify major forces and the underlying trends that would impact the BPS in the future. Based on this work, it has become clear that in the space from manufacturing to patients, three mega forces have emerged that will shape the distribution and delivery of biopharmaceutical products in the United States. What is happening in the United States is a leading indicator for what will also take place globally, although the dynamics are certain to be different. The three primary forces are as follows:

1. Compensation forces: Increased use of inventory management agreements, fee-for-service (FFS) models, pay-for-performance, and pricing pressure applied by government agencies and third parties will shape the way that products are sold, delivered, and administered in the future.
2. Channel forces: The increasing threat of direct sales models by biopharmaceutical manufacturers and the threatened entrance of third-party logistics providers (3PLs) and other competing entities in the channel.
3. Product forces: Increasing levels of product diversity requiring specialized handling and delivery coupled with increasing concerns about the pedigree (i.e., legitimacy) of goods being distributed in the BPS. The rise of personalized medicine will also impact how drugs are shipped to individuals.

These forces are discussed throughout htis book, but they are explored first in this chapter.

MYTHS OF BIOPHARMACEUTICAL DISTRIBUTION

As my research continued, I increasingly became more aware of the disparity between perception on the part of manufacturers and the reality of the distribution network. Part of the problem that exists with this perspective is the relatively low knowledge of the forces at work in the biopharmaceutical supply chain network. In a sense, FFS is a natural maturation of the biopharma supply chain from its origins as the "Wild West" of gambling on price increases, to a more formal and structured set of distribution agreements governed by performance metrics, cost transparency, safety, and regulatory requirements. This maturation is a natural growth and outcome of the increasing challenges being put forward in the new environment. In an effort to dispel some of the old myths of biopharmaceutical distribution, the myths associated with each of the three forces are discussed, and some counterbalance is provided based on facts collected while developing this book.

Compensation Forces

As noted in Chapter 1, wholesaler compensation for distribution has changed dramatically in the past eight years. In years past, wholesaler compensation relied on a system that was entirely reliant on inventory appreciation. This was known as "forward buying" and involved having wholesalers purchase product in advance of announced price increases to customers. For example, if Wholesaler A had advance notice that a manufacturer would be increasing price to $20 per case from $18 a case on January 15, they would "forward buy" up to 50 weeks worth of product on January 1 at the current (lower) price of $18 a case. After the announcement was made on January 15, wholesalers then would be able to sell their product at a "discount" of $19 to pharmacy chains, GPOs, and hospitals, which was now technically below market price but still make a tidy profit of $1 a case.

This arrangement was beneficial to both manufacturers and wholesalers. Indeed, manufacturers selected wholesalers not on the basis of lowest cost of distribution or highest service level but instead on the basis of which wholesalers were willing to buy the greatest share of that year's production. The practice also allowed manufacturers to overstate earnings at the end of December based on purchase orders issued by wholesalers for 12 to 20 weeks worth of product issued prior to January 1, thereby allowing enhancing share price. Everybody was happy.

Forward buying distribution services also allowed pharmaceutical manufacturers to manage the complexities of unpredictable demand and lumpy capacity and served as a key transition element for distributing pharmaceutical products to a wide array of fragmented hospitals and pharmacies. This model was effective for many years and provided a valuable service to the pharmaceutical companies, which did not possess a core competency in distribution strategy and technology. However, in 2005–2007 wholesalers' position in the channel was challenged due to increasing pressure for pricing controls, lower inflation, average selling price (ASP) regulation, and other external variables. As a result, pharmaceutical distribution companies had to adopt a different model, one identifying an FFS model. This model has by and large been adopted by the industry and represents an industry standard approach.

In 2003, this practice was put under intense scrutiny based on the New Jersey attorney general's disclosure of "channel stuffing" on the part of a major pharmaceutical company, Bristol-Myers Squibb. Following these actions, the U.S. Securities and Exchange Commission (SEC) forced several large pharmaceutical manufacturers to restate earnings due to failure to disclose forward-selling practices. The practice of selling wholesalers up to a year's worth of inventory and then counting these sales in the current quarter distorted earnings and sales growth figures (Frederick, 2005). Many manufacturers quickly eliminated this channel policy and mandated that no more than one month's worth of inventory could be sold to any wholesaler. Such agreements quickly became known as inventory management agreements (IMAs). In addition, the rebates previously used to drive sales have also come under government scrutiny. A 2005 Office of the Inspector (OIG) report found that when rebates were included, the government was overpaying for many drugs (OIG, 2005). Many pharmaceutical benefit managers (PBMs) understood the role of rebates and forced wholesaler prices to reflect rebates in their pricing.

IMAs and changes in government regulation caused a major shift in the way wholesalers were able to charge for their services. In 2005 the Big Three wholesalers decided that they needed for the first time to charge a fee for their distribution services. This is a standard approach used in every distribution network in the world yet was a major change for the pharmaceutical industry. The FFS model was obviously very, very different from the inventory speculation model that previously financed distribution activities.

Myth 1: Distributors have been subsidizing providers through cost minus pricing.

Fact 1: Wholesalers provide invaluable services to providers that reduce costs in the channel and allow them to stay in business.

This myth is largely driven by the impression that "cost-plus" buying is still regularly occurring. It is not. For the most part, profit margins at retailers and wholesalers are going down, not up. Instead, FFS is similar to activity-based pricing where customers are charged for each logistics activity based on their level of usage. Examples include storage fees per pallet, delivery charges, and pick-and-pack operations. However, the nature of these contractual agreements, specifically how and for what activities wholesalers should be compensated, caused a major stir in the industry. This means that the FFS approach in fact creates stability in the supply chain to provide medicines at the right place and at the right time for patients and will help to save lives.

One of the core issues at the root of the discussion was, "How did you come up with the fee?" There is some debate among industry participants about the origin of this fee and which of the Big Three identified this fee approach. There is general agreement, however, that Cardinal Health (CAH) was the first to develop an integrated total cost model as the basis for calculating an FFS. The total cost model was more generally known as the Next Best Alternative (NBA) model. (As one industry executive stated, "this had nothing to do with basketball!") Initially, an average cost to serve of 1.85% was applied to all companies equally by CAH. This figure was challenged by many, and indeed was not based on a solid bottom up costing model. Following the challenge by many customers, CAH then worked with a major consulting company to develop the Next Best Alternative (NBA) model that broke down the different costs to serve the top 107 manufacturers of pharmaceuticals. The model was customized to each manufacturer's unique requirements and effectively calculated the total cost to serve each customer through other channels other than CAH. For each manufacturer, a variety of parameters was used to build up a cost model, using the "lowest available cost" to a manufacturer, which determined that it would self-distribute to its customers. The model used a pull-down menu that covered a number of different logistics parameters, including the following:

- Net sales (less chargebacks)
- Product mix (sales, lines, units)
- Classes of trade (retail, nonretail)
- Number of outlets
- Manufacturer locations
- Inventory locations
- Hospital criteria
- Number of therapy days
- Inventory costs
- Administrative costs
- Warehouse efficiency
- Customer service
- Other costs

Needless to say, the model was very complex but provided a reasonable basis for estimating the NBA to using a wholesaler. Using this baseline, CAH developed a cost to serve for each customer that took the NBA and discounted it by 20%. This provided a thorough, data-driven approach that was brought into negotiations. However, the model inherently provided higher costs to some manufacturers than others, an issue discussed in Chapter 4. By and large, this approach has been successful, as manufacturers have grudgingly agreed to this fee, at least in the short term.

> Myth 2: FFS benefits only wholesalers, and manufacturers end up paying more.

> Fact 2: FFS provides many benefits to all parties in the supply chain, including smoother demand flow, less inventory in the channel, and higher service levels.

Structure of Fee-for-Service Inventory Impacts

Inventory positioning models assume a positive inventory holding cost. Yet for the past decade, biopharma wholesalers garnered 90% of their profits from inventory appreciation—in effect a negative holding cost. In addition, forward buying played a role in creating secondary wholesalers. Incentives to forward buy often led to overbuying. Traditional wholesalers, such as Cardinal (CAH), McKesson, and AmerisourceBergen (ABC) found themselves with high levels of inventory that they could not sell. Their efforts to sell these drugs created an unregulated secondary market with a network of smaller wholesalers. These secondary wholesalers were not constrained by previous pricing agreements between manufacturers and primary wholesalers.

Compensation is earned by wholesalers through performance of wholesaling services for manufacturers rather than through speculation about future price increases. Examples of services wholesalers provide to manufacturers include:

- Sophisticated ordering technology
- Daily consolidated deliveries to healthcare providers
- Emergency shipments to providers 24/7/365
- Consolidated accounts receivable management
- Contract and chargeback administration
- Returns processing
- Customer service support
- Inventory management
- Licensed, environmentally controlled, Product Development and Management Association (PDMA) compliant,* secure facilities

---

* Regulatory compliance with the PDMA is discussed at http://www.bio-itworld.com/archive/011204/strategic_pdma.html

To receive these services, manufacturers (which are now playing the role of a "supplier" to the wholesalers) are required to pay a quarterly distribution service fee (DSP) equal to a fee percentage times the wholesale acquisition cost (WAC) sales times product sales.

In these contracts, the DSP fee is adjusted by deducting the following:

1. Inventory appreciation, or the difference between the value of inventory preceding a price increase and the value after a price increase
2. Pricing credits for products supplied to the wholesaler at prices less than the current WAC
3. The net value of any deals or promotions on product acquired from the supplier. This is calculated by multiplying the difference between the WAC and the acquisition cost before cash discount, based on invoice amounts or rebates less any deals or rebates passed on to customers.

The basic fee in FFS contracts is expressed as a percentage of the WAC multiplied by product sales and is inversely related to sales volume. Not surprisingly, FFS contracts are less popular with some smaller manufacturers.

As with the traditional buy-and-hold models, inventory appreciation lowers the DSP fee, which means that traditional methods of rewarding wholesalers through inventory appreciation are still present. There are other services, or "extras," that can be added to the basic services offered by wholesalers. For additional fees, wholesalers can commit to maintaining high (97%) percentage fill rates or allow manufacturers to participate in a National Logistics Center.

An extremely significant feature of FFS contracts is that there is a large variance in the DSP fee *percentage* charged for services rendered by wholesalers. Small and medium-sized manufacturers of pharmaceutical drugs are charged a proportionately greater percentage of their WAC than large suppliers for the services supplied by wholesalers in an FFS contract. The DSP base percentage of WAC can vary from 3.5 to 7% depending on sales volume, with the lowest-volume manufacturers paying twice the DSP fees of high-volume manufacturers.

In the balance, however, the fact remains that wholesalers are providing a service that is badly needed by manufacturers, which have not typically had a strong record for world-class logistics and distribution systems. Their core competencies have focused on research and development (R&D) and on marketing, as well they should. Thus, FFS allows wholesalers to have a more stable business model through stabilized demand and inventory levels, improved service levels, and lower risk. These cost savings and benefits will be passed on to manufacturers in the former of lower FFS rates and improved service.

> Myth 3: Switching to a manufacturer direct model would have no disruptive effect on the supply chain and is easy to deploy.

> Fact 3: Direct shipping would probably take manufacturers 6 months to a year to establish a service that is currently available and would cost more to operate than the current service.

There is no question that FFS is a more efficient model than having direct shipment by manufacturers to patients. Replacing wholesalers with direct distribution by manufacturers while maintaining equivalent service levels would add an estimated $10.5 billion per year to industry costs, equivalent to an 11.6% increase in manufacturers' total costs.[*]

One of the major risks associated with a direct model is that manufacturers are less well equipped to deal with major supply chain disruptions, as they have less buffer inventory in the channel and do not have experience in dealing with the complexities of the current biopharma network. The likelihood of a drug shortage is much higher under a manufacturer direct model. A drug shortage can have many potential causes, such as manufacturing disruptions, a shortage of raw materials, a voluntary recall, a decision to cease production of a particular product, or inaccurate demand forecasting. It has also been suggested that investment buying contributed to shortages as large suppliers were purchased by wholesalers or retailers.[†]

There is evidence to suggest that drug shortages have become more prevalent during the period when IMAs began to be implemented. The *New York Times* reported that "...drug supply disruptions in the United States have become routine."[‡] Shortages are also lasting longer today than in the past. At this point, information in the public domain is not sufficient to directly link shortages of specific drugs to inventory management agreements between manufacturers and wholesalers.

---

[*] *The Role of Distribution in the U.S. Healthcare Industry,* Healthcare Distribution Management Association, 2004.

[†] Ensuring Product Availability, Healthcare Distribution Management Association (2003). Available at www.nwda.org/issues_in_dist/pdf_product/hdma_datf_whitepaper.pdf

[‡] "In American Healthcare, Drug Shortages Are Chronic," *New York Times,* November 1, 2004.

In addition, manufacturers we spoke with were often not aware of the hidden costs and risks associated with wholesaling including the following:

- Credit risk
- Returns
- Damaged goods
- Losses on counterfeit or gray market goods that are discovered in the channel
- Information technology (IT) infrastructure
- Distribution costs

As the transparency of costs (without an effective estimate of the hidden distribution costs) associated with service continues, it will become imperative for wholesalers to better track and document these costs and to build a business case defining the value of the services provided. It may become necessary to share and build more visibility into NBA cost models to illustrate the total costs of distribution that have been mitigated in the past through service agreements and that have become more transparent under the FFS model.

Perception of Manufacturers to FFS

In general, manufacturers have accepted the FFS model but may well be exploring options in the future. As for the others, the rule is that generally the larger the manufacturer, the more likely they are to resist. Smaller manufacturers are more likely to sign FFS agreements as they have fewer options.

The following sections contain comments and observations received from different groups of manufacturers, which are depicted in Figure 2.1.

Manufacturers—Stable Group

- Believe that the wholesalers provide a valuable service
- Believe the fee is appropriate
- Admit that they do not have the capabilities to run such a complicated network
- **Compliance** is the key for this group
- "I think there might be value [in bypassing the wholesalers], and we are studying it and still in the middle of negotiations. However, I personally think that it would be too much of an effort for us."

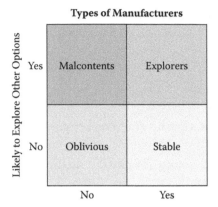

FIGURE 2.1
Perceptions of manufacturers to FFS agreements.

- "We believe that in 5–10 years the end user will be more of the customer rather than the wholesaler. Ideally, we would like for the wholesaler to be an extension of the manufacturer."
- "I don't know how we would be able to bypass wholesalers—we have contracts with chains—but we ship through wholesalers. The current environment is efficient. If pharma companies could get together and collaborate—maybe."

Manufacturers—Explorer Group

- A good portion of this group has signed agreements. However, they wish to find other options to improve negotiating power in the future. They do not have a viable structure to explore other options. They have approached PBMs to discuss options and are discovering that PBMs are not open to the idea of shipping direct.
- **Upper management pressure** is the key for this group.
- Most explorers have an exaggerated estimate of their capabilities.
- They are in the discussion phase with retailers and 3PLs, with no clear strategy or idea of the total cost to deploy such an effort.
- Cost is not the only consideration for this group. Issues such as risk mitigation are important to explorers.
- "We do go direct to the warehouse today. We would have the capability to go direct, but I am not sure if we would. However, the recent

events have forced us to look at alternatives models on how to partner. There is a potential in 3–5 years that we would go direct to the consumer. Even though there is a higher cost, it is not the only issue we look at, although not an insignificant one."

Manufacturers—Malcontent Group

- Most of this group has signed the FFS deals. However, they have initiated active negotiations/strategies with 3PLs to bypass wholesalers.
- **Channel control** is the key for this group.
- Companies are openly challenging the FFS model, using a rationale that they are paying too much, but are often unaware of the true costs of bypassing wholesalers.
- In addition, they believe that the returns being generated through these agreements are simply being passed on to pharmacies and not being reinvested into the channel to make it more competitive, despite the fact that wholesaler margins have decreased in line with expense efficiencies.
- "I know XXX (a 3PL) has put its name in the hat—we talked with [the people there] about it. They are very interested, since they are already doing it with hospital groups in the metro New York area."
- "We have spoiled the customer to save us money, and it is hard to get them to see how it is better if it is slower—do they really need same day or next day service?"
- "Will we ever get to engage with our end customers directly? Probably not. Our culture emphasizes security and brand protection. There is a potential that we could go direct in 3–5 years. We would have the capability to go direct to stores, but I am not sure if we would. We probably would continue to have an intermediary for hospitals and pharmacies."

Manufacturers—Oblivious Group

- Consists of small emerging players who outsource their entire distribution network to third parties. Most of them are focused on growing the business, clinical trials, or expanding the business.
- **Business maintenance/expansion** is the key for this group.

Channel Forces

As wholesalers FFS model became under more scrutiny, there emerged a whole set of "me-too" players that believed they could disintermediate the channel and compete with wholesalers. This included manufacturers that believed they could self-direct to pharmacies and hospitals, third-party logistics providers like UPS and FedEx, group purchasing organizations, and pharmacy benefits managers.

Traditionally, patients—the final consumer—received biopharma products from two sources: hospital or retail pharmacies. These outlets functioned similarly, carrying a fairly large amount of inventory that was then dispensed upon a demand trigger—a prescription or scrip. Even as retailers, hospitals, and manufacturers reduced safety stocks, forward buying and reliance on secondary channels for emergency shipments ensured that there was an abundance of product in the BPS. The channel also remained intact due to the relationships between pharma sales representatives, doctors, and retailers. Pharma representatives provided education on the latest drugs and provided samples. Doctors tended to prescribe these drugs based on pharma education and experience—their own and their peers. The prescriptions could then be filled only at a licensed pharmacy—often chosen based on geography or the doctor's recommendation.

Recent changes have greatly impacted the channel. The retail pharmacy market has greatly consolidated such that the top five pharmacy chains now control approximately 85% of the retail space and therefore approximately 20% of all drugs sold. Choices and prices have also been reduced by PBMs to contain costs for their clients and ensure their own profitability. In addition, the increased proficiency of 3PLs and greater acceptance of Internet-based sales have added another method for pharma products to reach patients.

> Myth 4: Distribution is all about shipping pharmaceutical products from point A to point B.

> Fact 4: Many hidden costs associated with distribution that are implicit in the FSS model are largely absorbed into the model.

One of the research outcomes in working on this book was the surprising nature of the "naïve" views of what goes into biopharmaceutical distribution costs and the relative low understanding of the complexity of the offerings provided by wholesalers.

In our interviews, we discussed many of the critical services offered by wholesalers, shown in the following table. Many of these activities involve assuming a certain degree of risk and investment on the part of wholesalers. Many of these factors are *not factored into alternative proposed models of distribution being put forward by other parties.*

Activity	Associated Risk
Forecasting demand	Forecast errors
Specialized data systems and personnel	
Inventory management systems	Specialized information systems
Ordering systems	Specialized information systems
Purchase order systems that bill only for shipped items	Specialized information systems
Carrying 20 or more days of inventory for pharmacies at no cost for high-moving drugs	Underage and overage
Delivery 5X per day, 24/7, 365 days a year	Specialized distribution assets
Warehouse and cost structure to ship to multiple locations	Specialized distribution assets
Business continuity requirements (multiple warehouses distributed nationally to decrease probability of delivery disruptions or inventory loss)	Assets deployed for mitigation rather than efficiency
Credit, billing, collections—particularly collecting receivables and taking on credit risk	Cash flow
Returns and recalls	Liability
Providing pedigree	Liability

Third-party logistics providers (UPS, FedEx, and Deutschpost) have been keen to enter this market. However, our research results suggest that 3PLs are not able to offer these services but are primarily able to offer only point-to-point offerings in this space. This was validated in our interviews with three major 3PL providers that are actively engaged in pursuing market share in the pharmaceutical wholesaler space.

The largest 3PL developed some early successes in pilots in the New York metro area but does not seem aware of the complexities associated with the channel. A second 3PL initiated early pilots as well and approached the market with a cautionary approach, focused on building consensus and identifying opportunities. The third 3PL has decided to focus on niche services such as cold chain and track-and-trace in an effort to target the growing biotech sector.

There is no question that despite the challenges 3PLs are aggressively pursuing a strategy of bypassing wholesalers. We believe that at some point 3PLs will enter this space in the next decade. This will largely be a "manufacturer push" initiative, and there will be some start-up problems in identifying the first pharmacy to consider it. However, the current mood of manufacturers is to actively explore this option despite the irrationality of the requirements. It also appears that 3PLs are approaching this market with an intent to invest, although the specifics of the channel requirements are also not well understood.

3PLs claim that their costs will be lower than the fee that is currently charged by the wholesalers. In addition, they believe that the supply chain design would be simplified as by eliminating the wholesaler and playing the role of a 3PL, the distribution centers (DCs) currently operated by the manufacturers could be eliminated.

They claim these following advantages over the wholesalers:

- Better shipment level data
- Improved security/drug safety
- Easier-to-roll-out radio frequency identification devices (RFID)
- Increased simplicity
- Activity-based costing will better represent work done
- Will allow manufacturers to build direct relationships with retailers

Wholesalers, on the other hand, believe that 3PLs will face these problems:

- Existence of unions
- If 3PLs do not take ownership, manufacturers would be forced to retain liability for the product for a longer period.
- It will be very difficult for a 3PL to take a saleable return back because it would probably have to be thrown away. There is no regulatory way for them to reinsert saleable products back into the supply chain, which would increase waste.
- They believe that 3PLs are not as well positioned to deal with business continuity planning as wholesalers.
- Retailers would not accept reduced service levels.
- 3PLs do not have the level of reach that wholesalers do, especially in remote areas.
- Lack of relationships with retailers
- Difficulty in providing a unified ordering interface for customers
- Customers do not want to have multiple order/receipt points

- Lack the scale, size, and experience of wholesalers
- Lack of ability to provide these value-added services
  - Returns
  - Contract administration
  - Chargebacks
  - Demand forecasting
  - Absorbing bad loans

Here are some comments made by manufacturers about 3PLs:

- Three manufacturers believe that the 3PLs could handle BPS distribution
- Another believes that *"none of the providers have all the capabilities of a wholesaler but believe that its only a matter of time"*
- *"A 3PL cannot replace the function of a wholesaler"*
- Another manufacturer does not believe that a 3PL would be the right choice as it understands its customers better than the 3PL
- Yet another manufacturer believes that although none of the 3PLs are capable of handling its distribution business independently, it would like to see a distributor model with multiple providers

All in all, considering the complexity of the distribution network and the familiarity that wholesalers have with the model, it is unlikely that 3PLs would be able to offer the same level of service at a lower price.

We believe that evidence is mounting that a group of 3PLs will launch a focused attack on the traditional space held by the Big Three wholesalers. The likely scenario is that a group of one or two manufacturers will contract with a 3PL to initiate service to pharmacies using a centralized distribution center concept. They will in effect "park" their inventory and ship to pharmacies and hospitals direct using a third-party network. Despite the challenges and barriers, we believe there will be a pilot effort with a select group of pharmacies but that this may not be sustained. At most, this channel would grow quickly but lose momentum as pharmacies resist having to go through additional channels.

Myth 5: Retailers and hospitals would prefer to buy direct from manufacturers.

Fact 5: Our research suggests that retailers are refusing to work with manufacturers due to the increased transactional complexity and cost associated with doing so. Hospitals rely on wholesalers for a whole set of value-added activities including direct to bedside replenishment that is changing the face of pharmaceutical distribution, reducing patient errors, and simplifying their inbound logistics and pharmaceutical costs.

My interviews with pharmacists reveal that for the most part they are not willing to accept lower service levels at the same or higher cost. The feasibility of the model proposed by manufacturers to lower service levels at the same cost is not an option that the pharmacists are willing to accept. Even if a "first-mover" strategy were adopted, the likelihood of this model being accepted by pharmacists is low. Extracts from one of the pharmacy interview comments from a senior executive provide validation of this parameter:

> If manufacturers started shipping through UPS, it would increase our costs. There is a lot of saber rattling going on, based on the pharma community's desire to go direct to retail and cut out wholesalers. I have worked in pharma, then at Eckerd, then here. My observation is that the pharma guys are focused on manufacturing and R&D and bequeathed logistics to wholesalers—and they are now flatfooted. They have very little sophistication, have no relationship and technology, all of which now resides with the wholesalers.
>
> The big challenge is that we receive a [wholesaler] order every day. It comes in a nice [container], sorted by our aisles, and is easy to receive. We probably would get our quality level to a point where blind receiving could occur and selection without detailing. If we were to switch to UPS, we now would get into large unbundled shipments from different players with different activities. Now we would have to carry safety stock on all those piles, and there would be no forward DC's immediate response to stockouts and lower service levels. Is the pharma community going to be willing to share the costs that we would incur associated with not going through wholesalers? Probably not. If I have to now incur larger safety stock carrying costs as a safeguard against lower service levels—will you, Mr. Pharma, give me financial incentives that will also offset my incremental labor cost associated with more purchase orders? The big question is whether there is enough money for the pharma companies to get enough, give us enough of an incentive, and give us something to sweeten the pot and still make a return on it. Because in the end, it will be more costly. We will have to carry more safety stock and more receiving labor, have to suffer from lower responsiveness from wholesalers, and have to carry more inventory. What is the impact of that math penalty—what goodness will offset that? I don't think that they [pharma] know that right now. Will they find a way to manage all the complexity, all those transactions, the whole chain of customer

information, the track and trace capability, RFID initiatives, etc.? I doubt it. The wholesalers are a lot more nimble. Could the large pharmaceutical companies do it? Probably. But what about the mid-level ones that we are still having to keep in inventory? Will they have the critical mass?

Direct distribution is not a likely scenario. Distribution to stores using 3PLs is not likely because retail chains do not want to be receiving 10 shipments a day from multiple manufacturers—they want to deal with as few as possible. In addition, there is a lot of special handling and biosensitive materials—as well as new requirements for serialization tags. The wholesalers do a good job of maintaining those elements to ensure they are not compromised. For this reason, pharmacies will not be able to go to individual delivery unless going direct to customer. Manufacturers are also not interested in selling direct[ly] to customers. There is a physician prescription interaction [that] they are not interested in becoming part of.

Hospitals are also unlikely to adopt a direct shipment model, even though some have made some progress in the metro New York area, possibly made feasible because of the high concentration of retailers in this area. One of the chief hospital pharmacists we interviewed noted that:

It would be highly unlikely that an alternative channel would emerge. There would have to be a substantial incentive to do that. The shakeup in the wholesale industry and pricing—if that turns out to create a big opportunity or liability, it will take that kind of a change to create much difference. Right now everyone is saying we are making our decision on cost—the old model of contract cost minus some percent. I wouldn't see organizations wanting to make major changes unless they felt they had to.

Group Purchasing Organizations

GPOs share the belief that manufacturers are not capable of bypassing wholesalers and are generally satisfied with the level of service and cost savings provided by wholesalers to their hospital customers. However, significant potential conflict is beginning to be created by wholesalers that have allegedly "auto-substituted" their generic manufactured products for hospital-requested original products when stockouts occur. There is also conflict created when wholesalers have attempted to "direct source" pharmaceutical products to hospitals, offering them a 2–3% savings over the GPO administration fee. In such cases, GPOs tell their clients that they are exposing themselves to undue risk, as GPOs are legitimately representing their hospital customers' best interests.

It is a growing possibility that mail order will soon be bypassing retailers and creating channel conflict. There are already signs that retailers have been caught by surprise and are now launching their own. Mail order is now the fastest growing sales channel for prescription drugs. Mail order also threatens the retailers' high margin "front-end" merchandise, because customers who receive drugs in their mailbox are not in their local drugstore shopping for cosmetics and candy. The lion's share of mail order sales is being generated by PBMs. Highly automated and hugely profitable, PBMs can fill and mail a prescription for as low as $2.50, a fraction of what it costs drug stores.

> Myth 6: Wholesalers are using sales data to exploit manufacturers and have a high incidence of chargeback errors.

> Fact 6: Data accuracy provided by wholesalers is critical in providing estimates of chargeback requirements, required for Sarbanes–Oxley compliance. Further, chargebacks provide an important set of data for marketing and trade relationship research, monitoring, and performance.

Another recent set of events points to another imminent challenge to the FFS market being developed by manufacturers and third-party auditing firms: chargeback audits. Chargebacks comes about through the difference between the WAC (the price the manufacturer charges the wholesaler) and the price that might have been negotiated between the manufacturer and a wholesaler's customer. In cases where the contract price is lower than the WAC, the wholesaler will bill the manufacturer for the difference—the chargeback.

This recent threat involves third-party auditors actively promoting a business model for auditing wholesalers based on the premise that wholesalers are actively engaged in overcharging manufacturers for falsified records associated with, for example, damage and product expiration. This practice is not only a nuisance for wholesalers in terms of accommodating these probes but also damages brand reputation and customer perceptions through the negative implications of these false accusations. In several cases I explored, audits of wholesaler chargebacks were minimal in scope, and in each case the difference was readily paid by the wholesaler to the party requiring the audit. There have also been stories in the press promoting chargeback audits as a way for manufacturers to discover another "blockbuster" in revenue generation. Conferences are even being held on the subject, an indicator that this issue is under increasing debate and scrutiny among manufacturers.

Generics manufacturers perhaps have a vested interest in obtaining greater insights into chargeback audits. Many generic companies create deals with certain customers whereby end prices are 20% of WAC prices. Due to lack of visibility into end channels, many generics have no way of accurately predicting their chargeback reserves, which poses a problem for quarterly reporting and compliance to Sarbanes-Oxley requirements. They would perhaps value a chargeback audit report provided to accurately create and report on chargeback reserves.

Product Forces

There are several important product forces: the increasing number and use of generic drugs, increasing differences in logistics service requirements for over-the-counter (OTC) and prescription drugs, increasing numbers of drugs requiring specialized handling, and the proliferation of reimported and counterfeit drugs. In addition, major challenges are emerging with respect to how personalized medicine will impact biopharmaceutical distribution.

> Myth 7: Medicare legislation will drive increased transparency of distribution value chains leading to simplified models of distribution.

> Fact 7: Average manufacturer price does not factor in the many hidden costs associated with distribution. Stockout costs associated with shortages are infinite, thereby skewing many standardized inventory models.

The BPS is fragmenting along different product lines coupled with associated service expectations. Retailers have increasingly merged OTC and generics products into their existing networks of distribution centers along with branded drugs. Manufacturers and wholesalers ship product to these warehouses, and order fulfillment to retail locations is handled internally. This contrasts markedly with the case of specialty drugs, new drugs, and branded drugs. Perhaps the greatest differences occur for drugs that require climate control. The cold chain (the supply chain for the ever increasing number of vaccines and plasma-based drugs that must be refrigerated), is driving a new role for wholesalers. This creates a conflict in the channel because a single manufacturer often produces high-selling branded drugs, OTC drugs, as well as cold chain drugs.

The theoretical effects of distributing such diverse products on inventory and transportation decisions are fairly well understood. Models based on economic order quantities and traveling salesman problems can come to solutions under simple circumstances. Although these models quickly become intractable given the variability of demand, lead times, product characteristics, and customer characteristics typically found in the BPS, the input variables and problem characteristics provided guidance for our research. Economic order decisions are based on three inputs—ordering and delivery costs, demand characteristics, and lead-time characteristics.

The traveling salesman problem describes a problem where a salesperson wishes to make sales calls to multiple cities while minimizing total distance traveled. The problem is a subset of assignment problems that are typically solved using a branch-and-bound algorithm. Interestingly, although the basic algorithm was proposed in the 1960s, realistic problems quickly overwhelm the fastest computers, and new algorithms and heuristics continue to be proposed. The problem is formulated by assigning a delivery cost function to customers. In more complex problems product commodities and customer types can have individual cost functions. Constraints then relate to delivery windows—certain times in which deliveries can be made, assigning specific vehicles to certain products or customers, and frequency of delivery required by customer or product. Such straightforward distribution models, however, implode when the realities of the ever changing and dynamic nature of the BPS are forced to fit into these scenarios. At issue are the challenges associated with calculating and uncovering many of the hidden costs in the network. The other challenge is the cost associated with a stockout. For many who work in this network, a stockout cost is essentially infinite. As one industry expert noted, "It's a patient, not just a package." That is, stockouts for medicines are considered unacceptable, and many of the traditional inventory models that consider stockout costs and assess probabilities of stockouts fail when stress tested against the resistance to drug shortages in the chain.

A complex issue in the pharma and biotech supply chain is the rebate structure and pricing structure that is under intense scrutiny, especially in the cases of Medicaid and Medicare.

Once the true costs of acquisition become available and open to the public, it is highly likely that increasing pressure on wholesalers will be imminent. Unfortunately, these estimates fail to account for the significant value-added services of wholesalers and do not reflect a number of hidden risks associated with management of distribution channels. Some of the hidden costs and risks associated with these channels include the following:

- Credit risk
- Returns
- Damaged goods
- Losses on counterfeit or gray market goods that are discovered in the channel
- IT infrastructure
- Distribution costs

As the transparency of costs without an effective estimate of the hidden distribution costs associated with service continues, it will become imperative for wholesalers to better track and document these costs and build a business case defining the value of the services provided. It may become necessary to share elements of the NBA model to illustrate the total costs of distribution that have been mitigated in the past through service agreements and that have become more transparent under the FFS model.

The most important point to note here is that service fees have never been addressed in calculating average manufactured price (AMP). Medicare office policy dictates that if the service fee was a bona fide fee at fair market value and was not passed on to a customer, it can be excluded from the calculation. However, manufacturers still include the service fee in AMP, as they are not clear about this position. It is important that manufacturers consider dropping the fee from their AMP to pass value on to their customers.

As the share of generics in the market increases, it is also likely that retailers will not be able to maintain the current margins they enjoy on generic drugs and will be forced to accept lower reimbursements from the government. This will negatively impact their margins and levels of service. Combined with the increasing pressure to move to 90-day prescriptions, retailers stand to lose margins based on these changes.

A retail pharmacist noted:

> Among progressive HMOs, there is a huge potential for differentiation. I am a big advocate of telling people that drugs are cost-effective from a total cost standpoint—but most people look only at the immediate price.

They don't get down to the total cost of healthcare, which is critical for understanding the impact. From an HMO standpoint, there is also a touchy issue of the cost–benefit of having people die. If people die at 70 versus 75, there is a benefit to HMOs, so there is a huge fight around that argument. On the purchasing side, GPOs are increasingly being out of date. I hear a lot of people asking the question, what do we need GPOs for? What does Premiere do that McKesson can't offer? Are GPOs becoming less of an issue? In terms of physician practices, GPOs do have an advantage.

Hospitals are also aware of the high costs of running their pharmacies but also recognize that they have little ability to control costs in this area, based on the politicization of healthcare. A major director at a large California hospital system noted:

Under Medicare, it is possible that hospitals will pay more—and there is lots of anticipation along these lines. However, there are so many politics on reimbursement issues it is hard to tell, as the reimbursement costs seem unpredictable and arbitrary. And hospitals are under extreme pressure to reduce costs.

At the University of California, we are a large network of hospitals, but we still don't know where the power base is going to be based on politics and are aware of the continued public scrutiny of healthcare costs. We are also aware of the competing interests in the marketplace. We believe it is better to be loyal citizens to a GPO versus going out on our own, because we don't know any better. However, we wish to maintain a competitive environment and will continue to have a lot of back-and-forth dialogue on this issue. We believe that collective participation turns out to be better in the long run. At some point we are not ruling out that we could do something on our own.

Myth 8: Other industries such as retail can provide similar distribution capabilities at a much lower cost.

Fact 8: The BPS is becoming increasingly complex, with specialized handling and personalized medicine requirements.

Some would argue that pharmaceutical wholesaling is similar to other wholesaling industries. On average, gross domestic product (GDP) growth has increased across all wholesaler industries by 7%, consistently year over year. This level of growth is the same in 2003 as it was in 1987. The entire U.S. wholesale distribution industry is approximately $3.2 trillion, of which pharmaceutical wholesaling is second only to the grocery and food service wholesaler–distributor industry. In this respect, the size of the wholesaler market is on a par with other industries such as oil and gas, computer wholesalers, industrial distributors, and electrical wholesalers (Fein, 2005).

Additional research, however, suggests that the wholesaler model in the pharmacy distribution industry is unlike any other. To begin with, many wholesale markets are fragmented, which promotes competition. The level of consolidation in pharmaceutical wholesaling is not common, since most wholesale industries are not dominated by a Big Three. Rather, many mom-and-pop operations exist. This is still the case in some states that have marginal requirements for secondary wholesale requirements, but increased scrutiny is also driving out this model.

Even though biopharmaceutical wholesale growth is growing steadily, it is largely tied to drug sales and the aging population. We believe that Medicare will actually increase the level of revenue growth, as more seniors will purchase prescription drugs that are affordable.

The major difference between pharmaceutical distribution and other wholesale industries is that no other industry has been driven toward buy-and sell-side margins, whereby customers (e.g., retailers) were essentially benefiting from Just-in-Time (JIT) delivery to store locations and not paying for the service. Every other whole industry operates on a performance-based fee for service arrangement. Thus, the FFS model is actually moving the industry much more toward an industry norm.

In general, Fein (2005) suggests that the current model in BPS is unlike any other industry. Due to the fragmentation and complexity in the channel, the lack of capability on the part of manufacturers to vertically integrate, and the unwillingness of pharmaceutical retailers and hospitals to develop distribution capabilities through multiple channels, the wholesaler model works best in this environment. For example, one industry analyst noted that a different model was once proposed and developed on a pilot basis in Canada (unsuccessfully). One analyst interviewed noted that this initiative had failed due to a fundamental lack of understanding of the role of wholesalers in the channel:

> It is not very likely that manufacturers can do it alone. If you think about precedent—the drug industry tried to do this in Canada 6 years ago in a 3PL model called the Canadian Pharmaceutical Distribution Network. It didn't work, and they gave the work to a wholesaler. This group represented

a handful of ex-pharma executives that formed a venture for a 3PL model. When it failed, the wholesaler who took it over [McKesson] immediately set delivery schedules and performance back to its former levels, and their market share has grown as a result. The direct model failed and went back to a wholesaler that was the only one capable of managing this level of complexity.

There are many benefits associated with an FFS model consistent with wholesale industry practices. To begin with, pharmaceutical manufacturers should recognize that they can use fee structures to leverage their influence and encourage true supply chain partnerships to improve customer service and create value in the chain as well as to eliminate cost from the chain. Successful fee-for-service agreements can reward concrete actions by wholesalers to build manufacturer brands, lower healthcare supply chain costs, and speed the availability to patients of beneficial new products.*

Such channel compensation programs represent powerful tools for driving change in the channel, greater collaboration, information visibility, and improved responsiveness, at a lower cost to all channel participants. In the end, this will benefit the ultimate customer, the patient buying the drugs. Removing the "veil" around mysterious buy-and-sell margins will enable all parties to truly move toward supply chain integration and collaboration. We believe some of the potential outcomes of such a movement, which is now a standard method of working in retail channels, are to establish initiatives around transparency to customer sales and inventory, control over secondary market activities, price integrity, anticounterfeit initiatives, supply chain security, and reduction of manufacturers' supply chain costs. The replacement of lost profits from investment buying with FFS agreements is a step in the right direction toward achieving supply chain distribution provider excellence in the channel.

We do not mean to imply that controlled investment buying should disappear. Indeed, competition among wholesalers is critical to ensure fair market pricing and service. Although inventory levels have shrunk to a level not seen, investment buying may now be a function of strategic inventory positioning to drive superior customer service, profitability, and recognition of potential market opportunities as a function of market intelligence to exploit shortages that may occur with competitors. We believe that the level of inventory reduction has reached a point where a

---

* Adam J. Fein, "Getting what you pay for from fee-for-service," February 2005. Available at http://www.eyeforpharma.com/print.asp?news=45205

disproportionate risk of shortages may become an issue. As one wholesaler executive noted:

> We are below 30 days of inventory. We are actually down to 20 for branded manufacturers. We need 21 days for cycle stock and safety stock—we need 14 days for those not on the National Logistics Center program. We have built a very efficient model as long as there are no hiccups. There is no buffer for supply chain disruption. If demand were to increase, it's not in the pipeline. We used to complain about transport costs for company transfers—we could burn it down and transfer—we can't do that now. It is an incredibly operationally efficient model. But we have put so many proactive controls in place, and I am proud of that. But a crisis always creates havoc. One of our large retail accounts went from dock to dock to pulling from replenishment. They pulled too much, and we ran out of stock on a ton of product—it was catastrophic! We found that we run so efficiently [that] not only did we not have inventory [but] we [also] didn't have headcount in our headquarters to manage it. There were no peripheral people to pick up slack, and it piled up on desks. It is amazing how we have migrated to this efficient model. You don't realize how efficient and lean your supply chain is until you get into crisis mode.

This level of efficiency has also been applied to new requirements in the chain. Some of the emerging technologies and trends include cold chain, pedigree, serialization, prevention of counterfeit product, shipping direct to patients for oncology products and biologic products, serialization, and radio frequency identification tagging. Many of these will require development of new capabilities within the network, which will require increased collaboration among manufacturers, wholesalers, retailers, and hospitals. We will cover many of these emerging areas in Chapter 6. However, our position is that the current model is still the most robust and capable of addressing these changes.

For example, consider the case of cold chain. This requirement is such that a product shipped from a manufacturer to a retailer needs to be maintained in a temperature-controlled environment, in which the temperature of the product is measured throughout its journey and any deviations in temperature for a given period of time is considered a failure, whereby the product must be scrapped. In the grocery industry, for example, yogurt has a very low price point, with the assurance of cold chain control throughout its delivery cycle. Biopharmaceutical distribution involves a much higher price point, transporting a high-end life-treating drug, and receives the same level of supply chain touch as yogurt. Yet biopharmaceutical wholesalers charge a lower distribution cost for transporting these drugs than for transporting yogurt. This example is illustrative of the level of efficiency that exists in the market today.

CONCLUSION

Extensive analysis of the literature and multiple interviews with industry participants were used to assess the current and future state of the BPS.[*] This research suggests that compensation and regulation are consistently powerful forces in the industry. We believe product forces will emerge as a more powerful force in the next 10 to 15 years.

Compensation

FFS is a relatively recent addition to the BPS lexicon, in response to changes in inventory management policies enacted by many pharmaceutical manufacturers coupled with lower margins experienced by wholesalers. FFS is based on applying activity-based cost accounting to the prices charged to customers. By linking actual value-added activities to the prices charged for services, activity-based pricing provides service companies with a mechanism for justifying prices as well as increasing openness and trust in interorganizational relationships. The wholesalers in our research as well as the 3PLs have offered a variety of activity based pricing models where they are compensated for logistic services. However, reactions to FFS are not uniform. Interestingly, manufacturers, the type of firm our focus group thought would be most impacted by FFS, in many cases view this pricing mechanism as unfair or at best another pricing gimmick.

The following insight from a 3PL underscores the possible reason manufacturers may be reluctant to accept FFS:

> The wholesaler model is just at a high-level fee for service, and manufacturers have no idea what they are paying at a comprehensive level. We asked

---

[*] Rosetti, C., Handfield, R., and Dooley, K., "Forces, Trends, and Decisions in Pharmaceutical Supply Chain Management," accepted for publication in *International Journal of Physician Distribution and Inventory Management*, July 2010.

them how many shipments they make, and large manufacturers had no idea. They sell in bulk to wholesalers and buy market-service data but have no direct shipment-level detail. So they have no concept of what is actually happening in terms of sales and service for their product.

Some manufacturers are aware of the infrastructure required to maintain these service levels, but most neglect the risks associated with owning the assets necessary to maintain these service levels. This may explain why many of the BPS members feel the fees charged in the FFS model are too high. Those that reject the FFS model believe that vertical integration or a switch to 3PLs is a viable alternative. Many manufacturers have explored alternatives, not because they are not happy with the service but because they truly fail to understand the complexity of the channel. Multiple observations from multiple channel participants reflect the fact that there is a poor understanding of the true complexity and cost of the services provided by wholesalers.

Regulation

Interestingly, regulators and analysts view FFS as an integral part of Medicare and Medicaid reform. Many experts are of the opinion that new emerging healthcare regulation will demand accountability at all stages of the BPS. If this is the case, then a form of activity-based pricing will be required to receive government reimbursement, creating a whole new set of requirements for transaction visibility and collaborative cost sharing information.

As wholesalers' revenues have switched from being derived from inventory speculation to fees based on efficient operations, there have been trade-offs in inventory and staffing levels. This has impeded the ability of wholesalers to act as a buffer between supply and demand and in worst-case scenarios to offer continuity in the pharmaceutical industry supply chain.

A closely related issue with the previous proposition involves the complexities associated with reimbursement in the channel and the muddied and complex set of regulatory requirements that have evolved in the channel in response to the healthcare crisis in the United States. In addition to the FFS model between manufacturers and wholesalers, U.S. supply chain participants must also contend with Medicaid and Medicare reimbursement. The reality of the regulatory policy climate is that all members will be impacted dramatically.

Channel Forces

Channel forces include alternative channels, logistics infrastructure, and service. My analysis reveals that alternative channels are not an influential theme, but logistics infrastructure and service are indeed very important themes. Three viable alternatives merit discussion: (1) the entrance of alternative wholesalers in the channel; (2) direct sales; and (3) product focused channels. In considering the first option, there are three distinct possibilities: (1) consolidation of smaller wholesalers; (2) entrance of 3PLs as a new entrant in the channel; and (3) vertical integration by a manufacturer of a smaller distributor. Each of these appears to be somewhat unrealistic, given the frank evaluation and exploration of these possibilities in our interviews with subject-matter experts in the BPS.

Although 3PLs appear to present a viable alternative, my research results lead me to believe that the 3PLs are unable to offer logistic services on par with the wholesalers. They excel at point-to-point distribution, but current service levels require holding inventory, something 3PLs seem reluctant to do.

Perhaps the most innovative alternative channel being explored is direct shipment combined with patient management. A cancer drug manufacturer initiated a program in the mid 1990s in response to significant channel problems. One of the senior executives from this company stated that product manufacturers should accept responsibility for owning the supply chain. With this ownership comes the responsibility of ensuring that necessary value-add services are provided to patients. The services offered by this company include real-time data regarding administration of product, compliance, and ongoing monitoring of patient health. This service will be limited only by the human factor: many patients are willing to pay a higher price to discuss pharmaceutical side effects, problems, and issues with a caring pharmacist through direct clinical intervention.

Logistics infrastructure was an influential theme in both the interviews and the press. In general, logistics infrastructure remains with the wholesalers, a few PBMs that have invested in highly automated warehouses for their mail-order business, and large retailers. Manufacturers have neglected logistics for over a decade, and the opinion is that they cannot build these skills back up quickly.

Other retailers I interviewed agreed that a reduction in service levels is not likely to be acceptable through alternative channels than wholesalers:

> The majority of retailers receive two or three orders per week. That is a very good level of service. At [Large Retailer] the difference between three and five a week was not that significant, but it was often the kind of thing we would look at as a tiebreaker. We first looked to see if they had to have best bottom-line price. If they had three deliveries a week and were better on price, that would be better. The majority of retailers have a secondary supplier where they can pick up shorts, in cases when the primary has an out of stock or demand that is out of stock.

Trepidation in the BPS about manufacturers playing larger role in logistics service may be well-founded. In our conversations we learned that when manufacturers are designing distribution centers (DCs) they are focusing on efficiency and trying to curtail service.

Service is another theme that will pose challenges. The recent period of wholesalers competing on service is being challenged by increasing complexity and cost uncertainties in the channel. The previous trends all point to a new period of lower service in the BPS where logistics infrastructure and service requirements will be points of contention. Manufacturers that attempt to gain greater control of the BPS through forward integration will be pushing for lower service levels. The three large wholesalers cannot reduce their margins and clearer pricing agreements, perhaps forced by the government, will remove rebates—perhaps the last form of alternative revenue. These forces all should result in hospitals and retailers being forced to accept lower service levels.

Product Proliferation and Customer Segmentation

The last set of forces I evaluated was product related. One element involves changes in BPS management to effectively deliver new types of drugs to customers. In addition, lower prices in certain drug categories change inventory management decisions. Generics and OTC drugs are driving a large part of these price changes. Finally, increased drug pedigree concerns are driving new technological solutions to the old problems of track and trace—knowing where products are in the BPS.

One of the major problems facing the BPS is the proliferation of products, many of which require specialized distribution networks. When Pfizer spun off its OTC drug line to Johnson & Johnson, Pfizer stated that there was not enough synergy between the resources required to develop new brand name drugs and the continued support of OTC medicines. In addition, generics are increasingly being sourced directly by large retailers that are treating these drugs the same way they procure other commodities. Last, a new host of biological and human plasma based drugs require a completely different supply chain. Referred to as the cold chain, this family of drugs must be kept in controlled environments and has a very specific shelf life often tied to temperature and humidity of its surroundings. The fact that production and consumption now occur globally has only increased the complexity of the BPS.

Interviews with one of the largest cold chain providers reinforced two big problems: scale and scope of product problems facing the chain:

> To meet these requirements, [cold chain distributor] established DCs and partners with [container company] to develop a skid-mounted shipping container easily moveable by forklift, with a compartment for dry ice and a battery-powered fan and control system. This covers temp control but also required customized transportation. The company went with a specialist trucking firm with nine customized trailers all standardized, which includes a backup refrigeration unit if the main fails. The trailer becomes the secondary packaging.

Therapeutics are "boutique" drugs customized to patient requirements. Manufacturers are currently creating drugs that would be customized based on success of clinical trials in a subpopulation. The segments would correspond to therapies best suited for specific individuals. A patient seeking treatment would be tested and segmented into a category of treatment, and the physician would then recommend the therapy best suited to the individual's particular condition, including recommended dosage. The BPS then plays an important role in creating specific "boutique" customized therapies to align with, for example, individual requirements and genetic characteristics. In this manner, a customized set of therapies that is most effective would evolve. However, this requires follow-on technologies that must be used to monitor patients as they follow through with prescribed therapies. An executive at a major PBM described his company's vision for sustained profitability using therapeutics:

> The next generation will be designer drugs. Are there certain medications that would work better in the African American population? If you are a manufacturer and you have four varieties of Zoloft—you have to serve more of the population through diverse product offerings that are specific to segments of the population.

These statements appear to point toward a BPS that is moving toward niche markets that cater to specific individuals, or at least subsegments of the general population. These examples contrast sharply with the recent moves by large retailers to improve operational efficiency.

Further, the share of generic drugs is likely to increase sharply in the next two to three years. Since wholesalers are more likely to carry branded products, it is likely that there will be a reduction in revenue for whole-sale distribution. Some estimates are in the range of 10% reductions. This is driven largely by the pharmacy benefits managers, who will purchase directly from generics manufacturers rather than wholesalers. One PBM executive we interviewed noted:

> From the data I have seen and IMS data,* a lot of branded product will come off patent, and the trend will continue. We are also seeing a new type of single source generic coming into the market—with some exclusivity for some period of time. That hurts us—we have guaranteed generics discounts we make to our customers that is based on the assumption of lower cost. If a single-source generic comes to market, however, it is difficult to get to a discount generic market price. For example, [Large Manufacturing] could single source and not allow others to manufacture the generic. In terms of the average wholesaler price, we would get only 25% off instead of 80% but would still have to reimburse our market at an 80% discounted price.

Therefore, it appears that generics are following the path of OTC medications, where brand names are being supplanted by store brands and active ingredients are more important than the manufacturer. Coupling this with price pressures from PBMs and retailers, there is strong evidence that the BPS is fragmenting.

There are several managerial implications surrounding balancing risk-adjusted compensation in the BPS. In the immediate future manufacturers should count on further increasing inventory levels. As the executive at a manufacturer currently using a direct sell model for some of its products pointed out, manufacturers will need to accept the responsibility of ensuring that their products are arriving to customers when they need them. Recent evidence shows that manufacturers are already increasing inventory levels; however, macro indicators of inventory in the BPS show that this has not been a strategic reaction. Increasing inventory levels at the manufacturer level are almost exactly equal to inventory reductions at

---

* IMS Health is a consulting company that tracks pharmaceutical manufacturing and sales.

the wholesale level. Inventory has just been shifted up the chain. If manufacturers wish to ensure supply chain continuity, they will need to treat inventory more strategically—either by compensating BPS partners to carry it or by changing their manufacturing processes toward more flexible production standards. However, if manufacturers take this approach, they will have to engage in some form of collaborative planning such that the BPS can ensure that drugs reach patients when they need them, even during disasters.

3

Regulatory Trends

INTRODUCTION

Any actions in the biopharmaceutical supply chain (BPS), regardless of their scale, scope, or breadth, are subject to regulatory requirements by various government agencies. Hence, ensuring compliance to the letter of the law remains a particular challenge for companies in the BPS. Not only are such laws changing on a regular basis, but the interpretation of these regulations are also difficult to interpret and are subject to wide variations in what it means to be "compliant." Further, government officials struggle to be able to even explain what these regulations mean. A host of consulting industries has arisen from former government regulators who have found it profitable to take on the task of explaining regulations to participants in the supply chain and defining in specific and measurable terms what it means to comply with these regulations.

A text describing every possible regulatory requirement for the BPS is beyond the scope of this book. Rather, we have attempted here to identify the major regulatory issues that participants in the distribution channel need to be aware of as well as emerging areas of regulation that require monitoring over time. By becoming involved in the legislative process, organizations can help to influence regulations and ensure that they are reasonable and that the cost of compliance is not excessive relative to the potential hazards.

A COMPLEX REGULATORY DISTRIBUTION ENVIRONMENT

Distribution of pharmaceutical and biologic products takes place in a market that is extensively regulated. Untested or adulterated drugs are a significant threat to public safety, so the U.S. Food and Drug Administration (FDA) was created in 1927 to oversee pharmaceutical safety and is among the oldest federal regulatory agencies. FDA regulations form a significant part of the legal environment of the market for pharmaceutical products. Failure to comply with these laws could lead to large fines or imprisonment.* The Prescription Drug Marketing Act (PDMA) of 1988 was enacted to ensure that patients were not victimized by counterfeit, adulterated, misbranded, subpotent, or expired drugs. The integrity of drug distribution in the United States is primarily protected through state licensing laws of wholesalers, pharmacists, and physicians; those who ignore the rules can lose their license to practice. As counterfeiters have become more sophisticated, the FDA has become increasingly receptive to electronic means of establishing pedigree through track-and-trace technologies.

The regulatory control for pharmaceutical marketing and promotion begins with the clinical process. When the FDA approves a drug for commercial sale in the United States, it provides approval based on very specific pathological conditions, otherwise known as indications. The treatment of these indications is proven effective by three phases of controlled clinical testing on animals and subsequently humans. As the approved drug is promoted, pertinent information for prescribers must be contained on the drug's label. The drug "label" specifically describes what indications the drug is approved for and all relevant safety information such as potentially interactive drugs and other medical conditions that might affect the drug's safety or efficacy.

The FDA's Division of Drug Marketing, Advertising, and Communication (DDMAC) is the regulatory arm that oversees the industry's promotional activities. DDMAC approves promotional materials prior to drug launch and provides ongoing surveillance of materials throughout the drug's life cycle. DDMAC also responds to complaints about promotional items and activities (Figure 3.1). DDMAC operates under Title 21 of the

---

* See AUA05, available at http://www.auanet.org/coding/codingtips/oig.cfm, which recounts how TAP Pharmaceuticals was fined nearly $1 billion for conspiring with doctors to bill the government for free samples of Lupron.

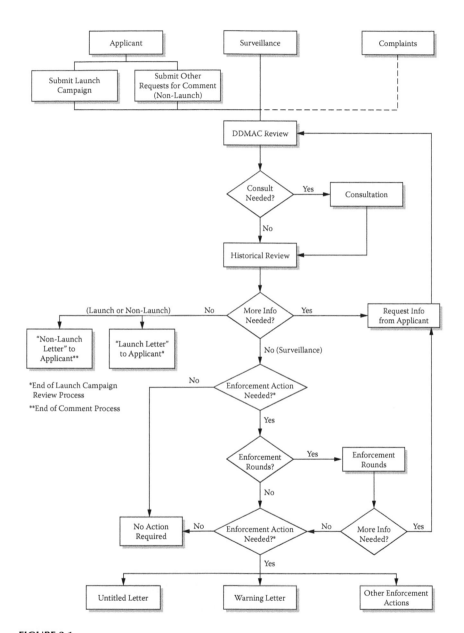

FIGURE 3.1

DDMAC promotional material review process. (From: http://www.fda.gov/cder/handbook/ddmacrev.htm. With permission.)

Code of Federal Regulation (21 CFR). The following sections are specifically enforced by DDMAC:

- 21 CFR 99: Dissemination of Information on Unapproved/New Uses for Marketed Drugs, Biologics, and Devices
- 21 CFR 200: General (Sections 5, 7, and 200)
- 21 CFR 201: Labeling (Sections 10, 100, and 200)
- 21 CFR 202: Prescription Drug Advertising
- 21 CFR 312: Investigational New Drug Applications (Section 7)
- 21 CFR 314: Applications to Market New Drug or Antibiotic (Sections 81, 550, and 560)

REGULATORY ENVIRONMENT FOR WHOLESALERS

Prescription Drug Marketing Act (PDMA) of 1988

Congress passed the PDMA in large part to deal with the problem of counterfeit drugs. Among the basic provisions of the PDMA is a requirement that states license wholesale distributors of prescription drugs. Primary distributors—distributors that have ongoing relationships with manufacturers—are considered *authorized* distributors within the meaning of the PDMA. Under the PDMA, *unauthorized* wholesale distributors are called *secondary* distributors. Before selling a pharmaceutical drug, the PDMA requires secondary distributors to provide purchasers with a statement, also called *pedigree*, identifying each prior sale of the drug so that the purchaser could theoretically trace the product back to its origin. With some exceptions, the PDMA prohibits the sale of prescription drugs that have been purchased by a hospital or other healthcare entity or have been donated or supplied at reduced price to a charitable organization. Relative to unauthorized wholesale distributors, authorized distributors have a significant regulatory advantage in that they do not have to prove pedigree for most of the pharmaceutical products they purchase.

The United States has a comprehensive system of laws, regulations, and enforcement against drug counterfeiting. In recent years there is evidence that drug counterfeiters are increasingly well organized and make use of increasingly sophisticated technologies to profit from counterfeiting. Responding to an emerging threat, the FDA formed a Counterfeit Drug

Task Force (Task Force) in July 2003. Among the conclusions of the Task Force were the following:

- Track-and-trace and product authentication technologies should provide much greater security in the years ahead. The adoption and common use of reliable track-and-trace technology would help secure the integrity of the drug supply chain by providing an accurate drug pedigree (secure record documentation that the drug was manufactured and distributed under safe and secure conditions).
- Relative to paper documentation, radio frequency identification (RFID) tagging was initially identified as a possible reliable means of product tracking and tracing, making copying of medications extremely difficult and unprofitable.
- Authentication technologies (e.g., color-shifting inks, holograms, fingerprints, taggants, or chemical markers embedded in a drug or its label) can be used as a critical component of any strategy to protect products against counterfeiting.
- The FDA envisions continued close cooperation with the states as they license and regulate wholesale drug distributors. The FDA works with the National Association of Boards of Pharmacy to coordinate and refine licensure of wholesale drug distributors. Model rules for state licensing boards make it more difficult for illegitimate wholesalers to become licensed and do business.
- The FDA is recommending increased criminal sanctions against manufacturers and distributors of counterfeit drugs. In addition, the FDA is recommending:
  - Adoption of secure business practices that result in steps that would ensure business partners are legitimate and taking steps to avoid persons of unknown or dubious backgrounds.*
  - Members of the supply chain, producers, distributors, and dispensers should, with assistance of the FDA, draft a set of secure business practices.
  - Procedures should be in place that call for prompt reporting of counterfeit drugs to the FDA.

---

* The Healthcare Distributors Management Association (HDMA) developed a document titled "Recommended Guidelines for Pharmaceutical Distribution System Integrity," which presents some recommended "due diligence" steps that should be taken by prescription drug wholesalers. Available at: http://www.healthcaredistribution.org/gov_affairs/pdf_anti/Guidelines%20for%20 Rx%20Distribution%20System%20Integrity%20FINAL%20Board%20Approved%2011-5-03.pdf

- The FDA intends to work internationally with the World Health Organization to interdict drug counterfeiting at borders of the United States.

Hatch–Waxman Act: The Entry of Biosimilars and Generics

Increasing healthcare cost and reimbursement of high-priced prescription drugs forced payers and the government to closely monitor and control the overall healthcare expenditure bill. Between 1984 and 1990, efforts at cost containment were at the top of legislators' minds. Biologics was in the crosshairs of this effort during this period.

The Drug Price Competition and Patent Term Restoration Act of 1984, referred to as the Hatch–Waxman Act, paved the way for the entry of generic drugs, allowing them to enter the market simply by demonstrating bioequivalence to the innovator drug. This act also gave incentives to branded drugs through a number of exclusivities. This act had major repercussions for the industry around generic drugs. In addition, the act allowed drug formularies to be introduced into managed care. Drug formularies are a list of all the drugs (branded and generics) classified in various tiers based on which reimbursement and copay levels are decided by the payer. Formularies were used by payers from this moment forward as a tool to encourage the use of generics and discourage higher-priced drugs.[*]

As a result of this act, generic substitution rose from 22% in 1985 to 42% in 1994 and close to 60% in 2004. As this occurred, branded companies started to provide discounts, aggressive direct-to-consumer marketing blitzes, and other measures to battle generics, which were for the most part ineffective in controlling the penetration of generics into markets.

Medicare Modernization Act of 2003

In 2003, President George W. Bush signed the Medicare Prescription Drug, Improvement, and Modernization Act (MMA). Of particular interest to BPS participants are recent changes in Medicare B and its impact on oncology and how Medicare D affects regulations regarding distribution of free samples.

---

[*] Wendy H. Schacht and John R. Thomas, "Patent Law and its Application to the Pharmaceutical Industry: An Examination of the Drug Price Competition and Patent Term Restoration Act of 1984," Congressional Research Service, Report for Congress, updated January 10, 2005. Managed Care and a Changing Pharmaceutical Industry, Michael P. Roland, Health Affairs, 1990.

Medicare

There is no question that the problems facing Medicare revolve around the massive increase in costs. Unfortunately, biopharma companies are often quite unfairly blamed for the escalating healthcare costs in the United States. In fact, administrative costs are responsible for between 20 and 31% of U.S. healthcare spending.[*] Another 33% of all expenditures go to hospital spending, and costs for prescription products account for just 10.1%. Yet the public is convinced that pharma are still at the root of all evil; almost two-thirds of respondents polled by the PricewaterhouseCoopers Health Research Institute believe that prescription medicines account for between 40 and 79% of all healthcare costs in the United States.[†]

Changes in Medicare contained in the 2003 MMA were designed to make Medicare more oriented toward prevention and to allow for more compensation for physician services, particularly in oncology. Medicare compensation is still tied to the average selling price, which is updated on a quarterly basis, but other changes, such as lowest cost available (LCA) policies, will exert downward pressure on Medicare compensation for pharmaceutical drugs that are not patient administered. Free sample distribution became the subject of more intense scrutiny under the Medicare Part D law, which began in 2006. A firm is subject to prosecution under federal anti-kickback laws for distributing free samples if it can be shown that the firm stands to benefit from distribution of the free samples by creating a preference for the firm's products among recipients or by being added to a formulary of a pharmacy benefit manager (PBM).

The full impact of the Internet on prescribing and dispensing of pharmaceutical drugs is unknown at present. If state authorities continue to be hostile to Internet prescribing, rules could be declared unconstitutional for interfering with interstate commerce. It seems likely and inevitable that websites and mail-order companies will occupy an increasing market share of wholesaling and retailing in the future because of convenience factors and the increasing percentage of the U.S. population that is computer literate. Legitimate drug dispensing websites are desperately trying to distinguish themselves from the marginally legal and illegal "pill mills." As legitimate websites become distinguishable from those that do

---

[*] Bernasek, Anna, "Health Care Problem? Check the American Psyche," *New York Times*, December 31, 2006, Business Section, p. 3.

[†] PricewaterhouseCoopers Health Research Institute, "Recapturing the Vision; Restoring Trust in the Pharmaceutical Industry by Translating Expectations into Actions," 2006.

not follow the rules, interstate barriers erected by state licensing authorities may collapse as they have in Internet wine and automobile sales. Reimportation of pharmaceutical drugs from Canada will continue as long as there are substantial price differences. Currently Canadian websites are trying to make themselves congruent with U.S. laws, but U.S. Food and Drug Administration (FDA) and Drug Enforcement Administration (DEA) officials are negative toward reimported and other drugs from Canadian websites because compliance with Canadian law does not satisfy the requirements of U.S. law.

At the heart of complaints from small manufacturers about fee-for-service (FFS) contracts is the fact that they are being charged a higher rate by wholesalers to handle their products than for large-volume manufacturers. Volume discounts are a common feature in the U.S. economy and are normally not in violation of the Robinson–Patman Act unless they substantially lessen competition or tend to create monopoly. Also, it is an absolute defense if a seller can show that it is cheaper to service high-volume manufacturers relative to low-volume manufacturers. Additionally, under the Robinson–Patman Act, a purchaser (wholesaler) is not liable for *inducing* price discrimination unless the seller's (manufacturer) prices are also in violation of the act for price discrimination. The chances of a government suit against the wholesalers for violating the Robinson–Patman Act seem remote, but that does not entirely eliminate wholesaler liability under the Robinson–Patman Act. Manufacturers could claim that their FFS contracts with wholesalers are illegal and therefore unenforceable.

Distribution of pharmaceutical drugs is very heavily regulated under the Prescription Drug Marketing Act, and regulatory changes make for legal uncertainty.* One of the most significant legal changes is the Medicare Prescription Drug, Improvement, and Modernization Act of 2003 (MMA).† Changes in Medicare compensation for healthcare providers and manufacturers require cradle-to-grave documentation for free or reduced price samples so that federal anti-kickback statutes are not violated.‡ The regulatory environment for wholesaling pharmaceutical drugs relies heavily on state licensing codes of doctors and pharmacists, but the Internet and direct mail present unprecedented challenges to enforcement. In spite of regulatory obstacles, it seems likely that alternative channels

---

* P.L. 100-293, codified at 21 U.S.C. 301 *et seq.*
† P.L. 109-60, codified at 21 U.S.C. 355 *et seq.*
‡ P.L. No. 99-634, codified at 41 USCS §§ 51 *et seq.*

associated with UPS, FedEx, and other possibly unauthorized wholesalers along with websites will play an increasingly important role in distribution of pharmaceutical products (more on this in Chapter 6).

The other significant legal and technological change has to do with combating counterfeit drugs through pedigree requirements. Pedigree regulations basically require wholesalers to document a paper trail from the manufacturers to healthcare providers. Until now, pedigree regulations have been satisfied through paper records. In the period around 2006–2007, many consulting companies heralded the application of new technologies in the form of radio frequency identification (RFID) tags and other identifying markers as a means of establishing electronic pedigree. After significant investments were made by wholesalers, manufacturers, and others in the supply chain, it became clear that RFID was an infeasible technology that would satisfy the requirements for an electronic pedigree. Some of the problems associated with RFID included the cost, existing technology required to read the tags accurately in a pallet or container, as well as the middleware required to enable tracking and storing of the information and linking it to a pedigree database.

Reimportation

The MMA allows for importation of drugs from Canada by wholesalers and pharmacists under certain conditions, which include a certification by the Secretary of the Department of Health and Human Services (HHS) that reimportation can be accomplished without any additional threat to the public due to counterfeiting and that there will be a significant cost savings. To date the Secretary of the HHS has not made such a determination, but a number of states have passed legislation that implies approval for reimportation. Of course, federal law has priority over state laws when a conflict exists, so the impact of state laws that facilitate reimportation is very questionable.

In the past, Americans took bus trips to Canada to stock up on cheaper Canadian drugs, but more recently reimportation is accomplished through websites that are owned by Canadians but cater to Americans. Most of the drugs obtained from foreign websites are reimported, which means these drugs have been approved by the FDA. In spite of the initial approval of these drugs for commercial sales by the FDA, the DEA has taken the position that reimported drugs are illegal. Similarly, the FDA is of the opinion that non-U.S.-based drugs are unlikely to comply with "the technical information required for domestic approval, such as source of ingredients, place of manufacture, labeling and packaging of containers" (Terry, 2004). Also, reimported drugs comply with the packaging and other requirements of their destination, which is likely to be different from U.S. requirements. There is also fear that drugs purchased from Canadian e-pharmacies may have originated from other (non-U.S.) sources.

By 2003 there were about 150 Canadian e-pharmacies that exported price-controlled drugs to the United States. This source of pharmaceutical drugs has been bolstered by opportunistic politicians in the United States who have passed state laws facilitating reimportation, especially for seniors, at reduced prices.* By and large these drugs are being sold to people who have valid prescriptions from U.S. doctors in traditional patient–physician relationships.

Medicare B: Impact on Oncology

Part B of the Medicare Program is government-sponsored and -administered medical insurance. Among the medical expenses paid for by Medicare Part B are medical and surgical services performed by physicians, durable medical equipment, outpatient hospital services, and independent laboratory services.† New HHS regulations were instituted in 2004, many of which pertained to reimbursement for oncology services. Medicare rule changes were designed to make the program more prevention oriented.

There is clearly a trend here toward squeezing of distribution costs not just in wholesalers but in physician's offices as well. But this has been refuted publicly. According to former CMS administrator Mark B. McClellan, for years Medicare has paid too much for drugs and too little for physicians' services offered to patients as a means to promote healthy lifestyles and refinements in administering these drugs in physicians' offices. These services include payment for staff time to prepare pharmaceuticals and for doctors' supervision of their staff in the preparations. "As a result of the AMA's recommendations, Medicare payment rates for drug administration services were more than 120 percent higher than two years earlier, and physicians will have more opportunities to bill for the administration services they are providing" [CMS04]. In addition, the CMS has made it

---

* Iowa, Illinois, Vermont, and Minnesota have all requested a variance from federal law to set up importation programs from Canada [Te04].
† See http://www.hgsa.com/professionals/refman/chapter2.shtml.

clear that oncologists can bill Medicare separately for managing significant adverse drug reactions related to chemotherapy administration.

In the final regulations, CMS has established new payment rates for most Part B drugs at 106% of the average selling price (ASP), which will be updated on a quarterly basis. Collaboration between CMS and specialty treatment groups in oncology are expected to exert downward pressure on drug prices. Often there are lower-priced generics available even though Medicare continues to compensate at higher rates that reflect prices of branded products. In some states, implementation of low cost alternative (LCA) policies have resulted in much lower prices for cancer-treating drugs when much cheaper generic alternatives were available.*

According to the National Opinion Research Center at the University of Chicago, about 40% of the drugs in the research pipeline are eligible for Medicare Part B coverage based on non-self-administration. The NORC also contends that a large number of biological agents are in the development process and are distinguishable from chemical agents for a number of reasons. Biological agents typically have a wide range of therapeutic relevance and more lengthy FDA approval times, are administered by injection or infusion, and have no real process for approving generic equivalents. There is some evidence of a trend toward physician-administered pharmaceuticals. Manufacturers, however, are seeking to reformulate administration of drugs from doctors' offices to home.

The concept of Medicare payments tied to therapeutic outcomes has gained significant momentum in recent years and has also become a focal point for controversy in many global one-payer government countries in the European Union and Asia Pacific.

Medicare D: Free Samples

Looming, but not yet instituted, is the new Medicare Part D, which provides substantial help to 43 million American seniors in paying for medications (Duke, 2005). According to Elizabeth Duke, administrator of the Health Resources and Services Administration, "The law has created several reimbursement challenges for safety-net providers—healthcare facilities that serve the nation's uninsured and other vulnerable patients."

---

* See Jacqueline Strax, "Lupron Kickbacks Betrayed Prostate Cancer Patient Trust," available at http://psa-rising.com/upfront/lupron-scam-mar01.htm

Beginning January 1, 2006, safety-net providers that participate in the prescription drug-pricing program, which provides low prices on pharmaceutical products, may receive Medicare reimbursement for medications dispensed to beneficiaries as long as the facility contracts as a network pharmacy with a Part D prescription plan sponsor. Vicki Robinson of the HHS Office of Inspector General (OIG) said that many facilities have expressed concern that some beneficiaries will not be able to come up with the out-of-pocket expenses required under Part D (Duke, 2005). Robinson warned that some types of cost-sharing assistance provided by drug companies may be illegal under laws that prohibit giving inducements to beneficiaries. "If the cost-sharing assistance comes directly or indirectly from a drug company that stands to benefit from the beneficiary's use of its drug, the long-standing fraud and abuse laws aimed at preventing kickbacks to the federal health programs may operate to constrain the way in which such drug company assistance was provided."* On the other hand, there is nothing in Medicare or the OIG rules that prevent a drug company from providing free drugs to uninsured patients.

According to Robinson, prior to the passage of the MMA, lawyers enforcing federal anti-kickback laws showed very little interest in patient assistance plans (PAPs) that provided free drugs directly to uninsured patients "because there were no federal program dollars involved." However, the passage of Part D "changed the landscape by creating a new federal healthcare program benefit to which the fraud and abuse laws now apply." Robinson contends that drug companies have a substantial financial interest in influencing decisions pertaining to drugs covered under the program. Under the federal anti-kickback statute, it is unlawful to "buy" federal healthcare program business. If a pharmaceutical firm's purpose for providing free drugs to a health center, hospital, or clinic is to induce more orders for the company's products, including placing the manufacturer's products on a formulary, or to prescribe the company's medication to Medicare beneficiaries, such acts could generate civil and criminal liability, according to Robinson.

Possible Robinson–Patman Liability for Price Discrimination

Depending on how the transaction is viewed, FFS contracts are possibly in violation of the Robinson–Patman Act, which makes illegal some forms of

---

* Such kickbacks would be illegal under the federal anti-kickback statute.

price discrimination.* Price discrimination takes place when sellers offer the same goods at different prices to different buyers and where it can be shown that the effect of such discrimination may be to substantially lessen competition or tend to create a monopoly in any line of commerce. There are two absolute defenses under the Robinson–Patman Act: (1) that the price differences are due to differences in cost; and (2) that the price differences are to meet an equally low price of a competitor. These defenses are absolute in the sense that, even if a seller's discriminatory prices substantially lessen competition, the defendant is not liable if either (1) or (2) can be proved.

It is very unlikely that current FFS contracts would generate a suit by the Federal Trade Commission or the U.S. Department of Justice for violations of the Robinson–Patman Act. If FFS contracts are viewed as the sale of *services* by wholesalers to manufacturers, then the Robinson–Patman Act has no relevance because it does not apply to services, only goods (commodities). In addition, if wholesalers are viewed as *purchasers* of pharmaceutical products and manufacturers as sellers, the U.S. Supreme Court has held that liability for *buyers* under Section 2(f) of the Robinson–Patman Act for "knowingly inducing or receiving discriminatory price" requires a showing that sellers were violating Section 2(a), which prohibits price discrimination by sellers.[†]

On the other hand, the history of the Robinson–Patman Act, passed in 1936, was to correct loopholes in the original Clayton Act of 1914 that allowed large manufacturers (of food) to discriminate in price by differentially offering services to large and small purchasers (Clark, 1995). Although the original Clayton Act of 1914 made price discrimination illegal, when the effect "may be to lessen competition or tend to create monopoly," it created loopholes that could be exploited through discriminatory offerings of services. A large seller trying to skirt the impact of Section 2 of the Clayton Act could offer the same price to all purchasers but could offer free or reduced-price services in a discriminatory manner to large purchasers. Thus, each of the six sections of the Robinson–Patman Act mentions discriminatory or illusory offering of services or access to facilities by sellers, which are, in substance, disguised price cuts.[‡]

---

* The Robinson–Patman Act of 1936 amended Section 2 of the Clayton Act of 1914. The amended Section 2 of the Clayton Act and the Robinson–Patman Act are often used interchangeably.
† *Great Atlantic & Pacific Tea Co. v. FTC*, 440 U.S. 69, 76 (1979).
‡ 15 U.S.C. Section 13(a)—(f).

For example, Section 13(e) prohibits discrimination in the "furnishing of services or facilities for processing, handling, etc."* In addition, Section 13(f) of the Robinson–Patman Act prohibits "knowingly inducing or receiving discriminatory price. It shall be unlawful for any person engaged in commerce, in the course of such commerce, knowingly to induce or receive a discrimination in price which is prohibited by this section."

In the pharmaceutical industry it is the wholesalers that are offering services for sale on a discriminatory basis to sellers or manufacturers of pharmaceutical products. If purchasing drugs and offering the services discussed above are viewed as a single transaction, then wholesalers are paying higher prices (or are offering the same services for lower distribution service provider [DSP] fees) based on the volume of sales, which are facts similar to those that led to the passage of the Robinson–Patman Act of 1936. In effect, the playing field is not level; large-volume manufacturers get price discounts relative to smaller-volume manufacturers. The Robinson–Patman Act was passed so that small retail groceries would have a level playing field with large grocery chains that demanded and received price discounts from food processors and manufacturers that were not received by the mom-and-pop stores. Discriminatory offers of services or access to facilities by large wholesalers to large manufacturers at reduced, or zero, prices appears at least superficially to resemble market conduct that was outlawed by the Robinson–Patman Act. Although a suit by federal antitrust enforcers against large wholesalers appears unlikely, FFS contracts might be ruled illegal in breach of contract suits by wholesalers against small manufacturers. If the contract is ruled illegal under the Robinson–Patman Act or under state unfair trade practices laws, the contract would not be enforced. It is possible that small manufacturers could file for a counterclaim, in a private antitrust action they would have to show that sellers, other manufacturers, had also violated the Robinson–Patman Act.

Other Important Drug Distribution Laws

Under the federal anti-kickback law it is a criminal violation to directly or indirectly make payments or anything of value to induce or reward

---

* At least one law firm [SW04] has rendered an opinion that if Cardinal Health separately enters into agreements with manufacturers to provide distribution services from it buy–sell agreements, it does not incur potential liability under the Robinson–Patman Act.

referral or generation of federal healthcare business.* This statute is a constraint on marketing and promotion of products that are reimbursable by federal healthcare programs (American Urological Association, n.d.). The reach of the anti-kickback statute is broad enough to affect sales, marketing, discounting, and purchaser relations procedures that are common and legal in other industries.

The False Claims Act is violated when a person knowingly presents to the federal government a false or fraudulent claim for payment that makes use of false statements or conspires with others to obtain a false statement or claim paid for by the federal government.† Firms that distribute free samples to physicians knowing that recipient physicians are submitting vouchers to Medicare and Medicaid for reimbursement violate the False Claims Act, as do the physicians. Violations of this sort were present in TAP Pharmaceuticals litigation in which TAP was required to pay $885 million in fines in 2001 to settle charges that it conspired with physicians to bill the government for free samples of Lupron, a treatment for prostate cancer sold by TAP Pharmaceuticals.

LEGISLATION THAT ENDED THE FORWARD-SELLING MODEL FOR WHOLESALERS AND MANUFACTURERS

As noted in Chapter 1, Chris Christie, then-U.S. attorney for the State of New Jersey, was a leader in halting the prior practice of "forward selling" to wholesalers. Forward selling involved the practice of manufacturers selling wholesalers up to a year's worth of inventory and then counting these sales in the current quarter, thereby distorting earnings and sales growth figures. This practice was brought to light by Christie and was challenged by the Securities and Exchange Commission (SEC). Christie gave a presentation on the history of this practice at a conference that took place in Philadelphia in 2005.‡

Christie began by noting that the extent of the "channel stuffing" carried out by Bristol-Myers Squibb (BMS) was massive and amounted to almost $1.8 billion. He also identified the long road that led to this problem and

---

* P.L. 92-603, codified as 42 USC § 1320a-7b(b) (1994).
† P.L. No 92-603, codified as 42 U.S.C. 1320a-7b(b)(1994).
‡ Presentation by Chris Christie, CBI Conference, December 12, 2005, Philadelphia, PA.

the behavior and leadership that enforced it. The end result was a deferred prosecution agreement, which began by having the executives at the company admit all of the facts, including the "sales acceleration" policies, extended postdating of invoices, and other pricing agreements that were used to induce wholesalers to take on more sales in prior periods. The amount of excess occurred from mid-1999 to 2001 over about 8–10 quarterly reporting periods.

There was extreme pressure from the senior leadership team at BMS to *double-double*, a term that referred to the objective of doubling earnings and doubling earnings per share starting beginning in 1994, which translated into driving an average annual growth rate in excess of 10%. The double-double approach began in 1994, continued throughout the 1990s, and was reaching its stated targeted objective of doubling growth toward the end of 1999. The next major growth initiative occurred in September 2000, when management announced the *mega double*—a plan to double year-end 2000 sales by the end of 2005. Instead of taking seven years, the objective was targeted for five years, requiring at least a 15% compounded annual growth per year. This incredible objective driven down by senior management into the ranks is what ultimately caused channel stuffing. There was enormous pressure from the top down to reach sales every quarter *no matter what*. At the same time, the sales organization was enjoying a decade-long winning stream, which dictated that sales members "always hit their numbers," and BMS did not want to place this track record in jeopardy. A culture was promoted that budgeting went only from the top down, and any bottom-up dissent from employees jeopardized their career. No excuses were allowed. In effect, this strategy created a corporate culture that did not encourage truth-tellers, although some people in the organization tried to tell the truth. This culture was pervasive throughout the company, and senior leadership was successful in communicating a clear vision and goal for everyone. There was also no question that people understood the mantra driving the corporate culture engine.

The problem with the strategy and where it started to derail is that the approach ignored the fundamental concept of disclosure or, very simply, telling the truth. BMS executives were stating blatantly false sales numbers on conference calls with analysts and were filing false SEC quarterly reports. Nowhere in these releases was there any hint at all to analysts that excess inventory was involved. In mid-2001 the channel stuffing was discovered but was underreported in the company's amended financial disclosures. After being challenged, executives were asked to release another disclosure error, but they instead had to release two more statements, one that was an internal disclosure and another for investors.

But once the attorney general's office began investigating, other things executive management had done began to surface. Leadership team members manipulated corporate reserves for merger and acquisition purposes. They bled merger reserves into earnings to boost amounts. The New Jersey state attorney's office was familiar with this practice, having seen it at Cendant, which was involved in one of the first major accounting fraud cases. In that case, the president was convicted and served 10 years in prison for merger reserves fraud. BMS was also guilty of selling product to wholesalers, with lag times based on accrual of rebate claims to boost the numbers. All of these actions were inappropriate in the light of a failure to disclose.

In the end, it became clear that channel stuffing was the primary vehicle to manipulate earnings and failure to disclose case. The leadership team not just at BMS but also at other manufacturers proved susceptible to this practice, and even though there were safeguards to prevent it from happening in the SEC structure, senior leaders allowed safeguards to lapse when it butted against the pressure to double-double.

Ultimately, when the state attorney's office became involved, a three-year investigation ensued. The team reviewed 5 million documents and performed countless interviews with both current and former BMS employees. Lawyers in the New Jersey attorney's office worked with the new management team to determine how to make amends and resolve the issue. A deferred prosecution agreement was the result. The office requested that the federal courts defer prosecution on that complaint, with the contemplation that the case be dismissed if the leadership team complied with all elements of the agreement reached with the U.S. attorney's office (which they did). This approach was seen as a justifiable midpoint between walking away versus doing nothing. Christie's goal in this case was a payment to shareholders as a means of making them as close to whole as possible due to the misconduct. The office negotiated a $300 million payment to a shareholder compensation fund to settle class action and SEC action and brought a total of $842 million back to shareholders who owned stock during that time. This was viewed as a significant accomplishment for both investors and employees.

In the end, this was a landmark case that drove all participants in the BPS to rethink their forward-buying and -selling strategies and one that ultimately led wholesalers to adopt an FFS distribution model, which is consistent with most of the compensation distribution models found in other industries.

THE OBAMA HEALTHCARE REFORM ACT

The Healthcare Reform Act passed in 2009 by President Barack Obama is likely to provide healthcare insurance coverage for some 46 million uninsured Americans (15% of the total population). Many of the provisions in the act related more to the insurance industry and included the following issues* (which are still in various stages of debate prior to their rollout at the time of writing of this book):

- Implementing tax credits for health insurance premiums
- Mandating all individuals to carry health insurance
- Mandating firms with more than 50 employees to provide health insurance for employees
- Providing federal financing to states to cover extension of Medicaid
- Closing the Medicare prescription drug "donut hole" coverage gap
- Strengthening provisions to fight fraud, waste, and abuse in Medicare and Medicaid
- Eliminating pay-for-delay, which occurs when brand-name pharmaceutical companies pay their generic competitors to keep their drugs off the market for a period of time—generally seems like a good idea, but one economist says eliminating these payoffs may make it less likely generics will be developed in the first place
- Increasing the threshold for the excise tax on the most expensive health plans
- Broadening the Medicare Hospital Insurance (HI) tax base
- Creating a new Health Insurance Rate Authority
- Invest in community health centers

The reform, in all probability, is likely to expand the revenue basket for providers of medical products and services, including pharmaceutical companies. However, the Obama program also calls for significant cost reductions, which would adversely affect the branded pharmaceutical industry in terms of both discounted pricing and contracted use of branded drugs.

One of the major issues in the act relates to Medicare Part D, which is likely to become the key issue for the branded pharmaceutical industry. Medicare Part D, which relates to prescription drug plans, went into effect

---

* Sources: Which Healthcare Companies Could Benefit From Obama's Government Healthcare Plan? By: iStockAnalyst | Mar 02, 2009, http://www.istock.com.

January 1, 2006. Obama's new legislation is likely to lead to the planned elimination of the noninterference clause in the Medicare Part D prescription drug program, which funds drug coverage for some 44 million elderly Americans. Under the present system, the government is prohibited from engaging in Medicare drug pricing negotiations with pharmaceutical manufacturers. Negotiations are handled strictly by private-sector managed care and pharmacy benefit management firms.

Obama and congressional Democrats favor changing the program to allow or possibly require direct government negotiations with drug manufacturers, which is expected to sharply lower the program's cost. Another likely money-saving tactic will be greater use of inexpensive generics through new incentives.

The outlook for the biotech sector under the Obama administration seems brighter. Increased funding for the FDA and National Institutes of Health (NIH) should help the FDA stay current on science-related research and approve new drugs on schedule and allow the NIH to conduct clinical studies and promote innovative research through new grants. In addition, the Obama administration is expected to support the advancement of embryonic stem-cell research, which may open new avenues to treat serious diseases.

The rise of biologics occurred for diseases where small molecules were not very effective, specifically in oncology and inflammatory diseases. Payers, though initially reluctant, started reimbursing for the higher-cost biologics-based therapy, primarily because they were the only good treatment option for patients with certain disease conditions. As part of the Healthcare Reform Act, Congress helped pave the way for cheaper versions of biologics, often referred to as "follow-on biologics." After a company has had 12 years of exclusivity on a biologic, other companies can produce similar versions of it, known as a *biosimilar*. However, the process involved in producing a biosimilar is more complex than that involved in producing a traditional generic drug.[*] The Pharmaceutical Research and Manufacturers of America (PhARMA), the major trade association for prescription drug companies, was brought to the table for the negotiations. In return for certain protections important to the industry, big pharma publicly supported the measure and made a commitment to provide $80 billion over the next 10 years to help pay for the costs of

---

[*] http://pharma.about.com/od/Government_IP/a/How-Are-Pharma-Companies-Preparing-For-Proposed-Changes-To-U-S-Healthcare.htm

reform. The reform act included greater market protections for the bio-pharmaceutical sector and greatly expanded healthcare access to more Americans—32 million previously uninsured Americans will be enrolled, and 16 million people will be added to the Medicaid rolls.

The drug industry has transformed from a business that tries to sell pills to the masses to one that markets very expensive treatments to small groups of sick people—and that changes previous assumptions about payment from Medicare. The thinking here from recent writers is that the flood of generics is protecting pharmaceutical manufacturers from the healthcare reform debate. Drug costs are only a 10th of healthcare spending anyway, and they are expected to grow at only 2% a year going forward. There is a real possibility sales will shrink.

As noted in *Forbes Magazine*, until last year "...the top-selling category in the industry was cholesterol medicines, which are prescribed 200 million times a year, according to prescription-tracker IMS Health. But they have been surpassed in terms of dollar sales by antipsychotic medicines, which are prescribed just 50 million times a year. An expensive medicine that serves a small population can mint money—and it's pretty tough for even the harshest government system to say no to it."[*]

While the most significant changes to the industry do not take effect until 2014, pharmaceutical companies have begun to change their sales models. Pharmas will be negotiating with more cost-conscious public and private buyers. The reform necessitates that pharmaceutical companies change their marketing techniques to survive. There will be less emphasis on marketing to physicians and key decision makers and more emphasis on reaching other decision makers, such as insurance companies, formulary gatekeepers, pharmacy chains, and physician extenders such as physician assistants and nurse practitioners.[†]

State Licensing Codes

Internet-based prescribing and dispensing are poised to become major components of healthcare delivery in the United States; in 2003, 18% of online households purchased prescription drugs online, and that number has been growing but plateaued at about 22%. Primary regulation of prescribing pharmaceutical drugs lies with the states through their

---

[*] "Why Pharma Wants ObamaCare," Matthew Herper, *Forbes*, August 20, 2009.
[†] Ibid.

licensing of doctors and pharmacists. State licensing boards have sought to restrict and outlaw website prescriptions if there is not a "valid" patient–practitioner relationship. Although some restrictions against "pill mill" websites are certainly justified, state licensing boards are often needlessly negative toward advances in healthcare through Internet technology. Massive imports of pharmaceutical drugs through Canadian websites will continue unabated so long as U.S. patients furnish copies of their prescriptions to Canadian e-pharmacies, and there are huge price differences for identical products across country borders.

E-health businesses that are available because of the Internet can be divided between Internet prescribing, usually accomplished through a survey of the "patient," and Internet dispensing. Internet dispensing, including mail orders, which are increasingly difficult to distinguish from mail-order dispensing, is the fastest-growing segment in the pharmacy industry. Legitimate e-pharmacies, such as Drugstore.com, are desperate to distinguish themselves from rogue websites and are eager to recapture business lost to Canadian pharmacies. Internet dispensing often makes use of electronically transmitted prescriptions that are written by traditional healthcare providers. PBMs are increasingly part of the managed care bundle. Healthcare plans seeking to control costs contract with PBMs such as Medco Health and ExpressScripts to manage fulfillment of patient benefits packages through online pharmacies.

Internet *prescribing* has been attacked by state regulators based on state statutes that require a "proper physician–patient relationship," before a prescription can be written and fulfilled. These regulators contend that an electronic, online, or telephonic evaluation by questionnaire is inadequate for the initial evaluation of a patient or any follow-up evaluation. On the other hand, states do not have jurisdiction or the power to enforce their medical laws against out-of-state and foreign businesses. To stop Internet *prescriptions*, some states make it illegal for an in-state pharmacist to fill a prescription that the pharmacist knows, or should have known, was issued on the basis of an Internet-based or telephonic consultation without a "valid" patient–practitioner relationship.

Direct Mail

Mail-order companies typically buy product from manufacturers or, more commonly, from wholesalers. According to FDA sources, in 1998 mail-order pharmacies accounted for about 11% of total prescription sales to consumers. Most (65%) of the product sold by mail-order pharmacies was obtained from a chain store, warehouse, or another mail-order company and virtually all of the rest (31%) was obtained from wholesalers. According to one mail-order pharmacy, "Mail-order prescriptions work best for ongoing medication and refills. It is a convenient way for your medication delivered to you in the mail."* Mail-order companies increasingly overlap with e-pharmacies and other website medicine. As with websites, mail-order companies dispense drugs to those with prescriptions. Relative to other forms of retail drug dispensing, mail-order companies offer convenience, standing in line at pharmacies is avoided, and in some cases it is more private. Direct mail is also a less expensive vehicle for vendors, sending directly to customers and avoiding several layers of middlemen.

CHALLENGES TO ENFORCEMENT—COUNTERFEIT DRUGS

Virtually all analysts agree that the U.S. pharmaceutical market is freer than most of the rest of the world from counterfeit drugs. On the other hand, a cost of a market that is mostly free of counterfeit drugs is constant vigilance. Counterfeiters are innovative; protection requires the latest in track-and-trace technology. Although there are a number of culprits in the battle for drug integrity, many have pointed to *secondary* wholesalers as the major vulnerability and violators. Drug counterfeiters have been able to:

- Sell their wares, some of which has been stolen (diverted) or obtained by bogus healthcare personnel
- Relabel drugs to hide the fact that these drugs have expired, overstate their strength, or pass off a substance as a pharmaceutical product
- Make use of the Internet to market products that are mislabeled or completely fraudulent

Pedigree requirements are, of course, supposed to counteract the threat of counterfeit drugs to the supply chain. For unauthorized distributors,

---

* http://www.healthcenter.caltech.edu/pharmacy.html

pedigree requirements are satisfied by providing purchasers with a "statement identifying each prior sale, purchase, or trade of such drug." In theory pedigree requirements create a paper trail of the drugs in question back to the manufacturer. Incredibly, FDA pedigree regulations have still not been implemented even though the Pharmaceutical Distribution Management Act (PDMA) was enacted in 1988. Pedigree requirements were enacted in Florida in 2006 and are due to be enacted in California in 2015.

State boards of pharmacy are increasingly demanding paper trails that establish pedigree. Several states including Florida, California, and Nevada have enacted or are implementing state pedigree requirements, typically based on paper records. There is resistance to both paper and electronic pedigree programs from manufacturers, wholesalers, and retailers, especially smaller firms. Among the concerns expressed by participants in the pharmaceutical supply chain is the fear that data sharing may violate confidentiality requirements in their contracts. Also, there is a concern that the compliance burdens of establishing pedigree differentially affect smaller mom-and-pop entities. At least one large retailer, CVS, announced that it will no longer purchase from wholesalers that receive drugs from secondary wholesalers.

In response to the growing menace of counterfeit drugs, the FDA established a task force on this issue. In particular, the task force singled out electronic track-and-trace technology (radio frequency identification [RFID]) as the most promising. This position was later reversed based on the difficulty of implementing RFID. Electronic pedigree "should accomplish and surpass the goals of PDMA and is potentially a more effective solution to tracing the movement of pharmaceuticals than a paper pedigree."

RFID tags are small electronic tags that can be passive or independently powered by batteries. These chips transmit data to readers via wireless data communication. Tag-reader capability enables these items to be identified wherever readers are located in the supply chain. Identification data are then gathered, analyzed, and stored in a database so that the pedigree can be confirmed from the point of origin to the destination. The amount of data gathered through RFID is virtually unlimited and can be encrypted depending on the application need, complexity, and cost of the chip. Use of RFID is widespread in other industries for inventory management, electronic toll collection, and shipping containers.

SUBSEQUENT LEGISLATION IN ANTICOUNTERFEITING AND PEDIGREE: A CASE STUDY

In June 2006, Florida put legislation into effect that a pedigree (either electronic or on paper) has to be provided for the sale of all prescription medications sold to customers in that state. Numerous other states followed suit in the following months and years.

Pedigrees are not required for over-the-counter (OTC) medications. However, an electronic pedigree (e-pedigree) must contain product information ([national drug code] NDC number, lot, expiration) as well as the chain of custody for the product from the manufacturer to the customer. The burden of initiating pedigrees currently falls on distributors. Manufacturers are not required to provide pedigrees upon sale.

Product received from an alternate source (another distributor) must have a pedigree provided to receive the product. Pedigree can be provided electronically or on paper. Today, most are still provided on paper. Pedigrees must include all changes of ownership, including returns.

An organization called Axway's e-pedigree product for storing and transmitting e-pedigrees between business partners was implemented in June 2006. Harvard Pharmaceuticals was one of the first implementations to go live. Axway's e-pedigree product was integrated with Harvard's warehouse management system (WMS) and website to provide an end-to-end e-pedigree solution. The e-pedigree system functions as a repository for pedigrees but does not create the data.

Alternate source is a challenge in pedigree. If you are an authorized distributor of record or an alternate source, you cannot just generate a pedigree. You have to create a pedigree from the original pedigree. Harvard thus had to create exit points within its WMS to match the paper pedigree to an electronic pedigree and send it to customers.

There is not a clear set of guidelines on pedigree formats. In California a pedigree has to be electronic. In Florida, it has to be both paper and electronic. This means having to receive a paper document, append a signature, and then sending outbound both a paper and electronic pedigree. Upon shipment the manufacturer initiates that pedigree, but "marries" a paper pedigree with a profacta pedigree.

The WMS has to be modified in several places to track additional information about inventory and to generate pedigree data for submission to the e-pedigree system. This included import and export data and document-handling systems. Harvard's modifications were accomplished via exit points, which did not involve changing base application logic. The customer website was modified to enable customers to view and print pedigrees for their orders. E-pedigrees were accessed by the website via an HTML.

The system requirements proved to be highly onerous. Harvard added a flag to receipt lines that indicated whether an item required a previous pedigree to be received in. The university added logic to check-in that prevented product from being received if a pedigree was required and no validated pedigrees existed.

Code was also added for receipt putaway that stored pedigree information about the product that was put away, if the item required pedigree tracking (RX items only). Serial numbers are recorded if a pedigree is required to receive product. Age (in days) was recorded for returns.

The company modified allocation logic to enforce pedigree restrictions. These restrictions included:

- Verifying data needed to generate outbound pedigrees exists for product being allocated
- Not allocating product to Florida customers if product was tied to a return pedigree that was returned more than 7 days after purchase
- Applying logic only if item required pedigree tracking

They also codified the closed container process to generate outbound pedigree data files when a container was closed. Inbound pedigree records were updated in first-in, first-out (FIFO) order. A pedigree web interface was used by customer service to apply return pedigrees to previously shipped pedigrees. Product cannot be returned without an existing shipped pedigree.

The Harvard team created a custom program for updating outbound pedigrees when the lot that was shipped did not match the lot of record on pedigree. The existing warehouse management system (Manhattan Associates) had to be modified with "hooks" to pull out data for pedigree. This was bolted on to Manhattan to generate pedigrees. California regulations are coming up in 2015. California pedigree laws have been delayed four times, but even so serialization is being pushed by manufacturers.

There must be a specific method and rigorous framework for the creation of pedigree data. The idea behind a pedigree model is that everyone holds on to the data. The challenge is that many smaller players do not have the capability—so it is being pushed onto manufacturers to maintain that data. Ideally, the pharmacy should maintain a product's pedigree data, but this not realistic. So the manufacturer needs to be able to create and hold the pedigree and make it available to the customer upon request, even three years from today. It will have to maintain that data within its systems (not in an archive system) and be available upon demand.

A number of manufacturers have invested significant amounts of money on RFID and product serialization and have seen little benefit or return from this investment. One company we interviewed noted the following:

> We have a number of contract manufacturing organizations that we are working with. If have to put a unique ID on every bottle of drug, we have a real challenge. This means that we have to get blocks of numbers to contract manufacturers, but we can't let them generate random numbers on their own. So we have to generate the IDs internally, which means we need a centralized way of getting serial numbers to people and companies. But during the manufacturing and packaging process, there is only one point at which you have visibility to the product, which is at the point of manufacture when a product becomes finished goods. And somehow we have to get that data into our system and merge them with our information on packs, pallets, containers, and other logistics systems.... This is an enormous challenge. Serialization started in California, but we are sure this is not just a fad, as others are waiting, and it will sooner or later become a federal mandate.

To make matters worse, pedigree systems are different in Europe and require a system of record outside of the warehouse management system, involving nested serial numbers and encased serial numbers. Once a distributor moves cases from a pallet and it is processed in the system, each and every product on that pallet needs to be scanned.

Arguments have been made that serialization can help promote inventory visibility and tracking. Theoretically, the vendor or manufacturer producing a product would include a serial number data, and once received by the customer it would be scanned and matched against a serial number sent ahead of time. This would assume that there is a high level of control on auditing. But anything less than 100% accuracy could involve fines, destruction of goods, and other major headaches for supply chain participants. The whole concept of serialization and pedigree will remain a challenge for some time to come.

REBATE, PRICING, AND PAYMENT STRUCTURES FOR MEDICAID: A SIGNIFICANT THREAT ON THE HORIZON FOR WHOLESALERS

A complex issue in the BPS is the rebate structure and pricing structure. Again, this is a highly regulated issue that is under increased scrutiny in today's market. This is especially true for reimbursements of Medicaid and Medicare.

The primary issue revolves around the calculation of estimated acquisition costs, which are shown in Figure 3.2. Several key terms are useful to define here:

- Average manufacturer price (AMP): The average unit price paid to manufacturers by wholesalers for drugs distributed to the retail class of trade minus customary prompt pay discounts. The AMP is statutorily defined and calculated from actual sales transactions. Manufacturers must report AMP to CMS quarterly for the Medicaid drug rebate program.
- Average wholesale price (AWP): A price published in national drug pricing compendia issued by private companies such as First Databank and Medi-Span, based on pricing information provided by manufacturers. Its calculation is not defined in statute or regulation. It is generally considered a price for retailers.

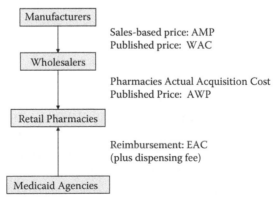

Medicaid Drug Distribution Chain Example

FIGURE 3.2
Relationship of AMP, WAC, and AWP.

- Estimated acquisition cost (EAC): The state Medicaid agency's "best estimate" of the price generally and currently paid by providers for the drug. Within federal parameters, each state establishes its own EAC formula in its state plan. In general, states reimburse pharmacies for drugs at the lower of EAC plus a dispensing fee or the pharmacy's usual and customary charge to the public.
- Multisource brand drugs: Innovator multisource drugs. Brand-name drugs that have generic equivalents.
- National drug code (NDC): The 11-digit code that Medicaid uses to identify unique formulation of each drug, including the manufacturer, strength, and package size.
- Generic drugs: Noninnovator multisource drugs.
- Single-source brand drugs: Single-source drugs. Brand-name drugs that have no generic equivalents
- Wholesale acquisition cost (WAC): A price published in national drug pricing compendia issued by private companies such as First Databank and Medi-Span. It is now statutorily defined as the manufacturer's list price for the drug to wholesalers or direct purchasers in the United States, not including prompt pay or other discounts, rebates, or reductions in price, as reported in wholesale price guides or other publications of drug pricing data.

While states must reasonably reimburse pharmacies for prescription drugs provided to Medicaid beneficiaries, they often lack access to pharmacies' actual market prices. Due to this lack of data, they rely on estimates to determine Medicaid reimbursement. Most states base their calculation of estimated acquisition costs on published AWP, which are the subject of much debate by the OIG, which alleges that Medicaid is paying too much for prescription drugs. Robert A. Vito, regional inspector general for evaluation and inspections in Philadelphia, commented:

> Our analysis comparing actual pharmacy acquisition costs to AWP for calendar year 1999 revealed that pharmacy acquisition costs for brand name and generic drugs were 21.8% and 65.9% below AWP, respectively ... and that the difference between actual acquisition costs and the amount the Medicaid program would have paid using the States' average estimated acquisition cost formulas was $1.5 billion in 1999.

The OIG released two reports[*] in 2005–2006 that further indicate that the published prices Medicaid uses to calculate reimbursement amounts for prescription drugs do not approximate pharmacy acquisition costs. The first report finds that for Medicaid-reimbursed drugs overall AMP was 59% lower than averaged published prices such as AWP and WAC.

Rebates are provided by manufacturers to various entities in the channel, including PBMs and wholesalers as an added incentive to buy their product. This dynamic is changing today. With increasing legislation around drug pricing, transparency is a big issue. In the past, a greater portion of rebates were kept by PBMs. Today, there is more of a migration of rebates passing through to the end payer.

One PBM we interviewed noted:

> We have adopted an above-the-board policy to develop an agreement pass through on all new products, so everyone knows the exact amount of the rebates coming from the manufacturer. We will now pass on 90% of the rebate to customer. We have an open-books policy that allows the payer to come in and audit our contract down to the wholesaler NDC numbers.

Another form of rebates is rebate administration fees. To obtain the goal of positioning a manufacturer's product in second-tier status, rebate arrangements may be made to allow the product to be placed on a second tier instead of a third tier. This is becoming more transparent as the OIG is pushing for increased fraud prevention and abuse legislation.

The OIG study published in June 2005[†] contains some findings that highlight the fact that reimbursements and unbundling of WAC-based reimbursements is inevitable in Medicaid legislation (Figure 3.3). The OIG found in its audits the following key high-level results:

- At the median, AMP is 59% lower than AWP. Forty-nine states use AWP to estimate pharmacy acquisition costs. The median State EAC formula is AWP minus 12%. For 98% of Medicaid-reimbursed NDCs, this median state EAC formula would reimburse at a price higher than AMP.

---

[*] Medicaid Pharmacy—Actual Acquisition Cost of Brand Name Prescription Drug Products (A-06-00-00023) and Medicaid Pharmacy—Actual Acquisition Cost of Generic Prescription Drug Products (A-06-01-00053).

[†] Medicaid Drug Price Comparisons: Average Manufacturer Price to Published Prices, OIG, June 2005, OEI-05-05-00240, Washington, DC.

OIG Audit Report (June 2005)

Table 1 AMP to AWP Comparisons by Drug Category: AMP = AWP − X%			
	Median	Average	Weighted Average
Single Source Brands (3.5 NDC's)	23%	25%	24%
Multisource Brands (2.4 NDCs)	28%	40%	36%
Generics (18 NDC's)	70%	65%	74%

FIGURE 3.3
OIG audit report.

- At the median, AMP is 25% lower than WAC.
- Generic drugs exhibit the largest differences between average manufacturer price and the published prices. For generic drugs, AMP is 70% lower than the AWP at the median.
- For generic drugs, AMP is 40% lower than WAC at the median.

Additional comparisons of OIG audits of ASP to AWP add additional fuel to the fire for control and regulation of reimbursements.[*] The findings of this study suggest the following:

- The median percentage difference between ASP and AWP is 49% (based on 2,077 drug codes). Even when factoring in the discounted AWP most states use to calculated the estimated acquisition cost for Medicaid drugs, ASP is still substantially lower.
- The difference between ASP and AWP was greatest for generic drugs. For 704 single-source brand codes, ASP is 26% below AWP at the median.

The OIG concludes that there is significant interest in changing Medicaid reimbursement for prescription drugs by aligning pharmacy reimbursement more closely with pharmacy acquisition cost. The changes proposed in recent federal policy has made Medicaid reimbursement consistent with Medicare by basing reimbursement on actual sales transactions.

---

[*] Medicaid Drug Price Comparison: Average Sales Price to Average Wholesale Price, OEI-03-05-00200, June, 2005, Washington DC, Office of Inspector General.

IMPACT OF MATERIAL HANDLING LEGISLATION ON PHARMACEUTICAL AND BIOTECH DISTRIBUTION

Cold Chain

The Medicines Control Agency (MCA) of the Department of Health regulates the medicinal products for human use in the United Kingdom on behalf of the UK Licensing Authority. In accordance with Directive 2001/83/EC on wholesale distribution of medicinal products for human use, UK legislation requires that medicinal products are stored, transported, and handled under suitable conditions. Good distribution practice (GDP) requires that storage areas for medicinal products should be maintained within acceptable temperature limits and that products are not subjected to unacceptable degrees of heat or cold during transportation.

Similarly, the United States is driven by United States Pharmacopeia (USP) and FDA regulations such as 21CFR600.15. MCA and FDA inspectors assess compliance with the guidelines of GDP during routine regulatory inspections of licensed premises. It is estimated by the MCA that approximately one-quarter of all discrepancies reported are related to inadequate control or monitoring of storage and transportation temperatures. This can impact not only the efficacy of the supply chain and distributor but also product safety and quality. Products may be subject to recalls as a result.

In the event of a serious breach of GDP guidelines, withdrawal of the license may result. Largely as a result of MCA directives, quality assurance and packaging development staff in Europe are increasingly looking for validated cold chain shippers, which protect the product from physical- and temperature-related damage. The FDA is addressing the increased use of information technology in the life sciences arena with security requirements embodied in 21CFR Part 11. There is a growing use of data gathering (loggers), communications (Internet and mobile technology), and storage and retrieval (data management) as part of cost control and efficiency.

The impacts of Medicare Parts B and D will continue to play an important role in the strategic planning for participants in the biopharmaceutical distribution channel, including manufacturers of oncology medicine, as well as GPOs. Some of the commentary from one of the largest providers of biological oncology products is as follows:

At a recent meeting I attended with three of the largest GPOs representing 5,000-plus hospitals as well as patient groups and industry, significant discussions revolved around the current legislation around Part B. Taking into account the impacts of Part B, most of the reimbursement models have gone to an ASP plus 6% model. It is likely that the hospital outpatient reimbursement will also follow the ASP model, except that you would get an extra 2% for the pharmacists' time. The outcome of the meeting was that everyone agree to sign a joint letter to send to CMS requesting that they reconsider the decision.

Another interesting thing discussed at the meeting was the federal and states' movement toward reimbursement formulas. One of the insurers, BCBS [Blue Cross and Blue Shield] in one of the states, has gone to an ASP model for biopharma. However, ASP is a calculation net of discounts. If we offer a 2% prompt pay to distributor, this would be deducted from the price. This is especially problematic as it is not just a net price but in most cases there is a six-month lag. In some markets, we have seen reimbursement prices tanking while oncologists are seeing price increases. The lag time on reimbursements will always be out of sync with the market, since in many the acquisition price is higher than the reimbursement. Many oncologists' business models are based on the fact that their margins rely on profit from reimbursements on oncology and cancer-treating drugs.

The outcome is that patients will suffer. Oncologists either eat the difference or will refuse to see Medicare patients and refer them to hospitals. This will result in a migration of Medicare patients from physicians' offices to the hospitals. In the case of immune deficient patients, the last place doctors should send them is the hospital. They are far better to be in a home office or a care facility. The current regulations are driving the oncological offices to a point where they cannot afford to administer Medicare patients. So the patient will end up in the hospital, where they will be around patients with other diseases and increase the probability that they can get sick.

This is a direct prediction of Medicare Part B legislation—the forced migration of patients into hospitals. As this occurs, it is inevitable that there will not be enough bed space and not enough product to support the patients. We allocate critical products to our primary customers who have the ability to pay. The primary customers are the private clinics who have private patients who will pay. We produce enough for hospitals but not enough for them to be able to accommodate an influx of Medicare patients. They will not have access to enough product.

We believe that a direct distribution model to patients to allow them to self-infuse product is much more practical. We need to have the product follow the patient.

The Rise of Biologics versus Pharmaceuticals

Biologics work by targeting specific parts of the body's immune system to combat inflammation. They have proven very effective at relieving symptoms and helping people with ailments (such as Crohn's disease) achieve long-term remission. However, in part because the manufacturing process is more complex for biologics than for some other drugs, biologics have a steep price tag. Even people who have health insurance can spend a lot of money on biologics. Virtually all Medicare plans and some commercial health insurance plans put biologics in the "fourth tier" of their drug formularies. Rather than having a copayment, consumers must pay a percentage—typically 25 to 35% of the cost of drugs in this top tier.

This has led to an interesting debate on whether insurance companies will be willing to fund the higher cost of biologics. Some examples include the following:

- Recently approved biologic drug treatments for severe psoriasis cost more than the average annual house payment according to a recently published article (between $170K and $320K) over a 30-year period.[*]
- One year of maintenance treatment with biologics for Crohn's disease can add up to about $20,000.
- A recent study at the University of Toronto discovered that biologics are more effective than methotrexate in achieving a short-term response in juvenile idiopathic arthritis (JIA) patients with prior inadequate responses to disease-modifying antirheumatic drugs (DMARDs); JIA is the most common chronic pediatric rheumatic disease and can have long-term effects leading to disability in adulthood. The study population consisted of polyarticular-course JIA patients with a prior inadequate response or intolerance to DMARDs. However, this comes at a high annual cost, as the biologics in question are much more expensive than DMARDs, and treatments cost in excess of $26K–$44K more than the DMARDs. The study concluded that adequate long-term data with respect to both safety and effectiveness are not currently available, nor are utility estimates. Such data will be important to estimate value for money for treating JIA with biologic drugs over the long term.[†]

---

[*] http://www.natbiocorp.com/mc-biologics-cost-prohibitive.htm
[†] http://www.ncbi.nlm.nih.gov/pubmed/20740607

Why are biologics so costly?[*] There are several reasons listed by researchers.

- **The cost of making them.** Biologic agents are more expensive to make than chemical drugs like DMARDs. The materials needed to create them cost more, and the manufacturing process, which uses live organisms, is more complex.

- **The cost of research and development**. Developed through technology called *genetic modification*, biologics target specific parts of the inflammatory process involved in rheumatoid arthritis (RA) while sparing others. Drug makers say the cost of researching and developing these drugs makes them much more expensive than chemical drugs.

- **Less brand competition**. Because many of the biologics work in different ways to reduce inflammation, they face less competition from similar drugs. As a result, pharmacy benefit managers are not able to negotiate prices for biologics.

- **The way they are given.** Some of the biologics are infused in a rheumatologist's office or infusion center. By contrast, most traditional pharmaceutical drugs are taken by mouth at home. The fact that some biologics are infused also affects the way Medicare reimburses for them.

- **Lack of generics.** When a drug company applies for a patent, it has exclusive rights to make and market the drug during a certain period of time. After that time, other companies can make cheaper generics. All of the current biologics are still under patent protection.

- **Biosimilars versus interchangeable biologic**s: One of the pieces of legislation that is in debate at the moment is the Biologics Price Competition and Innovation Act (BPCIA), which seeks to provide an expedited approval framework for follow-on biologics.[†] This act will in all likelihood inform the final rules the FDA implements, and those rules will determine the business strategies of innovator companies and the extent to which generic companies use the BPCIA.

---

[*] Welch, B. *American Family Physician*, 78 (December 2008), 1406–1408. The Johns Hopkins Arthritis Center, "Rheumatoid Arthritis Treatment," *Arthritis Today*, "Drug Guide: Biologics." Kaiser Health News, "Checking in with Patricia Danzon on the Hot Topic of 'Biologics.'" David I. Weiss, MD, rheumatologist, Arthritis Associates, Hattiesburg, MS. Medicare.gov, "5 Ways to Lower Your Costs During the Coverage Gap," "Help with Medical and Drug Costs."

[†] Adapted from http://www.dlapiper.com/implementing-the-biologics-price-competition-and-innovation-act/

Under the BPCIA, generic biologics can be characterized as "biosimilar" to or "interchangeable" with innovator products. Both require clinical studies for approval, with interchangeability requiring a higher showing. Only those follow-on biologics designated as interchangeable can be automatically substituted by a pharmacy for the innovator's product. As a result, generic companies will have to market biosimilars to boost prescriptions and sales. Thus, when seeking approval, generic companies will weigh the cost of marketing biosimilars against the cost of the yet-to-be-determined clinical testing requirements for interchangeables. If those requirements are too onerous, the generic company may instead choose to pursue a biologic license application (BLA), which has the benefit of circumventing the innovator company's marketing exclusivity.

Patient safety is the biggest concern voiced by both innovator companies and patient advocacy groups, which note that little is known about biologics and any impurities or minor structural or formulation changes could have unanticipated effects for patients.

Another facet of the debate is Congress' intent: to make low-cost generic biologics available to consumers. Congress probably intended something less than full clinical trials for approval of biosimilars and interchangeable biologics. But motivated by patient safety concerns, the FDA is unlikely to implement the minimal requirements that generic companies seek. Ultimately, the FDA rules will likely provide a pathway less onerous than a BLA but more stringent than that advocated by generic companies.

The BPCIA includes a 12-year exclusivity period for innovator biologics to encourage continued innovation. The 12 years of exclusivity applies even if the relevant patents are found invalid or not infringed during the prelaunch litigation procedures of the BPCIA.

Given the time frame for FDA approval of biologics, 12 years of exclusivity may provide more protection than the patent system. But that does not eliminate the need for patents. Generic companies can still file BLAs, and in some situations it may be more economical or advantageous for them to do so. Innovator companies can expect generics to choose an approval pathway based at least in part on the existence of and perceived strength of the relevant patents. The more robust the portfolio, the less likely a generic will pursue a costly BLA and at-risk launch over the BPCIA with its prelaunch litigation process. The FDA's final rules are unlikely to end the debate surrounding the BPCIA. Whatever the rules may be, both innovator and generic companies will have to consider and pursue competitive strategies in the biologics market.

PAY-FOR-PERFORMANCE MANDATES

Perhaps one of the most challenging elements in the regulatory environment for the biopharmaceutical supply chain is the increasing focus on pay-for-performance that is being adopted by insurers and the Center for Medicare and Medicaid. Many of these are being targeted at biologics in particular.

One of the major impacts associated with the high cost of payment for biologics is also taking place in drug development.* The FDA recently approved for sale a new AstraZeneca PLC cardiovascular drug called ticagrelor, which had the potential to be a blockbuster drug. But regulatory approval is just the first step—the second is getting insurance companies and government health systems to pay for the expensive new drug. AstraZeneca, negotiating with U.S. insurers over the coverage of ticagrelor (brand name Bilinta), is faced with slow approval for reimbursement. To do so means assembling whole teams to shower insurers with data that they hope will prove that their drugs are worth paying for. In this case, this means showing that the drug prevents heart attacks, hospitalization, and other expensive problems. Pay for performance also extends back to the clinical trials phase and relates to the problem of understanding how payers look at value. For instance, there is resistance to ticagrelor in Europe, where a rival drug, clopidogrel, is available as a low-cost generic. Both treatments are designed to prevent blood clots, which cause heart attacks, but the generic costs about 3.5 euros versus 24 euros for ticagrelor. French health authorities ruled there was "insufficient evidence" of ticagrelor's benefits over clopidogrel received a preliminary recommendation in the United Kingdom. In Germany, when a company launches a drug, it gets to set the price for the first year, and then a government-appointed committee reviews data and decides whether the drug provides "additional benefit" over an older treatment. If it does, a price is negotiated. If it does not, the new drug gets priced at the level of the older drug.

This policy trend in Germany is likely to spread to other countries, including the United States, in the near future. Companies like AstraZeneca have established "payer excellence academies" to train sales and marketing staff about dealing with insurers and state healthcare systems. They are also signing deals with health insurers, such as Wellpoint, allowing it to analyze how its drugs have performed versus other treatments in the

---

* Jeanne Whalen, "Hurdles Multiply for Latest Drugs," *Wall Street Journal*, August 1, 2011, B1.

36-million-patient base that Wellpoint serves. More of these types of studies will be required for justifying the high cost of drugs in the future to regulators and payers.

―――――

CONCLUSION

The impact of regulation will continue to shape biopharmaceutical manufacturing and distribution in the supply chain. As noted in this chapter, regulation and legislation are impacting every dimension of policy and strategy in the chain, including the following:

- Pricing and reimbursement
- Statement of quarterly profits to the SEC
- Medicare payments
- Internet pharmacies and distribution
- Counterfeiting and e-pedigree requirements including RFID and serialization
- Material handling and cold chain requirements
- Insurance payments
- Pay-for-performance requirements

These regulatory fronts are not the only requirements being set forth for companies in the supply chain but represent some of the most challenging elements with which to contend.

To be able to comply with legislation, a new approach is required—one wherein industry participants need to be included with the federal and state governments as key participants in the supply chain. By creating visibility and transparency into costs, pricing, and requiring rates of return, participants not only can shape these outcomes but also can provide a higher level of care for patients and improved customer service levels, in a manner that will ensure sustainable industry returns.

A higher order of biopharmaceutical innovation focused on network integration will be required. Regulators will become an integral part of the discussion, involving transparency of data, sharing of information, common e-pedigree systems with costs shared by all parties (and ultimately therefore shared by patients), and monitoring systems that will help justify the high cost of emerging biologics through pay-for-performance metrics and ongoing systems of analytics that span not just distribution networks but indeed the entire clinical and commercial process in the manufacturing network as well.

These concepts are explored further in the last chapter of the book.

4

The Last Mile: Changes
in the Hospital Environment
That Impact the Life Sciences

THE HEALTHCARE IMPERATIVE

As noted in earlier chapters, the cost of healthcare is a significant concern not only to governments but also to patients and life sciences companies. This is most acutely felt in the hospital operating environment. Hospitals are facing mandates from local and federal governments to reduce operating costs, improve patient safety, reduce budgets, and cut Medicare reimbursements. This is especially true in many hospitals, which are facing a major problem in profitability. In the current healthcare operating environment, the financial health of hospitals is showing an alarming trend, as operating margins are shrinking at a rapid rate. In the last three years, the median operating margin of hospitals continued a three-year slide to 1.5% in 2008 compared with 2.1%, 2.5%, and 2.8% in 2007, 2006, and 2005, respectively[*]: In 2008, 29% of hospitals lost money on operations. Finally, according to new statistics from the American Hospital Association, the nation's 5,010 nonfederal community hospitals posted a $17 billion overall profit in fiscal 2008, down 61% from the previous year, amid a punishing recession that caused a $20.5 billion reversal in hospitals' investment portfolios.

---

[*] Evans, Melanie. "Moody's Report Shows Margins Slid in 2008," *Modern Healthcare*.

In light of these alarming facts, healthcare system chief executive officers (CEOs) are recognizing that a new operating model comprising a new set of competencies is required to be successful in the marketplace. Faced with a need to improve operating margin, there are three possible options for CEOs: (1) increase revenue through service line expansion; (2) reduce nonclinical or clinical full-time employees to cut payroll costs; or (3) understand supply chain cost drivers and optimize spending on external labor and supplies in medical and non-medical-related areas.

For more progressive healthcare providers and hospital systems, the latter category has become a key focus area for mitigating risk and improving operating margin. While many companies have sought to target reduction in prices paid through volume leveraging agreements with group purchasing organizations (GPOs), the fact is that many of the costs associated with sourcing services and high-cost technologies do not lie in the realm of volume leveraging.

One of the major areas for targeting improvements is in biological and pharmaceutical distribution, a major portion of hospitals' budgets. There are two major trends that will influence the profitability and cost-effectiveness of hospitals in the coming years: pharmaceutical replenishment systems that exploit automated barcode technologies, and creation of electronic records that will link to pay-for-performance and personalized medicine in the healthcare environment. Research conducted in developing this book shows that hospitals that engage in medical dispensing technologies have the potential, over a five-year period, to realize significant benefits that will contribute to meeting these mandates. This is an important step function that will form the foundation for the longer-term trend, the move to personalized medicine.

The combination of automated dispensing (AD) and system-based replenishment has been demonstrated to provide significant benefits over time to leading hospital pharmacies. The link to personalized medicine through electronic health records is a much more complex issue that will take place in the long term but that hospitals need to begin thinking about today. A framework identifying the journey toward hospital biopharmaceutical supply chain integration will be introduced, which illustrates the core elements required to develop a closed-loop distribution channel that minimizes trade-offs, reduces the likelihood of medication error, improves pharmacy inventory and productivity, and provides significant improvements in nursing and patient satisfaction levels.

PATIENT SAFETY AND TOTAL COST OF PATIENT CARE

Hospitals in the United States and Canada are under intense pressure from many fronts. These pressures often seem to conflict: how can a hospital management staff simultaneously reduce operating costs, eliminate medication errors, improve patient satisfaction, and retain their staff and improve productivity? Given the challenge involved in meeting all of these objectives, hospitals are now turning to third-party distributors for assistance. Consider the following:

- The Institute for HealthCare Improvement estimates the United States could cut 15 to 30% of its $1.4 trillion annual healthcare tab by operating more efficiently and improving quality. Eliminating medical errors alone would save $37.6 billion according to the Institute of Medicine. Medication errors are the most common mishap, and each may add more than $2,000 to the cost of hospitalization, translating to approximately $2 billion in annual spending nationally. Pharmaceutical costs are the highest line-item expense on any hospital's budget, but with the myriad failure points that exist, operational inefficiencies can create significant costs and waste.[*]
- St. Joseph's Hospital in Wisconsin recently hired a local accounting firm to install a hotline for staff to anonymously report medical errors and near misses, either their own or those of colleagues. Before the system was installed, the hospital collected 250 reports per month. Afterward, the number shot up to 3,000 a month. The cases confirmed what St. Joseph's had suspected: the hospital was not adequately addressing safety issues.[†]

The Patient Safety and Quality Improvement Act, signed into law by President George W. Bush in July 2006, allows doctors and nurses to report medical errors voluntarily and confidentially. Chief financial officers at hospitals are also demanding cost reductions, especially in medication costs for in-patient pharmacies. As one pharmacist interviewed

---

[*] Lewis, Russell, "Dockside to Bedside: A New Paradigm for Health System Medication Management," http://www.hctmProject.com
[†] 'Naik, Gautam, "To Reduce Errors, Hospitals Prescribe Innovative Designs," *Wall Street Journal*, May 8, 2006, p. A1.

noted, "Ideally we could save money on drugs by not buying them at all, but this would impact our patients' health and their rate of survival."

Insurance companies are also taking a tougher safety stance. Many health maintenance organizations, as well as Medicare, now refuse to reimburse doctors for certain procedures, and some insurers are granting easier patient access to hospitals' records of medical mishaps. More state legislatures are also mandating that hospital pharmacy records be kept for a minimum of three years, which includes a physician's signature on the scrip. Customer word-of-mouth is also driving patients to seek care in preferred hospitals. And with the advent of electronic health records passed in President Barack Obama's Healthcare Reform Act, the need to begin thinking about how to link patient outcomes to prescribed drugs and procedures will become increasingly important for hospitals to be paid for their services. And the movement toward pay-for-performance based on the efficacy of drugs and biomarkers will have a major impact on the development and distribution models in existence today and will no doubt drive massive change.

The other issue that impacts this discussion is the nursing shortage, which is reaching epidemic proportions. The need to provide a satisfactory work environment for nurses is becoming a critical element to reduce turnover and avoid temporary agency costs and nurse absences.

THE ROOT CAUSE: MULTIPLE HANDOFFS

Hospital pharmacies are now recognized as playing a key role in addressing these challenges. Not only are pharmaceutical costs at the top of hospitals' budgets, but they are also the number one problem resulting in medication errors that occur from the loading dock to the bedside—including central receiving, in the pharmacy, during distribution, at the point of administration, in charge capture and billing, as well as the analysis of clinical outcomes.

The number of handoffs that occur in the delivery of drugs has long been viewed as the "Bermuda Triangle" of healthcare. Dangerous errors and oversights can occur in physician order entry, dispensation, administration, and monitoring of the dose. Now, with growing evidence that communication breakdowns during such transfers are one of the single largest sources of medical errors, the Joint Commission on Accreditation of Health Care Organizations is requiring hospitals to establish standards for handoff communications—and break down long-standing cultural barriers among doctors, nurses, and pharmacists. "A hand-off is a precision maneuver, but in medicine, it has been left to happenstance," says Richard Frankel, a professor of medicine at Indiana University who is working on safety programs with the U.S. Department of Veterans Affairs (VA) medical center in Indianapolis.[*]

The most often bungled handoffs occur when a patient gets a dose of a drug that was already administered on a previous shift, or a nurse fails to administer a drug due to a stockout, or a nurse inserts a med into the wrong automated dispensing drawer. To address these problems, hospitals are seeking ways to reduce errors through improved standardization, automation, and fail-safe processes. This is an especially critical element for hospitals that are using computerized pharmaceutical order entry (CPOE) systems. A CPOE is an electronic system that captures a patient's prescription from the attending physician and keeps an electronic record linked to the dosage, frequency, and type of medication the patient needs to take, which is linked to dispensing stations and the central pharmacy electronically.

If the root cause of many hospital costs and medication errors is handoffs, how can hospitals address this issue while accommodating the challenges associated with maintaining customer satisfaction, improving pharmacy inventory turns, and reducing nurse turnover? Is there a magic bullet?

Of course, there is no such single solution. Hospitals have readily adopted the introduction of automated medication lockers and CPOE systems, which were heralded as a new era for hospital pharmacies. However, recent evidence suggests that the successful adoption of CPOE technology will also require some fundamental changes in the philosophy and structure of medical distribution.[†] Moreover, it is now clear that such systems must be accompanied by a fundamentally different set of business process redesign initiatives, driven by associate training, change management, and a roadmap for deployment.

---

[*] Landro, Laura, "Hospitals Combat Errors at the 'Hand-off,'" *Wall Street Journal,* June 28, 2006, D1.
[†] Pedersen, Craig, Schneider, Philip, and Scheckelhoff, Douglas, "American Society of Health System Pharmacies National Survey of Pharmacy Practice in Hospital Settings: Dispensing and Administration—2005), *American Journal of Health-Syst Phar,* 63 (February 15, 2006).

Life before Automated Pharmaceutical Dispensing

Prior to automated dispensing, filling a cart and picking medicines was the only way to distribute medicines to patients. This labor-intensive approach is still used in many hospitals today, especially in remote parts of the country. Medicines were stored in robots (central pharmacy automation units) that filled each nurse's cart. Many hospitals already suffered from staffing shortages, so they initially welcomed early technology that filled carts automatically and reduced headcount. An alternative technology was a robotic carousel that spun and then dropped meds into bins that were put onto carts. This approach was known as a *centralized* approach, since all meds were dispensed from a central robotic automation unit.

Automated Dispensing Market Penetration

The rise of automated dispensing was the development of a new technology called Pyxis, an automated dispensing cabinet manufacturer acquired by one of the largest wholesalers, CareFusion Health, in 2003. CareFusion made this acquisition with a vision to develop an end-to-end supply chain solution. Pyxis hit the market with a decentralized vision that at its core emphasized the need to store drugs closer to the patient bedside. These cabinets were deployed on each floor of a hospital that serviced beds within a pod. The technology was intended to fill medications: the physician would write the order, the order was entered into a patient profile system, the medications were delivered to the medical station, and the nurse pulled the meds and filled patient orders out of the med station rather than having to fill up a cart.

The decentralized model developed by CareFusion with its Pyxis machines changed the centralized model. Most hospitals using a centralized robotic system today recognize that these approaches are not cost-efficient. For example, many hospitals such as William Beaumont in Michigan have decommissioned robots:

> The American Society of Hospital Pharmacists (ASHP) supports the use of automated devices when it frees pharmacists from labor-intensive distributive functions, helps pharmacists provide pharmaceutical care, and improves the accuracy and timeliness of distributive functions.... When automated devices are not used appropriately, their complexity, design and function variations, maintenance requirements, staff-training

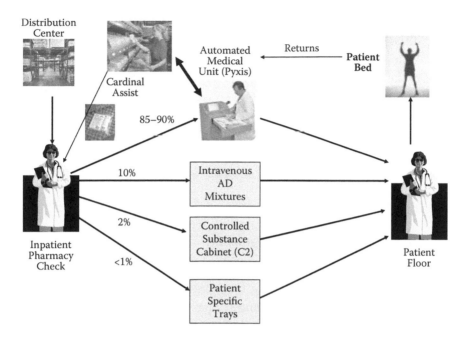

FIGURE 4.1
Route of patient medications in the channel.

requirements, and other factors can have undesirable effects and compromise patient safety.*

This ASHP study also found that automated dispensing units are used by 72% of hospitals and robots by 15%. The use of centralized systems is declining, from 80% in 2002, to 74% in 2005, and projected to be 50% in the future.

Prior to automated dispensing (AD), all doses were delivered via patient specific trays (nurses walking around and handing out cups of pills.) The technology changed the way meds are distributed to the floors and established a foothold as the technology leader for decentralized automation. The goal was to deliver 80–90% of doses closer to the bedside, improve patient safety, increase nurse safety and improve convenience.

In an AD environment, automated medical units (AMUs) permit about 85% of the fastest-moving medications to be delivered in an automated fashion (see Figure 4.1). The remaining dispensations include intravenous

---

* ASHP Guidelines on the Safe Use of Automated Medication Storage and Distribution Devices, *Am J Health-Syst Pharm*, 55 (1998), 1403–7.

AD mixtures 10%, controlled substances (2%), and patient-specific trays (1%). This created efficiencies for an in-patient pharmacy and allowed pharmacies to reduce the number of pharmacy technicians to fill patient trays, make adjustments, and deal with returns coming back from patients. The key components in an AD system consist of the following:

- A communication hub
- Profile of patient medicines required
- Scanner verification for med stations, which automates the pick process for a central pharmacy

Limitations to Automated Dispensing

AD allows approximately 70% of doses to be delivered the first time onto patient trays early in the morning for nurses on their rounds. All other meds are completed out of the central pharmacy. But many nurses and pharmacists new to the technology do not fully understand how to deploy it effectively and are unable to move beyond the 70% ceiling for dispensation. As one pharmacist noted:

> This is the way I was trained out of pharmacy school—nurses like it that way and didn't adopt the technology and were given no clear message on how to optimize it. I think that part of the sales cycle requires that wholesalers approach the customer to sell capital equipment.

To understand the challenges associated with using AD and manual replenishment, consider the typical drug use process. A paper order is issued by a physician—one goes to the pharmacy and one to the nurse and one stays with the patient. The pharmacy picks up the order, types the order into the pharmacy system, which interfaces with an AD machine using the patient profile, and fills the order; the nurse picks it up, matches it to the chart, and dispenses the drug. On manual dispensing units, the machine is just a box, effectively a drug storage unit. With an interface to a patient profile system, however, the system is linked into the patient's orders. During this manual process, there are multiple data entry points that create opportunities for errors.

The value proposition for installing an automated dispensing machine is fundamentally based on improving staff use. Medications can be delivered to the pharmacy, inspected by the pharmacist, and then filled into the medical stations as required. Even though med stations are still replenished two to three times per day because of stockouts, there are labor savings because a pharmacy tech is able to do this job, not a pharmacist (who is paid a higher salary). One problem with a stand-alone dispensing machine is that it is still labor intensive without a solid supporting infrastructure for pharmaceutical inventory management. There is also a disconnect in terms of roles: the pharmacy owns logistics—but nurses owned the stations. Adoption of the systems requires the chief nursing officer's approval as it creates changes in nursing staff skills for trays.

THE RACE TO THE BEDSIDE

The limitations to AD equipment revealed an important challenge for hospitals: nurses owned the product flow to the patient from the cart to the patient, and pharmacies had to design their systems to accommodate the reality of this fact. The true supply chain unit of analysis is no longer simply to the AD machine—it requires that wholesalers think about extending their reach all the way to the patient's bedside. "The race to the bedside" (pharmacy floor to patient) led to the development of automated inventory management systems for hospital pharmacies. The most prominent system was one also developed by CareFusion designed to work with its Pyxis machines, called auto-replenishment. This system was the product of leading thinkers who worked in the field of hospital pharmacy.

The Genesis of an Idea

In a back alley behind a bar after an ASHP meeting, a group of hospital pharmacists who were close friends began to talk among themselves about the challenges they faced in getting to the bedside. The pharmacists, being dedicated to patient satisfaction, asked a simple question: "Why are we spending so much time checking shipments, ordering drugs, and doing transactional work? As pharmacists, they knew they should be spending their time where they were best needed: doing clinical interventions. This line of thinking led them to a simple idea: what if it were possible to automate the ordering and replenishment of drugs into AD machines and bridge the gap between the machine and the bedside? This led to an ongoing set of discussions, several pilot programs in University of California hospitals, and an ongoing set of user group meetings around this new innovation.

The primary driver leading this group of pioneers to explore was described by one of the individuals, Rich Mendebril from Seton Hospital in California:

> Nurses don't care about logistics—they just want the product to serve the patient, with the least amount of paperwork as quickly as possible. When nurses have a scheduled administration at 9 a.m., they simply want the product available and want a simple way to capture the transaction with no stock outs. This was the true benefit of automated dispensing: it satisfied nursing level needs but was not connected with distribution and management. This is where the inventory management technology became married to the machine, in an effort to drive first-dose delivery to 85–90%. If our nurses weren't happy, then the patient wasn't happy. So automated replenishment was something that we came up with that nurses didn't ever know or care about but that ensured that they always had the right drugs when they needed them, reduced the probability of making medication errors significantly, and made their lives easier.

Although automated replenishment started out as an idea, it quickly grew into a fully deployed integrated supply chain system for serving hospitals around the country.

Automated Replenishment

Although automated dispensing automates the distribution, tracking, management, and security of medications, there are several challenges associated with this approach: managing inventory expenses; labor involved in refilling stations; station configuration; optimization of stocking and reducing stockouts; and, most importantly, opportunities to reduce handoffs that result in medication errors. Automated replenishment systems were designed to address this gap, by providing full functionality in generating reports to optimize inventory levels and minimize stockouts. The first ASSIST system was conceived by and developed by hospital pharmacists, who sought a system to manage the size and frequency of replenishments and truly understood the needs of a hospital pharmacy. Hospital pharmacies that learn to exploit the full functionality of automated replenishment systems discovered that they could increase the use (percent of formulary going through the system) of their hospital and derive significant benefits.

Specifically, hospital pharmacies I studied that used automated replenishment at mature levels realized:

- Improved inventory turns from 8 (6 weeks of stock) to 24 (2 weeks of stock on hand)
- Reduced picking of medications from 600 per day to less than 80 per day
- Reduced medication picking errors of 7 per day to less than 0.5 per day
- Reduced stockouts from more than 200 per day to less than 30 per month

These benefits have a significant impact on the total cost of patient care.

Although there is a defined learning curve for pharmacists who introduce automated replenishment, many of the pharmacists who have successfully deployed the system declare that they would never return to a manual system.

THE JOURNEY TOWARD AUTOMATED PHARMACEUTICAL DISTRIBUTION

In my research I identified three phases of maturity as hospitals begin with the introduction of automated dispensing and automated replenishment into their hospital pharmacies. This maturity is not a function of simple automation but of improved process efficiency, reduced numbers of handoffs, organizational learning, and exploiting the true reporting features of systems technology to improve hospital pharmacy operations.

Phase 0: Preautomation

Prior to implementation of automated replenishment, many hospitals were using dispensing machines as a means to store medications. Many hospitals have multiple dispensing machines, and the most common approach to improving stockouts in these cases is largely by increasing the number of machines. However, these hospitals are still very much in

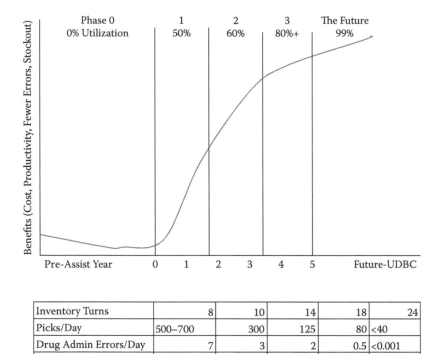

	Pre-Assist Year	1	2	3	4	5
Inventory Turns		8	10	14	18	24
Picks/Day	500–700		300	125	80	<40
Drug Admin Errors/Day		7	3	2	0.5	<0.001
Stockouts/month	>200		90	60	30	<1

FIGURE 4.2
Phases of automation.

a manual materials mode. The journey to hospital distribution maturity begins with hospitals that are in an early crisis mode. Although many hospitals (less than 2,000) have adopted dispensing machines, many have not experienced the benefits of optimizing the inventory of this equipment. A number of hospitals have recognized that they have failed to achieve the predicted benefits of the technology and indeed in some cases have begun to witness deteriorating performance in their efforts to improve productivity and efficiency. This has occurred not so much because of problems with the technology but because of the increasing complexity and demands placed on hospital staff, with little room for additional resources and personnel to deal with these issues. People are working harder and longer in the pharmacy but are spending much of their time receiving and inspecting and performing multiple pharmacy pulls and fills during the day (in some cases on multiple shifts) and have less time to spend on clinical interventions. Hospital pharmacies in these scenarios face the

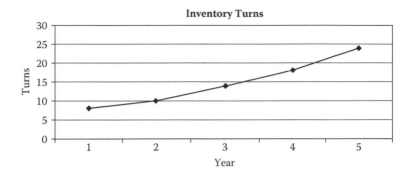

FIGURE 4.3
Inventory turns.

challenge of optimizing the pharmacists' time with patients instead of having to do multiple checks on inbound shipments of medications.

In a pre-auto-replenishment scenario, our research suggests that it is not uncommon for a hospital of 300 or more beds to experience very low inventory turns (less than 8 turns per year, or the equivalent of 45 days of inventory on hand), upward of 500–700 picks per day, and multiple stockouts. Predictably, medical errors are not uncommon due to the large number of handoffs and clerical work involved in a long working day.

Phase 1: Implementation of Auto-replenishment

The immediate benefit upon implementation of auto-replenishment is a drop in the number of picks that occurs. One Phase 1 hospital noted:

> In the past, I had to have people to do night and evening work filling machines. Previously we had two shifts, each doing 300 fills per shift. It would take about 3 hours per shift for pharmacists to check the fills in the morning and another 1.5 hours for the evening shift. Now [September 2005] we are up to 320 fills just in the morning and have completely eliminated the evening shift. Now we are just stocking the stockouts—and daytime I am using the techs to do stockout management, cleaning up—a value-added system for our nurses. We used to fill over 600 line items per day. At our peak, we filled about 400 line items during the day and in the evening about 270 line items—close to 700 line items per day. With auto-replenishment we are now down to 200–300 fills per day, which is a great improvement.
> Over 13 years ago, we put in machines; it was the original pilot site. At the time, nurses and pharmacists resisted the change, although now they love

it. When we put in auto-replenishment, they complained at first, and now it is just part of their daily workflow.

This same hospital noted the following pattern in the reduction of picks per day that occurred after deployment.

Month	Year	Phase	Picks per Day
December	1	Pre-auto-replenishment	700
November	2	Auto-replenishment implemented	550
March	3	Auto-replenishment working	420
December	3	Auto-replenishment functioning	400

Another area that auto-replenishment impacted in the early stages was stockouts. Auto-replenishment provides greater visibility and insights into stockouts as opposed to earlier systems and brings major issues to the forefront. As one pharmacist noted:

We never got a chance to measure stockouts in the past—issues such as manufacturing back orders, and others—difficult to measure. One gram of sulfazonin was out for a full year! Zosin was also on back order for a full year. These high-usage meds jumped right out at us, but it also allowed us to examine more closely their cohorts. As a result of auto-replenishment, we were able to cut back significantly the amount of time we spent on analyzing and managing stockouts. With auto-replenishment's reporting inventory management system, we can assess how much we have and if we have too much inventory of a given item. In the past, we didn't actually look at what you had on the shelf, now we can pull information and find out how much we stock. I have been tracking this number since 2002. Inventory turns was really bad. In May 2005 our turns were less than 10. With auto-mated dispensing we couldn't tell. The main pharmacy turns was really bad, but we couldn't tell exactly what they were. We are up to 12 turns now, which is marginally better, but need to do more to optimize the system.

Auto-replenishment also helped us to track the number of errors over periods of time. In September 2002 we had 189 in one month or about 6 errors per day. This was in large part because we were picking 600 instead of 450. We had about an average of about 56 errors per month or about 2 per day, and these were only picking errors. In October 2002 we had 220 errors per month and 158 in December.

As pharmacies begin to see improvements in these areas, they move to the next phase of improvement, which involves optimizing auto-replenishment and exploiting the reporting capabilities.

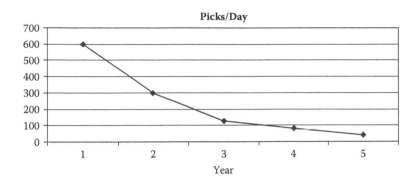

FIGURE 4.4
Picks per day.

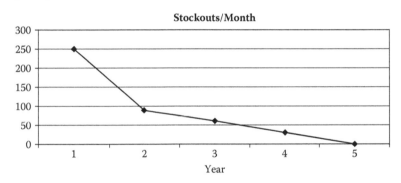

FIGURE 4.5
Stockouts per month.

Phase 2: Early Integration

Phase 2 companies have implemented auto-replenishment and are beginning to understand some of the critical weak points in their distribution system. As technician time is freed up, people can begin to better understand the reporting capabilities, and picking efficiencies begin to increase. Predictably, with fewer handoffs, errors also continue to fall. Hospital pharmacies that reach Phase 2 begin to see the benefits of auto-replenishment not simply in inventory benefits but also in operational efficiencies and improved nurse and customer satisfaction:

> We saw filling errors drop like a stone with auto-replenishment. We were not picking 75% less than in pre-auto-replenishment periods. In fact, we were challenged a couple of months ago by our finance officer and asked to justify the costs of what we were paying for the technology (approximately

$75K per year based on our profile). My response was simply—if we eliminated auto-replenishment we could afford to hire one pharmacy tech per day extra on a shift—and at this point if we went back to a manual system, we could no longer provide the same service levels even with the extra tech. And the system doesn't call in sick.

In general, hospitals in Phase 2 understand very quickly that if you pull fewer meds accuracy increases exponentially. Also, nurses experience fewer stockouts, simply because med replenishment is driven by what nurses are using directly via auto-replenishment.

Hospitals at this phase are also better able to manage their low turnover items:

> We are starting to look at things that are not used as well as those that are used too frequently and work on inventory max and min levels to reflect what we want to come in. Our techs are very conscientious and understand that the min should be low enough to do a quick count. If you boost your max level, it won't help you if you don't do cycle counts.
>
> Clinical interventions are out of the central area. We are doing more things with the same numbers of techs. As a matter of fact, we have increased the number of machines by one-third but not the staff.
>
> Auto-replenishment allowed us to make a big inventory reduction that offset reductions in drug budgets, and we have generated over $20M in inventory savings. Some of our areas at 18 turns, but none of our areas are lower than 12 to 14. We are at 12.73 turns for inpatient areas, and turns at other stations are at 23, 20, 16, and 5. The latter is the operating room pharmacy, since we need to stock what the surgeons prefer there and it can never be out of stock.

One Phase 2 hospital pharmacy experienced the following improvement levels:

- Program cost: $53,740 per year
- Savings:
  - Inventory reduction (02-04) $392,486
  - Carrying cost reduction (8%) $31,399 per year
  - Labor redeployment $87,600
  - Wholesaler delivery reduction $49,255

Clearly, the benefits of auto-replenishment were being seen with increased maturity and growth of the system. However, many companies

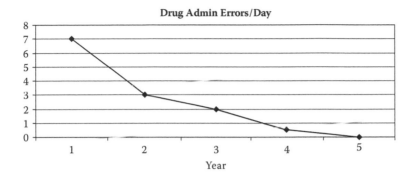

FIGURE 4.6
Drug administration errors per day.

in Phase 2 have not yet exploited the true reach of auto-replenishment by adding on the ParX inventory management system.

Phase 3: Auto-replenishment Integration

Exploiting the full capabilities of integrated auto-replenishment, automated dispensing, and multihospital integration is a major stepping stone in impacting total patient cost.

When several hospitals systems are combined with auto-replenishment, this represents the most powerful use of inventory replenishment automation. These systems are based on a simple hypothesis—stockouts can be eliminated through ongoing monitoring of usage patterns and development of automatically generated minimum and maximum inventory levels and reorder points. Automated systems can be programmed to automatically calculate inventory replenishment levels based on actual usage patterns over time. This allows users to override the recommendations but provides excellent guidelines for almost eliminating stockouts altogether while reducing pick times to lower levels. Additional benefits in inventory management and hospital efficiency continue to occur. As noted earlier, auto-replenishment can significantly reduce inventory and take it down from levels of two weeks' supply to two days' supply on the shelf. Further, auto-replenishment can cut down the cycle time from ordering to replenishment. In a typical hospital, it takes four hours from pharmacy dispensation to nurse administration. With auto-replenishment, this can be cut down to less than 30 minutes. One technician interviewed noted that he spends about 1.5 hours once a day filling the machines using the auto-replenishment deliveries compared with six times a day for the similar facility with no auto-replenishment. A recent 2012 interview with a CareFusion executive provided insights into the challenges that exist.

John Sobie, former vice president of marketing for CareFusion for the Pyxis business, was interviewed for this book and shared his thoughts on the progression of the Pyxis technology in 2012.*

> Through the late 90s, all of the focus in healthcare systems was on Y2K readiness, and then it became about medical administration errors and safety first. There was never much emphasis on the waste factors and the supply side of throughput and volume. In 2004, Pyxis had a technology advantage, but they didn't even know it! They had developed a bedside barcode administration device that closed the loop called "Verify" in the 1998–2004 period. Pyxis Verify could dispense medications, and have the caregiver scan the wristband on the patient and verify that it was the correct medication. This technology was ahead of its time. It was a bedside unit that provided incredible cost savings advantages. Unfortunately, Verify went by the wayside. Countless other innovations during this period including the smart generation of Cubie drawers, went out the window, and with that the emphasis on supply faded.
>
> Looking back, we went through Y2K, then the "do no harm" period, the "med prevention error" period, and are now back to the verification at the bedside (back where we were in 2004!). However to truly exploit the advantages of automated dispensing, you have to go whole hog. Once you do decide to automate supply, the total cost savings numbers are real! The West Coast hospitals in San Diego have deployed Pyxis in every location. It takes fortitude to put in wall-to-wall automation like this, as it involves grabbing all of the elements at once and putting it near the bedside. But with this type of automation, you can take out a box of bandages, and it is charged back to the patient automatically. The key is knowing what to put into the cabinets that makes sense—you don't put in cotton balls! You need to track the right end of the spectrum.
>
> Another huge innovation that Pyxis developed was the Jitterbug. This is a battery-powered radio frequency transmitter that is no larger than a gum-sized package. Once assigned to a specific device to a specific bin or location, every press of the button sends a signal that an item has been used. It can be used in an open shelf situation or in conjunction with a cabinet. You can use it for low, medium and high security solutions and you can do it for 20% of the cost of the barcode system.

---

* John Sobie, phone interview, February 2, 2012. Sobie was VP of Marketing at CareFusion until October 2010. He spent 18 years working in marketing for the Pyxis division at Cardinal Health, and two years at CareFusion.

When you talk to clinicians and IT people and show them the benefits of integration with billing and medication safety, verification, etc., there is no question that they WANT it. But there are real complexities associated with how to drive it together and whether the systems are truly interoperable. It is a dynamic market space.

On the medication side—the market is largely saturated. But the issue for automation providers is that it is saturated but not fully penetrated in the majority of their hospitals! They may have the machines on the floors, in the OR, or in the catheter labs, but they are not really exploiting the full range of technology. One of the best sales cases we have is a hospital like Sharp in San Diego. They are wall-to-wall automation, and they have senior management telling Pyxis that you must partner with integration providers to ensure that the automated systems are fully integrated with hospital patient billing and other systems. And if you don't, you don't get to play. They saved $14M in the first year on supply automation.

There is no doubt that automated dispensing will provide the lowest total cost solution every single time. One day, I get a call in from a current dedicated customer, and he says he was told by his new CFO to get rid of all dispensing machines, and he doesn't want to renew the lease. My response to him was "Sure thing. But you know what, in one year I will call you back, and you will want to renew the lease." That may have sounded arrogant, but I knew when I said it that when we implemented Pyxis at that location, we helped them reduce 35 people to 9, we eliminated backroom coders, and drove major savings in inventory. I told him that I predicted that inventory will go up, your lost charge capture will go up, and financially you will look very different and lose much of the operational excellence efficiencies you are enjoying today. Not even 6 months later, I get a call from him, and he tells me that they have inventory all over the place, the nurses are ready to kill him, they are hiring more people than ever to do manual labor, and he is about to lose his job! What did we do? We renewed the lease! And within the first 90 days, 75% of nurses said they love it and they are back on track. Those who embrace it stand at the forefront.

TOTAL PATIENT COST

The impact of auto-replenishment for hospital pharmacies that reach Phase 3 represents what many believe is the model for the future in healthcare. It is of no surprise that a study by Accenture in the 1990s found that, based on time and motion studies, hospital staff (including nurses) spent

30% of their time waiting for something to happen. This represents an opportunity to increase productivity by 30%.

It is also a well-known fact that pharmaceutical is one of the top hospital costs, followed by nursing time. Both of these parameters are directly and indirectly impacted by the deployment of such systems. However, these systems also attack a much more important set of parameters than hospital costs: the total cost of patient care (TCPC).

Total cost of patient care is a metric not often considered in discussions but comprises the hidden costs of mistakes that impact patient care. The elements that make up TCPC include the following:

- Lost nursing time
- Technician productivity rates
- Missed opportunities for pharmacist clinical intervention
- Nursing turnover costs associated with dissatisfied nurses
- Lengthened hospital stays as a result of slower healing rates attributed to missed doses and drug errors
- Legal costs associated with settling claims for drug errors
- Reduced revenues from dissatisfied patients, or lost revenue from returning patients
- Any other elements that negatively impact the rate at which patients become better while in the facility

Waiting for missed doses causes another problem—medical errors. There appears to be a strong relationship between missed doses and medical errors occurring. When nurses get distracted from their workflow (as when they wait for a missing dose), they are more likely to make dispensing errors. One hospital I visited has a voluntary mistake reporting system, which found that there are on average two drug administration mistakes every day. This does not include other errors in the drug use process (drug ordering, dispensation, administration, and monitoring). Many pharmacists believe that acceptable disposition is their only responsibility and that their job is done once they dispense the drug. However, their real job is to improve patient outcomes based on appropriate use—and if a drug stockout occurs the nurse is more likely to make a medical dose error.

Improved nurse and technician productivity, as a result of fewer stockouts, helps the patient as well as the hospital. One hospital I visited participates in a national benchmarking study. The study benchmarks over

800 hospitals in the country, and two of their primary metrics are labor hours per discharge and labor hours per patient-days. Against all other teaching hospitals, this Phase 3 auto-replenishment hospital was found to have one-third of the 50th percentile of labor hours per discharge and one-third of the labor hours per patient days. If one considers that over one-half of a nurse's time is spent administering drugs, it is not surprising that auto-replenishment is associated with these benefits.

My preliminary research finds that the rates of return and savings shown in Figure 4.7 are probable, given the dynamics of the hospital pharmacy environment. These savings are based on the fact that automated dispensing costs are significantly reduced, coupled with improved productivity of pharmacy techs, nurses, and inventory savings. While these numbers include both hard and soft savings objectives, they reflect the fact that improvements on all fronts can lead to a more efficient hospital with improved patient care.

Annual Savings by Category	PHASE 1	PHASE 2	PHASE 3	PHASE 4
Total Annual Savings on Reduced ADEs	$7,300,000	$1,825,000	$2,737,500	$910,675
Total Annual Labor Savings	$1,042,696	$312,996	$201,741	$215,677
Total Annual Inventory Savings	$275,215	$316,497	$178,889	$151,368
Savings (net of ADE Savings)	$1,317,910	$629,493	$380,630	$367,045
Grand Total of All Annual Savings	$8,617,910	$2,454,493	$3,118,130	$1,277,720
Annual Investment for Cardinal ASSIST	$54,000	$54,000	$54,000	$54,000
Payback and ROI (not incl ADE's)				
Pay Back Period (years)	0.040974	0.0857834	0.1418699	0.1471208
Return on Investment	2440.57%	1165.73%	704.87%	679.71%
Payback and ROI (not incl ADE's)				
Pay Back Period (years)	0.006266	0.0220005	0.0173181	0.0422628
Return on Investment	15959.09%	4545.36%	5774.32%	2366.15%

Notes: Medical Errors kill over 100,000 annually. Time Between Pre ASSIST implementation and Post ASSIST implementation is 5 years. Model assumes an annual salary increase of 5%. Use $5,000 for the ADE as a conservative number, but research shows it was $10,700 in 1996.

FIGURE 4.7
Annual savings.

A long-time Phase 3 hospital pharmacist noted the following:

> We were doing about 13 or 14 turns a year, and now we are at 17–18 since
> we used auto-replenishment. Before the system was released on the mar-
> ket four of us sat down and designed how to package the drugs and made
> decisions on tablets in packages of 10s and injectables in 5s. As the prod-
> uct developed and we stretched and pushed the envelope out we worked
> to exploit the capabilities. The physical part of the system worked well
> early on, and we were interested because we believed the wholesaler was
> an expert in SCM and inventory control. So we asked them to help us as
> users of the system to manage the inventory in our machines. Putting in
> these machines has an opportunity cost (patient beds), which makes the
> real estate very expensive. I thought we managed our inventory well on the
> equipment, but I found out I didn't and knew others were a lot worse than
> me. So we went to the wholesaler and told them we wanted more manage-
> ment reports to monitor our use of a drug in the equipment and the right
> quantity. If you run out of a drug and a nurse needs it—it is a stockout.
> Stockouts impact service and create many inefficiencies.

Every hospital manages stockouts differently. If it is a critical drug,
nurses will call the pharmacy and will have to find someone to pick and
bring it to them. The whole object is not to run out. The drug should always
be right there already stocked on the unit, so the nurse can get to it—and if
it is there, then there should never be a stockout.

But stockouts occur for a number of reasons. The most common is inadequate machine placement for a particular drug or underestimated use.
Or the trigger is set incorrectly for notifying the pharmacy that it needs
to be filled:

> The real value of the automated system for replenishment is the reports
> that we developed for managing inventory effectively. Inventory savings
> could be a one-time savings, but we use these reports to look at inventory
> quarterly—always running out of these things if nurses tell us. But when
> there is a run of a drug in a certain area we can look at management reports
> and can raise inventory or do something. We also used to get a lot of dead
> wood—drugs that aren't moving and shouldn't be there consuming real
> estate. That is the biggest problem that people in the hospital pharmacies
> have: managing the machine inventory and having drugs in there that are
> not moving. But using the system allowed us to adjust inventory and main-
> tain service to patient care areas.

We have rarely had a wrong drug delivered by the wholesaler using the
system. As long as you follow the protocol, use the drawers as extensively

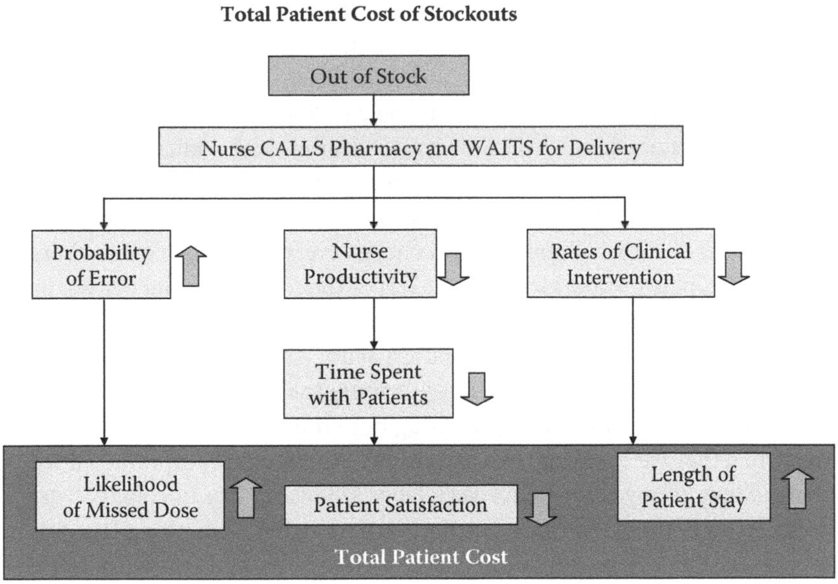

Total Patient Cost of Stockouts

FIGURE 4.8

Total patient cost of stockouts.

as you need to, you never make a mistake. For example, when you scan the barcode on the delivery the cubie drawer pops open and you can't put it in the wrong drawer. If you scan the matrix drawer, it works. With the new cubies, there is a cover over the drawer so people can't force drugs into a drawer where it doesn't belong.

Hospitals in Phase 3 also see a reduced number of emergencies and problems arising. They are better able to manage the flow of drugs into the pharmacy and out to the floor, without emergency rush orders. As one pharmacist noted:

Nurses don't know auto-replenishment from anything else. In their eyes, the drug is either there or it isn't. The mission for a great pharmacy distribution system in the eyes of nursing is very simple: if the order is in and the drug is in the machine, they have no idea. If the order is in the pharmacy system and the drug is in the machine, then there is no problem. It has been my battle cry for 30 years—our job is to make sure nurses have what they need when they need it.

One of my gauges of success is that there are no phones ringing. Walk into any hospital pharmacy in the country and listen for phones. If phones are ringing off the hook, someone doesn't have what they need when they need it. When I hear a phone, I can be doing anything, but it is a cue to me to see what is happening. We have five techs per day and another three at night. We take care of about 400 patients a day. Nothing is chaotic and the nurses like it because they have what they need when they need it.

No matter what hospital you are at, you can have a great pharmacy system with no automation. You have to do a lot of work—filling unit-dose cassettes, which takes three to four hours to fill plus two hours for a pharmacist to check it. With auto-replenishment we don't check anything, and I have techs check what another tech checks every day, which takes about 20 minutes, plus 1.5 hours to pick. The rest of the time we are out delivering medicine. I have not increased or decreased staff for 18 years.

When we started we used no computers at all. All of the time I have saved is because of automation, which has given me the chance to have three to four pharmacists per day doing nothing but clinical shifts versus 18 years ago when they were staffing. I have techs here today doing real value-added tasks. Some of my services are very labor intensive, like oncology. I use techs to do nothing but make chemotherapy batches, something that was hardly existent before. But I didn't have to hire people to do the extra work, and I still have the time to provide excellent service to nurses.

The true measure of auto-replenishment is shown by the activity that occurs when the system is not replenishing, on Sunday. A Phase 3 pharmacist notes:

On a day that we get a delivery, we have to pick 120 lines versus 350. Six days a week we have to pick only 125 lines per day versus 350 on Sunday. It would be more than that in the midweek—probably closer to 400. I may see a situation three or four times a year, typically on a Sunday, when one of my techs picks the wrong drug and puts it in the equipment, in the wrong spot or the wrong drug. Picking the wrong drug is not possible if it came through auto-replenishment. We are down to about four or five errors a year, but it used to be a lot more than that.

CHALLENGES ON THE HORIZON FOR BIOLOGICS AND PHARMACEUTICALS IN THE HOSPITAL PROVIDER ENVIRONMENT

Several pharmacists we interviewed believe that the time between pharmacy order and nurse delivery could be cut to zero with auto-replenishment. How? If auto-replenishment stations were configured correctly, replenishment would occur every day and there would be no special replenishment cycles. These individuals believe that every patient unit could be configured with the most frequently used set of drugs within that unit. In any particular unit of a hospital, anywhere from 450 to 600 drugs are used most frequently. If configured correctly, AR machines could be configured to hold these drugs all the time. In this manner, 98% of every physician order would already have the drug ready to dispense, already in the unit within that patient ward.

Creating this list would not be difficult. A list of every dose at 10 major hospitals representing major units (e.g., intensive care unit, critical care) could be created initially. This critical list would of course change by about 5% on an annual basis based on entry of new drugs. However if wholesalers could track these drugs and recommend the correct quantities and Pyxis drawers to locate them, then the machines would never stock out, and nurses would never be looking for a med. This would not only cut down on stockouts but would also improve the safety of average patients tenfold. By removing the chaos associated with 50% of nurses' drug-dispensing activities, the number of sick patients would drop, medical dose error rates would drop, and employee satisfaction would double.

The potential benefits to hospitals that are willing to take the time to invest in learning about the auto-replenishment systems is tremendous. The initial costs are low, but the major investment is the willingness to take the time to learn and take the journey toward hospital pharmacy dispensation automation. In the long term, we believe that this approach will be used by more hospitals in the future and will lead to the next major event on the frontier—unit-dispensed bar code medications.

At some point in the future, every medication will be packaged in a unit dose bar code. When a physician prescribes the drug, it will automatically generate a request to a nurse to schedule a dispensation from a precise location. When nurses pick the drug and go to dispense it, they will first scan the bar code on both the unit dose packaging and the patient's bracelet, which will confirm that the correct dose and drug is dispensed to the correct patient. Meanwhile, auto-replenishment is keeping track of the dispensation, which automatically triggers a reorder point, which in turn generates a delivery from a wholesaler DC to the hospital the next day, where the drug is replenished into the machine. The hospital can now review its ongoing drug usage, can track patient dispensations versus long-term patient care, and can drive continuous improvement into the healthcare system. This scenario is already happening today. The real challenge that remains is to close the loop with the patient, the payer, and the ability to track efficacy. "Closing the loop" on patient–drug–payer supply chains is critical to the next wave of change on the horizon: pay-for-performance.

Personalized Medicine and Pay-for-Performance

Attending the IDN Summit in Phoenix on September 13, 2011, one would not know judging by the relaxed atmosphere at the beautiful Arizona Biltmore that there was an underlying tension in the air. At this meeting of supply chain executives, there was a growing realization that massive changes in the reimbursement structure for hospital payments was about to occur. Several big themes dominated the conversation, the first of which was the Accountable Care Act of 2010, which contained over $155B in hospital payment cuts over 10 years. As part of the reform law, a new hospital inpatient value-based purchasing program will be implemented, with 2% of Medicare payments at risk by 2016.

What is the concern? The biggest issue is a new measure of hospital quality, called *Medicare spending per beneficiary*, which will penalize higher-cost hospitals under a formula that could take away far more than value-based purchasing. In this environment, supply chain groups are being called upon to expand their purview into areas once reserved solely for physicians and clinicians: surgery, cardiac catheterization, imaging, and others. But many clinical departments have legacy systems for inventory or no systems at all, which means performance measurement for them is a challenge.

Reimbursement Models

Payers are using a lot of tools to control the overall cost of biologics and new drugs in hospital therapy and are establishing a number of different restrictions in reimbursing drugs. Some of the major categories[*] are discussed next.

Pay-for-Performance (PFP)

PFP involves a negotiated agreement between the life sciences company and the payer, in which reimbursement is based on the performance of the

---

[*] "Changing Market Access Strategies in Pharmaceutical Industry," Ananth Consulting Group, Rjaram Iver, White Paper, August 2010.

drug for individual payments. Examples include the agreement between the National Health Service (NHS) in the United Kingdom and Johnson & Johnson for an oncology drug called Velcade. Under this agreement, the NHS will pay only if the Velcade treatments demonstrate a desired response measured by the reduction in tumor size.* Another example is the agreement between the National Institute for Clinical Excellence in the United Kingdom and Novartis for Lucentis, an eye treatment. Novartis agreed to cover the cost of treatment if more than 14 injections are required for ongoing treatment of the patient.

The United States is also focusing on pay-for-performance measures. This has already occurred with Aetna and Cigna, which have a lot of PFP partnerships with a number of hospitals. In August 2006, Aetna launched a national PFP program that would give incentives to physicians who improve the quality of care and reduce the overall treatment cost. This is also part of a broader program aimed at reducing the cost of payments for biologics and drugs bundled with physician fees to drive to a "bundled payment" outcome.

Step Edit Therapy

This tool has also been applied for a number of years and poses a threat to the life sciences industry and healthcare providers alike. In this approach, a typically less expensive or generic version of a drug is authorized first before another drug (e.g., the more expensive branded drug) can be authorized for use. The branded, new drug is authorized only when the earlier generic, less expensive version has been shown to not be effective. Step edit therapy is popular in countries where generics proliferate. Most payers in the United States use this approach for various therapies, but especially so in the case of biologics-based therapies.

Examples of step edit therapy include the case of Blue Cross of Idaho, which imposed a step edit on Byetta—a new medication for diabetes. Based on the guidelines, Byetta is placed on a "third tier" of approved formulary drugs and is authorized only when patients have taken at least two other agents or one combination drug with no effect.† Similarly, the Harvard Pilgrim Health Care program established a step edit on Vytorin. Patients are encouraged to maximize the statin dose before adding the drug to their regime.

---

* NICE website, http://swww.nicemedica/pdf/MyelomaDoHSummaryREsponderScheme.pdf
† Iver, 2010.

Price Capping

This payer strategy involves capping the price for various drugs for a particular treatment. Payers fix an upper cap on the reimbursement for a drug used for a particular treatment. This strategy has also been adopted by manufacturers. For example, Genentech capped the total cost of Avastin, a cancer treatment, for the approved indication at $55,000 per year for individuals below a certain income level. Amgen also capped a patient's annual copayment for Vectivix at 5% of the patient's adjusted gross income.

Outcome-Based Pricing

Biopharma companies have seen the writing on the wall and have begun exploring outcome-based risk sharing arrangements with payers. One example is an outcome-based agreement developed by Janssen-Cilag and NICE in the United Kingdom. NICE refused to approve the drug based on cost-effectiveness, so the company proposed to treat eligible patients for four months and be paid based on the contingency that patient outcomes result. If the drug achieves a specific response, patients are permitted to continue the treatment and NHS will cover the expense. Otherwise, Janssen must cover the cost and reimburse NHS for its expenses. In another example, Merck has signed with Cigna a deal whereby Merck's two anti-diabetic drugs, Januvia and Janumet, are reimbursed according to their performance. Cigna is seeking to develop a broader set of agreements with statin manufacturers that is pushing the boundaries even further. If the patient suffers from a heart attack while taking statins on a regular basis, manufacturers must pay for the treatment cost.[*]

Accountable Care Organizations

A major trend that is catching many healthcare providers by storm in 2011 is the notion of accountable care organizations (ACO). In the 429-page document developed by the Center for Medicare and Medicaid Services (CMS), ACOs are organizations whose primary care providers are accountable for coordinating care for at least 5,000 Medicare beneficiaries as a separate legal entity. These organizations are accountable to provide better care for individuals, better health for populations based on

---

[*] Paul Jones and Jan Malek, "Prospering in a Pay-for-Performance World," white paper, Cisco.

preventive services, and lower growth in expenditures, based on a vague concept called *patient-centeredness.*

This document becomes even more threatening to current operating models for hospitals, as a big chunk of Medicare reimbursement will be tied to something called *comparative effectiveness.* This means that there must be a firmer scientific basis for determining the clinical value and cost–benefit of devices, drugs, and interventions through comparative effectiveness research (CER). This is intended to avoid using technologies that are adopted into practice without sufficient evidence and that caused harm to patients, including high-dose chemotherapy, drugs like Vioxx, and bone morphogenetic protein, which has a risk of sterility in men. This is all well and good, except that there are no databases, poor performance metrics, no standards around the protocol or types of diseases, and patient characteristics that provide a precedent for measurement of whether a treatment is effective.

Another looming issue is bundled payments. Under this format, a provider is no longer paid in terms of a fee-for-service (FFS) while a patient is in the hospital. In an FFS model, each member of the medical team—the radiologist, the cardiologist, the anesthesiologist, and perhaps the consulting physician who works with the patient afterward (as well as the life sciences company providing the medical therapy)—is paid separately based on their activity. In bundled payments, a single fee is charged for the entire procedure, including possible readmission fees up to 30 to 90 days after the patient is discharged. And then consider the fact that today Medicare payments are about 50% of hospital revenues, and that in five years, they may be as high as 90% of revenues. All of these factors combined represent a real threat to hospital executives.

So how this all comes together is that ACOs are required to implement evidence-based medicine. This means hospitals are to be held accountable not only for the cost of the care they provide but also for the cost of services performed by doctors and other healthcare providers in the 30 days after a Medicare patient leaves the hospital.

There is also an impending conflict between the two schools of thought— CER and *personalized medicines* (PM)—on the effectiveness of different biological and pharmaceutical treatments on patients. The purpose of both methods is based on the principle of supporting high-quality, evidence-based decisions for optimal patient care. The difference lies in the fact that CER is oriented toward evaluating treatment effects across study populations, whereas PM focuses on using individuals' genomic information and other personal traits to inform decisions about their healthcare.*

While the purpose of CER is to determine which healthcare intervention works best for a given healthcare problem, the purpose of PM is to ensure that healthcare delivers "the right treatment to the right patient at the right time." Supporting high-quality, evidence-based decisions for optimal patient care is a laudable goal. However, like most other forms of evaluation of healthcare interventions, CER is usually oriented toward evaluating treatment effects across study populations, whereas PM focuses on using individuals' genomic information and other personal traits to inform decisions about their healthcare.

What this means is that CER does not investigate important differences in patient response to interventions (e.g., whether patient response to a cancer drug varies by certain genetic characteristics), its findings may be inadequate or misleading for patient care. This could have extended consequences if these findings are incorporated into product labeling, practice guidelines, reimbursement policies, or utilization management that could curtail PM.

For CER to contribute to PM, it must account for patient differences that influence the impact of interventions on health outcomes. These characteristics can include severity of disease, co-morbidities and risk factors, genetic characteristics, sociodemographic characteristics, health-related behaviors, and environmental factors.

Aligning CER and PM means that PM is subject to prevailing evidence requirements for screening, diagnostic, therapeutic, and other interventions. For genetic and genomic testing, health professional groups, guideline panels, and payers are calling not only for rigorous evidence of test accuracy but also for evidence of clinical utility—that is, impact of test results on clinical decisions and, ultimately, patient outcomes. This applies, for example, to gene expression profile testing to predict breast cancer outcomes, pharmacogenomic testing for guiding treatment for depression, and selecting treatments for colorectal cancer.

New Developments in Comparative Effectiveness

Comparative effectiveness (CE) is the synthesis of multiple date source research comparing the benefits and harms of different interventions and

---

* Saturday, October 31, 2009, "Can Personalized Medicine and Comparative Effectiveness Coexist? The Experts Weigh In," RPM Report.

strategies (drugs, devices, testing, etc.) to prevent, diagnose, treat, and monitor health conditions in "real world" settings (unlike randomized control trials, which are usually highly "artificial" and non-representative of average patients); CE typically does NOT include the dimension of cost in its analysis.

Comparative cost effectiveness (CCE) adds the comparative dimension of total cost over a clearly defined episode of patient care, and examines clinical outcomes inclusive of the economic impact of side effects and adverse effects (incidence, severity, duration, and populations identified via in-depth data extraction and additional research/data collection). CCE considers total healthcare resource consumption (time, HR, supplies), not only product acquisition cost. Additionally, CCE collects and presents cost/resource use data alongside comparative effectiveness data, and provides all facility decision makers with very practical and important comparative product data for clinical and product acquisition decision making.

One technology that is emerging on the horizon is being applied to support the principle of comparative cost effectiveness. This technology, developed by a team of economists with the Center for Applied Value Analysis, is an approach that involves examining the clinical differences between products and therapies relative to the actual clinical outcomes and costs. This type of analysis allows hospital administrators to determine whether one product versus another is economically feasible, or whether a given pharmacotherapy, device, or technology make economic sense. I witnessed an early demo of CAVA's online comparative cost effectiveness provided by their CEO, Josh Feldstein.* The system applies a predictive analytics platform that is supported by an extensive backend database that has captured massive levels of business intelligence support for hospital decision making. This approach allows facility specific, head-to-head value analyses of some of the most clinically challenging technologies of devices, pharmaceuticals, and technology.

In the example I observed, a cost model was run for three different medicines to treat thrombocythemia. The cost of the three treatments were somewhat lower for the generic, but with the additional documented costs associated with bleeding events and readmission of the patient, the cost of the branded manufacturer drug was five times lower given the likelihood of an adverse reaction! This is certainly not always the case for all such events, but the database is able to pull in information that comes closest to putting together a "total cost of ownership" model associated with a given

---

* Josh Feldstein, CEO, CAVA, February 10, 2012, http://www.cava.com

therapy or device. In some cases, "more expensive" is not always better, whereas in other cases, "you get what you pay for" is the rule of thumb.

CONCLUSIONS

This chapter has introduced some of the major changes that are occurring in the way that hospitals dispense pharmaceuticals and the massive changes that are occurring in the payer environment that will cause them to rethink their approach to healthcare.

Hospitals have increasingly collaborated with wholesalers to develop automated dispensing and replenishment of pharmaceuticals from their internal pharmacies. This has resulted in significant improvements in working capital, reduction of patient errors and improper doses, and a lower total cost of patient care. The application of unit bar code technology is further driving the dispensing process all the way to the patient's bedside, which will further reduce errors and drive improved compliance and monitoring of patient dosing.

The major threat on the horizon today for hospitals and biological manufacturers is the increasing pressure of payers to reduce the cost of biological treatments, particularly for diseases such as oncology and inflammatory diseases. Payers—including CMS in the United States, NICE in the United Kingdom, and the various agencies in Europe—are putting increasing scrutiny on the effectiveness of these expensive new treatments. Private payers such as Cigna, Aetna, and Blue Cross are also imposing new measures. To control these costs, payers are using a variety of different pay-for-performance strategies, including step edit therapy, price capping, and outcome-based payment.

Hospital and healthcare executives I interviewed at a recent IDN Summit conference held in September 2011 asked a lot of questions. For example:

- How do you know whether previous comprehensive effectiveness research (CER) study results remain relevant particularly if a new product with competing claims has entered the market?
- Do CER findings based on early use of a treatment truly apply to particular clinicians or facilities with extensive experience in more recent refinements?
- What is the source of CER? How are they disseminated? Can findings be extrapolated to a broader range of clinical indications and patients?

- How are supply chain leaders supposed to make decisions on procurement of these technologies and how to gather and critique available scientific evidence?
- How do you track and manage the multiple clinical care measures, patient experience measures, and information technology (IT) measures across a massive population base and coordinate this with Medicare reimbursement?

These are difficult questions indeed. In the future, it will be imperative for biopharmaceutical companies to change their approach to drug development to support CER and PFP. As hospitals move from a physician-focused model to a model where the payer has greater power over therapies and decisions, biopharmaceutical companies must begin to involve the payers not only in their sales and marketing strategies but indeed also in their development approach. Cost containment will continue to be at the top of the agenda. I believe that we may soon see payers and regulatory agencies closely involved in the drug development process, even at the level of basic research and development (R&D) and clinical trials. Payers will have the opportunity to comment and advise based on the study design and to direct the target of the research based on early clinical insights. This is already happening in some cases. In June 2008, GSK invited healthcare officials from the United Kingdom, France, Spain, and Italy to examine their candidates under development to gather feedback on their molecules to understand the likelihood of payment.[*] In 2007 Novartis began working with the National Institute for Health and Clinical Excellence in the United Kingdom on a Phase 3 clinical trial to identify whether it was likely to be reimbursed. These types of agreements are likely to occur more and more in the future.

---

[*] "Glaxo Seeks Guidance from Health Systems," *Wall Street Journal*, July 7, 2008.

5

The Blurring of Boundaries in Biopharmaceutical Supply Chains: The Case of Oncology Medicine

INTRODUCTION

In response to the massive structural and infrastructural changes that are occurring on the horizon, supply chains in the life sciences and biopharmaceutical industries are changing rapidly. The rise of pay-for-performance, bundled payments, increasing power of payers, personalized medicine, and shrinking public medical payment rates are forcing everyone in the supply chain to rethink their traditional roles. Nowhere is this more apparent than in the market for oncology medicines. As noted earlier, oncology is a growing field, one that relies increasingly on biological therapies as a cure. The field is also extremely fragmented and is under increasing pressure to provide results prior to payment (as we saw in the last chapter). As a result, participants in the supply chain are increasingly working closer together, and we are beginning to witness the blurring of boundaries among traditional group purchasing organizations (GPOs), wholesalers, hospital providers, and payers. Oncology medicine is a good indicative vector for the direction that the entire healthcare environment is headed, and is thus worthy of further study.

In this chapter, I examine the growing market for oncology treatments. I then examine the blurring between major GPOs and wholesalers and the increasing level of service being provided to physicians, clinics, and patients. Included in this discussion is the physician–GPO relationship, which is under increased scrutiny by regulators. Finally, I postulate what may happen given the shrinking margins occurring for providers in this market and what this future may bring.

The Oncology Market

The market for oncology treatments and distribution is growing rapidly. Cancer is the second leading cause of death in the United States, claiming over half a million lives annually, with the number growing. The disease is responsible for one of every four deaths and strikes approximately 1.37 million people every year. Although survival rates for the 15 most common cancers have been improving every year since 1993, the overall number of cancer deaths has continued to increase given the country's growing population and the aging of its citizens.[1] What is most alarming is that this state of affairs will likely change for the worse. The number of cancer cases in the United States is expected to double over the next 50 years to 2.6 million, the result of an aging and expanding population.

A number of underlying demographical issues underlie this growth. First, the U.S. population is living longer than in previous generations, and life spans are expected to continue increasing. According to the U.S. Census Bureau, both men and women are living longer in each age segment. As the aging population expands, cancer (or neoplasms) may become one of the leading causes of disease and death. In addition to living longer, the U.S. population is experiencing a dramatic shift in the causes of mortality. There has been a significant decrease in overall deaths due to heart disease and a corresponding increase of deaths due to cancer in the same time period for those 65 years of age and older.

The prevalence of the disease in a population has always dictated the cost of treatment options for these causes of illness and eventual death. For example, as heart disease became a leading cause of illness over the past few decades, drugs used to treat heart disease became the leading drug therapy cost drivers in pharmaceutical care. With the growth of cancer, oncology drugs are growing rapidly. Similarly, as cancer fast overcomes heart disease as the leading cause of death and disease in the United States, chemotherapeutics, biotechnology drugs, and other treatment options will correspondingly lead the way with increased use and higher treatment costs in the foreseeable future.

Other key trends point to how the market is responding to the growth of cancer-related treatments:

- Novel drug therapies and advances in radiation treatment have made many cancers survivable. That's good news for patients, and so is the fact that pharmacists are playing a more pivotal role in managing not only the clinical but also financial aspects of patient care.[2]
- As stand-alone, community-based cancer centers and physician treatment facilities proliferate, the demand for board-certified oncology pharmacists is growing. A recent study estimated that 70 to 80% of large oncology practices employ pharmacists and pharmacy technicians.[2]
- Pharmacists have proven to be a valuable asset for several reasons. Not only are they familiar with drug protocols as well as being experts on drug interactions, but oncologists also frequently rely on pharmacists for recommending dosage adjustments in patients for complex diseases. At many comprehensive cancer centers, pharmacists make key decisions in the preparation of injectable agents.[2]
- Increasingly, the pharmacist's role is expanding beyond clinical duties. For example, in many facilities pharmacists oversee drug purchases. Recently, a Congressional Medicare Payment Advisory Commission recommended that, to reduce costs and improve efficiency, community-based oncology practices should hire pharmacists to buy and prepare medications and recommend drug products based on price and clinical effectiveness.[2]
- More and more large community-based oncology centers are installing on-site retail pharmacies where a staff pharmacist not only fills oral prescriptions but in some cases also compounds intravenous medications.[2]
- The rise of oncology pharmacy as a board-certified specialty has been steady, and the demand for such specialists is expected to increase over the next decade. Oncology was the fifth specialty to be created by the Board of Pharmaceutical Specialties (BPS) in 1996.[2]
- The first crop of BPS-certified oncology pharmacists numbered 118. Now, just a little more than 10 years later, that number has climbed to 655, making it the second-largest specialty after pharmacotherapy, which boasts 3,688 pharmacists.[2]

Growth of Cancer Treatments

Of all specialty pharmaceuticals, chemotherapeutic drugs represent a large component of these expenditures, and this is growing at rates of 15 to 20% per annum. According to a 2004 CMS National Healthcare Expenditure Projection (2003–2013), U.S. specialty drug expenditures have gone from $35 billion in 2003 to $73 billion in 2008. Specialty drug spend will grow from representing 18% of total drug spend in 2003 to 26% in 2008. One of the major contributing factors to this upward spending trend in specialty drugs can be foretold by the domination of research and drug pipelines focused on by drug manufacturers. Another emerging area is the growth of "orphan" drugs targeting small populations of patients (at a very high cost per patient!).

Current research and development pipelines of pharmaceutical manufacturers point to a future where biotechnology-specific treatment agents will be a dominant force in the U.S. healthcare environment. Biotechnology drugs differ from conventional drugs because they focus on specific cellular mechanisms and targeted patient populations.

Other estimates of the growth of the market include the following:[3]

- Medco Health Solutions estimates an oncology spend of approximately $20-$25 billion.
- Medco Health Solutions estimates that of the more than 400 drugs in the development pipeline, 210 are for cancer and related conditions.
- Express Scripts forecasts the growth trend for cancer use will be approximately 40% through 2012 as a result of new drugs and combination therapy.

In a presentation by McKesson, David Vidic estimated that oncology drugs will grow to more than 50% of the pharmaceutical spend in the next few years, based on existing drug pipeline outlooks. My independent research leads me to believe that these figures may be somewhat overly ambitious. For instance, one managed healthcare provider noted:

> For oncology, we have seen a combined medical and pharmacy benefit in the range of 14% trend increase over three years. The growth rates for oncology pharmacy and medical combined in 2006–2007 was a 3% increase. Other numbers I have seen often cite an increase of 20% for specialty drugs. However, I believe that managed care providers are managing this growth fairly well, are clued in to the gamesmanship going on in the market, and

are closely monitoring what is happening on the medical side for payers, particularly with squishy J-codes.

(The latter reference to J-codes is explained later in this chapter.)

THE ONCOLOGY SUPPLY CHAIN

The evolution of the oncology supply chain is an interesting story. Prior to 1991, group purchasing organizations (GPOs) did not exist in community oncology practices, and very few oncology drugs were available. National wholesalers were set up to service hospitals; few were interested in shipping drugs by the vial to community doctors, nor were they equipped to do so. This gave birth to the first set of four distributors of oncology products: Oncology Therapeutics Network (OTN), Oncology Supply of Alabama, Florida Infusion, and PRN. Their focus was on providing a niche service to community-based oncology practices with next-day on-time medication delivery.* North Carolina then invited these companies to bid on being the sole drug distributor to oncology practices in the state, and OTN won the bid. Soon after, more states jumped on board, and a set of administrator-run societies became involved in the mid-1990s. Examples included the Southern Oncology Alliance of Practices, the Pennsylvania Oncology Hematology Managers' Society, and the Michigan Society for Hematology Oncology. Before long, manufacturers began negotiating drug contracts directly with these societies in exchange for an administrative fee for choosing their drug. The societies then offered their collective volume to the distributors. Doctors were thrilled to have access to great prices, as this allowed them to deliver high-quality care over and above the below-cost reimbursements that many of their patients had for infusion services.

A series of consolidations in the industry followed over the next decade. Cardinal Health acquired PRN in 1994 but later exited the specialty pharmaceutical space along with divesting in other businesses such as Pyxis and non-core wholesaler businesses. AmerisourceBergen, a wholesale distributor, expanded to include Oncology Supply (1996) and later purchased the International Oncology Network, which developed overseas in India and expanded to the United States. It also purchased U.S.-based Bioservices in 2003, a specialty pharmacy.

---

* Evolution of the Oncology GPO, Bryan Cote, *Oncology Business Review*, November 2007.

McKesson acquired OTN, a provider of contracts, tools, and services, and Onmark, customizable services including distribution and GPO services, in 2007. In January 2011, McKesson acquired the crown jewel: the U.S.-based Oncology Network, one of the nation's largest networks of community-based oncology physicians.

Today what exists are two primary channels of aligned parent company relationships that span wholesale: GPOs and specialty pharmacies. About 80% of the specialty pharmaceutical sales volume in the United States now goes through McKesson and Amerisource. It should be noted that U.S. Oncology Network (USON) is a physician practice management company that owns and operate practices—a business very different from McKesson's core business and one that does not necessarily have immediate financial appeal given what is going on with medical oncology payments, particularly for chemotherapy and supportive drugs. That said, by combining USON's Level 1 Pathways program, Innovent Oncology, with its analytics business and major market share in specialty pharma, McKesson may be seeking to corner the market on medical oncology in the future acute-care organization structure that is evolving.

Specifically, McKesson's Lynx technology platform is designed to provide practices with e-prescribing capabilities, practice management tools that include patient scheduling and billing system capabilities, inventory management and charge capture capabilities, and reimbursement reporting and analysis tools. USON's technology platform is designed to assist oncology practices in the areas of care delivery, drug management, and revenue cycle management. The iKnowMed electronic health record (EHR) is being used by over 900 of USON's affiliated physicians.[*]

These technologies are targeted at practice management services enabling practices to benefit from recent legislation passed encouraging the use of technology in healthcare. This legislation includes the American Recovery and Reinvestment Act of 2009 (ARRA) and the Medicare Improvements for Patients and Providers Act of 2008 (MIPPA). Both acts established incentive payments aimed at physicians to promote the use of health information technology (IT)—specifically EHRs and e-prescribing technologies—over the next several years.

---

[*] "McKesson Buys US Oncology: What does this further consolidation of the specialty pharmaceutical channel mean to manufacturers?," Don Sharpe, *Oncology Business Review*, posted November 22, 2010.

Specialty drugs now account for more than 25% of the total pharmacy benefit drug spend, and estimates suggest that this will climb to more than 40% by 2030. The medical benefit specialty drug spend adds an additional 22% to the total drug spend beyond the pharmacy benefit for most payers. Specialty drugs for cancer are even hotter—industry forecasters predict that biotech products targeting cancer will be among the top 10 selling pharmaceuticals in 2016.[*]

What this means to specialty pharmaceutical manufacturers is that consolidation of distribution and increased technology platforms will provide improved potential to capture and manage significantly broader and deeper volumes of drug-related clinical, claims, and distribution data. In the end, this can be used by all players (manufacturers and payers alike) to better track oncology prescribing regimens and trends. Although Amerisource still holds a majority of the market share (about 60%), McKesson's 25% market share is likely to grow. With the growth of biosimilars, both parties will be able to capitalize on the higher margins that will accompany these products.

THE GPO–DISTRIBUTOR–PHYSICIAN RELATIONSHIP IN ONCOLOGY

The industry, while moving toward a consolidated GPO–distributor–specialty relationship, is continuing to evolve. My primary and secondary research has led me to the following conclusions regarding some of the key service offerings that are facilitated by these partnerships that drive market share in the oncology market:

- The distributor can bring pricing programs and help to some degree with the administration. The GPO can work directly with the physician. For instance, USON has the Protocol Analyzer program, which can take a diagnosed patient, drop in options for treatment, look at revenue stream from that, and identify approved options. Further, the program highlights how it impacts the practice.

---

[*] Pharmacy Times, Oral Oncology Therapies: Specialty Pharmacy's Newest Challenge Published Online: Wednesday, May 18th, 2011, Randell J. Correia, PharmD.

- The partnership can provide support—education, buying opportunities, and preferred distributor services, such as next-day delivery, Web ordering, statements, and information on the Web. For a physician practice, these services have been developed to the extent that they are almost automated programs. Such programs can function effectively only when the GPO and distributor put their pieces together and make it a unified offering to the market. In the words of one wholesaler, "Putting together these offerings—that is how you get market share."

A bizarre anomaly developing in this market share is unprecedented in typical biopharma supply chains: the purchasing power of the distributor is now shared with the GPO. GPOs have a lot of pricing power that guarantees market share in certain hospital markets. Distributors are able to obtain the volume discounts that complement this strategy. However, the unique strategic application of direct to physician service offerings creates a situation where certain types of agreements can prevent volume discounts from occurring.

Manufacturer relationships with GPOs are common. For example, a particular manufacturer (e.g., Amgen) may want to understand how much market share one of their products (e.g., Procrit) has. Market share initiatives are driven by a GPO, which then takes ownership for delivering this market share in their customer base. There is then a compensation program that rewards them for being compliant and driving market share. This in turn provides an advantage on the distribution side. An affiliated distributor (McKesson) can go to a manufacturer and emphasize that its proprietary GPO (USON) represents the majority share of market, which provides significant leverage.

Actual estimates of pricing discounts are difficult to estimate. As distributors, there is a narrow window between what the manufacturer will sell it to and what CMS provides for reimbursement. According to an interview with one company:

> There is very little margin on discretionary pricing, as pricing is the same from all distributors. We bring the value-added service. All of our relationships are direct from manufacturers. We don't have agreements for oral—so buy from them—99% are direct from manufacturer.

Further discussions reveal that multiple relationships exist in this space between key supply chain participants:

We are a $15B business, and we have a relationship with administrators. The GPO forms the relationship with the physicians, and the GPO is involved with the treatment. The distributor is involved with working with the practice on the efficiencies of running the practice. That is where you get the double hit from the GPO relationship. The key is that the distributor relationship must be strong with the hospital administrator.

Services Provided by Specialty Wholesalers and Distributors

The service offering provided by these specialty companies is multifaceted.

Multiple services are provided to physician and oncology clinics. Some of the key elements include the following:

1. Daily functional services: The interface, technology, automated ordering, and automated machines are provided by the wholesaler, whereas the GPO provides the programs that can be attached to the hardware provided—so hospitals can get their information, their purchase requirements, and their market share. These elements are viewed as value-added services obtained at no additional cost by physicians.
2. Physician education: for example, webcasts for education, physician roundtables, updates, newsletters. While not as critical, these elements help to provide a solid foundation for retention of services and are perceived as value-added by physicians in the network.

Differentiated Services

Because there is such a small window in pricing (all distributors sell at the same price), value is delivered from the GPO side of this unique partnership. Wholesalers have a lobbying presence in Washington, DC, are aware of changes that are occurring, and position themselves as the voice of the oncology on Capitol Hill via newsletters, email blasts, and ongoing communication and alerts.

Ironically, while these elements are viewed favorably by the physician customer base, they do little to enhance bottom-line profitability. As one individual from a GPO noted:

As far as enhancing their profitability—from a product sell side—little can be done. The margins are so restrictive, and there is an extremely low ability on our part to impact their profitability. We can make them aware of changes and ensure that they are aware and compliant to changes of billing codes (we do a tremendous job on that side). This is especially true with private payers and anything with CMS, where we are their lifeline. But in the end, we cannot significantly improve their profitability.

PROFITABILITY IN THE ONCOLOGY MARKET

Numerous interviews with health maintenance organizations (HMOs), physicians, hospitals, and GPOs lead me to believe that the margins for distributors in the oncology market will remain relatively low. These estimates vary according to various sources, from less than 1% to 5%. A realistic estimate is on the order of 2–4%, which is primarily a factor driven by market share growth.

Personal interviews with executives, combined with a focused set of interviews with payers, do not provide a realistic estimate of what the true margins are within this market. For instance, an interview with one executive revealed the following:

> Margins for distributors are less than 1%. In terms of pure margin in oncology [income after expenses], we get about 80 basis points (0.80%). I have been doing this for 30 years; we used to make 3%, but that all changed recently. There are fees paid to the GPOs that enter the oncology price. The margins are better when you look at GPO fees, but they still don't get up to 3%, even if you look at the entire oncology price. The margins are in the 2% range, which includes all fees.

Profitability estimates from third parties are significantly different:

> These companies are just wholesalers—they don't do anything. They are developing a specialty pharmacy division, but there is not a lot of money in wholesale distribution. They make 2 to 5% depending on the drugs. From a margin perspective this is small. But when one considers that there are big players with large market share, the economics change. If they do $5–10 billion, that is a blip in the overall scheme of things. They claim they have 50% of the market space. I don't know what that means, other than you are an efficient distributor—but if you own 25% of the entire drug wholesaler business, they have almost no negotiation capabilities with the drug companies overall.
>
> But if you look only at the specialty market, it is a different story. On $5 billion, 5% is a lot of money. It is a volume gain; they make 2–3% and

some inventory investment purchasing and in a simplistic way they make 2% on wholesaler operations. For smaller operators, if you do a billion, you can't survive—it is just a volume gain. But once you start taking up space and you become an integral part of the chain, you begin to become a player. Wholesalers are being pressed by the likes of Walmart, so the only remaining revenue sources are the independent pharmacies and the small chains—and small pharmacy sees it that way. So wholesalers are targeting physicians whose margins are already pressed and focus on that market rather than the hospitals. Where else can they go?

CLASS-OF-TRADE (COT) PRICING[4]

In the COT system, a single stand-alone pharmacy, outpatient surgery center, or specialty physician may be able to get similar or better prices for certain prescription drugs than a large, multibillion-dollar national pharmacy chain.

The formation of the COT system stems from the Robinson-Patman Act of 1936, a supplement to the Clayton Antitrust Act. This act was originally intended to protect small retailers from competition from large chains. Pharmaceutical manufacturers' infrastructures are set up according to the COT of their markets as defined by each manufacturer. A company with oral and self-injectable products may lump specialty pharmacies into the same COT as mail-order pharmacies or pharmacy benefit managers (PBMs) and view home infusion companies as a different COT. Another drug manufacturer may lump specialty pharmacy, specialty infusion, and home infusion companies into the same COT, effectively blocking these companies from limited distribution contracts that are typically awarded to national companies.

For chemotherapeutic agents, oncologists enjoy one of the most favorable COT pricing from manufacturers. According to Joe Fleming, chair of Professional Home Care Services, "Hospitals and physician offices enjoy much better pricing on infusible products than do home infusion companies." Home infusion companies often enjoy better pricing than retail pharmacies and even large national retail chains. The more favorable drug purchase prices for oncologists often allow these physicians to make significant money on the medication portion of reimbursements from third-party payers. When COT pricing differences are coupled with the less sophisticated adjudication processes inherent to the J-code system,

TABLE 5.1

Drug Pricing According to Class-of-Trade Designation

Drug Name	Oncologist COT	Non-Oncologist COT 1	Non-Oncologist COT 2	Canadian Pharmacy
Lupron 7.5 mg (Leuprolide)	< $200.00	$634.29	$620.55	$456.45
Zoladex 3.6 mg (Goserelin)	< $200.00	$375.99	$382.95	$471.04

Source: Nee, C., 2007.

Notes: Based on actual purchases according to the various COT purchasers in December 2006. Classification of and pricings within each COT may differ by the qualifications set by respective manufacturers. The prices offered here are for comparison only and should not be used as final pricing.

payers are beginning to see that there are opportunities for better cost-containment strategies. These differentiated COT structures are illustrated in the example in Table 5.1.

Under the current oncology drug pricing system, oncologists qualify for a unique COT category established by the pharmaceutical companies that give them preferential access to some of the lowest cost anticancer and adjunctive agents in the marketplace. Oncology drug manufacturers are so protective of their COT program that they will individually certify each oncologist for participation in their COT program. Some drug manufacturers have gone the extra step of establishing direct purchasing programs, so that only oncologists can qualify for purchases at COT discounts. This is very important to understand since any other buyers who are not qualified oncologists cannot compete for the lowest prices regardless of their volume of purchases. (For an example of pricing by class-of-trade, see Table 5.1.)

Chris Nee, an expert on oncology distribution, notes the following:

> COT pricing has been around for a long time—around 30–40 years. What is happening now, however, is that there is a tremendous push from smaller oncology groups (which comprise about 60–70% of the practices in this country) that cannot afford to put out the time of money under the ASP model so they are pushing the patient to the hospital for release. The hospital does not have the COT, and pricing is higher than physicians, and as a result, some of the reimbursements are not covering the costs.
>
> Reimbursements are misaligned. Since Medicare pays so expeditiously and the margins for the doctors are so much lower under the ASP model, most are not willing to take the risk. And then many of them don't like the CAP [competitive acquisition program]. CAP has proven to result in a lot

of issues regarding delivery and appropriateness, a lot of red tape, timing, and in general it is very difficult to work with. Physician workflow isn't prepared to deal with the administrative burden, so the next best thing they can do is to push the Medicare patients into hospitals and resolve it with the government and hospital.

Nee also notes that the only physician offices that seem to be taking the CAP benefit are those that are not efficiently run:

Some of the companies I am working with have found a way to resolve this and are making improvements in physician office workflow. These are the ones that do not need CAPs. The typical small physician practice, however, is highly inefficient. For example, in many clinics family members are managing the program, and they have no experience in managing supply chains. All of a sudden they have to buy drugs from a CAP, buy from other sources for inventory, manage that inventory, and replenish it. Their lack of capability overloads the system, even in big practices. They may have to work with 10 different health plans as well as Medicare. If they are running a busy practice and the drugs are difficult to manage along with a lot of hassles of filling out forms, they say forget it. Let the hospital manage the hassle of reimbursement.

EMERGING RELATIONSHIPS IN THE ONCOLOGY SUPPLY CHAIN

To shed more light on this subject, it is important to first "follow the money" and develop an understanding of the history of chemotherapeutic payer and reimbursement systems, including Medicare, and its role within the overall market.[5]

CMS (formerly known as the Health Care Financing Administration, or HCFA) has always had a significant impact on how healthcare is practiced in the United States. During the 1980s, changes to the CMS reimbursement initiated the shift from providing hospital or inpatient-based oncology drug treatment to the oncologist office or ambulatory setting.

This movement was orchestrated by changing reimbursement to a scheme that favored office-administered therapies over hospital-based drug treatments. The main change was the move from an FFS reimbursement program for hospitals to a diagnosis-related group (DRG) program.

In the DRG program, all services and drugs are part of the payment based on a DRG determination. As drugs became more expensive, the DRG payment did not cover even the cost of the drug. Hospitals responded to the limitations of DRG reimbursement by decreasing the length of a hospital stay and transitioning patients to outpatient settings where anticancer drugs and physician services were paid for on an FFS basis. Moving the care of oncology patients to the outpatient setting alleviated the DRG challenge for the hospitals and made it profitable for oncologists to provide chemotherapeutic drugs and services in their offices.

Prior to 1997, CMS reimbursed ambulatory chemotherapeutic drugs based on an FFS schedule of 100% of the average wholesale price (AWP) to physicians. This reimbursement schedule was so profitable to the doctors that they often waived the Part B 20% coinsurance payment that the Medicare beneficiary should be paying. The drug reimbursement at 100% of AWP came under a lot of pressure as CMS gathered data from other pharmacy reimbursement schedules, mainly from PBMs and other managed care health plans, where reimbursements are based on a discounted AWP. This led CMS to reduce anticancer drug reimbursement from 100% of AWP to 95% of AWP in 1997. Even at a 5% discount from the previous level, oncologists enjoyed strong revenues and margins from the drugs they administered. In fact, the profit margin on the drug side was so pervasive that oncologists often placed little emphasis on the professional side of the overall oncology services. This was in contrast to the rest of the physician community, where the physicians spent most of their time fighting for increases and against rate decreases for professional service reimbursement from CMS and other payers.

Oncologists continued to enjoy strong profits from drug reimbursement until 2003, when the Medicare Modernization Act (MMA) was enacted to provide prescription drugs to Medicare beneficiaries. Although the MMA did not address the issue of chemotherapeutic drug reimbursement directly, it did put into motion a series of reductions to Part B drug reimbursements. The initial phase of the MMA called for a reduction in drug payments by CMS from 2003 through 2005. Based on the MMA, CMS has projected it would reduce drug reimbursement by 28% while increasing the drug infusion payment by 130%.

As part of the changes to the CMS payment methodology, three categories of drugs were created that provided differences in payment schemes from 2004 to 2005. Pass-through drugs are those drugs approved by the U.S. Food and Drug Administration (FDA) with or without a Healthcare Common

Procedure Coding System (HCPCS) code (or J-code). And as part of the non-pass-through drugs, three separate categories of drugs are identified:

- Sole-source: drugs with no generic equivalents
- Innovator multisource: sole-source drugs with generic equivalents
- Noninnovator multisource: generic drugs

In 2006, the MMA allowed for a new reimbursement plan for Part B drugs where the fees are not based on AWP but rather on a new schedule called the average sales price (ASP). The majority of the drugs reimbursed by CMS is based on 106% of ASP, or ASP +6%, methodology.

In addition to introducing the ASP +6% reimbursement model, CMS set up a system to award contracts to authorized medication dealers through a program called the competitive acquisition program (CAP).

COMPETITIVE ACQUISITION PROGRAM (CAP)[6]

The Medicare Modernization Act (MMA) established an alternative method called CAP for physicians to obtain many drugs covered under Part B. Since July 2005, physicians have had the option of making an annual election as to whether they wish to purchase these drugs on their own and be paid based on the ASP rate or to obtain them from a vendor. The vendor, in addition to being responsible for supplying the drug to the physician in the CAP, is also responsible for billing Medicare for the drug, collecting the coinsurance from the beneficiary, and coordinating secondary payer issues.

Participation in CAP is voluntary, and physicians who elect into CAP must abide by their choice for the year, except for certain rare exceptions. The benefit of participating for physicians is that they do not incur the expense of purchasing and billing for these medications, nor do they have to concern themselves with the Medicare payment rate for these products and trying to acquire them at the best possible prices in the market. The CAP program was initially viewed as a beneficial program for oncologists. However, challenges in the CAP program have caused physicians to question the risk and rewards of this program.

Due to the COT issues previously discussed, oncologists are able to order drugs for their patients and bill CMS as they have for decades. Financially, some of the larger oncology groups are able to negotiate better rates and maintain an adequate margin even under ASP. The increased hassle factor of CAP and continuing profit from oncology drugs have caused few oncologists to participate in the CMS CAP. This makes sense, as oncologists have traditionally performed these functions and are unlike other specialties where the provision of drugs is not part of the normal services of the physician.

Oncologists have also pointed to the clinical obstacles for their participation in the CAP. The oncology community at large views CAP as an untried and untested experiment. Oncologists have complained that they will not expose their patients to the risks it presents and that CAP has forced the creation of individual patient inventories, has increased the likelihood of treatment errors and delays, and has placed new and unreimbursed administrative burdens on clinics.

Wholesalers have also avoided the CAP. One executive we interviewed noted:

> The CAP applies to practices that are poorly run. ASP plus six works very well, but when they tested it there was little interest in the oncology community to adopt it. Essentially, ASP plus six took away any means of additional revenue. For practices that were interested in the CAP, what we found was that the practice was poorly run, and they could not take on a large receivable. On top of that if they had bill to a payer and they are taking on a payable and a receivable, and they have to manage the receivable to pay the wholesaler.

A further complexity in the oncology supply chain is the issue of J-code reimbursements.

J-CODES

Chemotherapeutic agents and oncology services by physicians have traditionally been reimbursed by the Medicare Part B reimbursement scheme. And since CMS is the largest payer for these types of services and drugs, many private insurance companies have similarly categorized cancer and chemotherapeutic agent reimbursements as part of the outpatient medical benefit and not the pharmacy drug benefit.

Because oncology services are reimbursed as a medical benefit or under Part B, CMS designed a payment scheme based on two coding systems:

one for the professional services rendered by the doctor, known as *current procedural terminology,* or CPT codes; and the other for *medications and related services,* or J-codes. Professional services and medications covered by CMS must have a CPT code or J-code as part of the invoice by the provider to CMS for services rendered to an eligible beneficiary under the Medicare program

In the United States, medications have traditionally been differentiated by commercially available dosage, quantity per package unit, manufacturer, and lot number through the use of a coding system known as the national drug code (NDC). The NDC is used in the outpatient or ambulatory setting by pharmacies and healthcare payers for reimbursement processes. The use of the NDC is very important in that the NDC numbers submitted by pharmacy providers for reimbursement requests to payers are very specific to the medication dispensed to the patient, according to a unique set of parameters. Those parameters include manufacturer, dosage, packaging unit per day-supply used, and lot number for each drug. In other words, the NDC is so specific that payers can specify exactly the quantity of drug to be reimbursed and the monetary amount they will pay.

J-Code Specificity Challenge

Compared with the NDC, the J-code has numerous inherent challenges to payers. Whereas the NDC is very drug-specific, the J-code lacks much of the specific information third-party payers require for reimbursement. The specificity challenge did not expose any major issues when most of the drugs under J-code were single-source brand medications.

However, as generic drugs become more prevalent, the lack of medication specificity presents significant challenges, as prices may be very different from the various generic manufacturers. In the case of generic drugs, the J-code in essence becomes a ceiling reimbursement price, and significant gaming in pricing can be maneuvered by manufacturers as well as practitioners to maximize reimbursement revenue.

Dosing Challenges

The commercially available traditional medications are based on specific dosage increments. For example, a traditional medication may be available in 5 mg increments from 10 mg to 40 mg. Patients' medication dosage requirements are based on increments of 5 mg. So, if 10 mg is not working based on the clinical requirement, the doctor may increase the dose in 5 mg increments based upon an established FDA-approved upper limit of 40 mg.

The dosing criteria for chemotherapeutic agents are different and are often based on weight, lean body mass, or body surface area of a patient. Thus, the dosage for a specific patient often is not based on the commercially available dosage form. If the patient needed 15 mg of J-0128 and the commercially available drug comes in 20 mg vials, then there is an inherent waste of 5 mg. This problem is magnified if the patient requires a 21 mg injection and the doctor has to use two 20 mg vials of the drug, leading to a waste of 19 mg.

Cost Challenge

Another challenge to dosing in the J-code system, compared with the NDC, is that every drug dosage costs the same regardless of the amount of dosage for that drug. An example of NDC pricing is shown in Table 5.2. Conversely, every unit of J-0886 (Epoetin Alfa) is the same price. Contrast that to traditional drugs where the cost of a 10 mg unit of a drug does not always double when a doctor uses the 20 mg dosage of the same drug (the cost doubles if the doctor uses two 10 mg doses of the drug). Because of market competition, drug manufactures may use flat or tiered pricing

TABLE 5.2

Average Wholesale Prices of Commercially Available Medications

Medications	Commercially Available Strength	Commercially Available Package	Average Wholesale Price (AWP)
Lipitor	10 mg	90 tablets/package	$260.05 ($2.89/tablet)
(Atorvastatin)	20 mg	90 tablets/package	$370.95 ($4.12/tablet)
	40 mg	90 tablets/package	$370.95 ($4.12/tablet)
	80 mg	90 tablets/package	$370.95 ($4.12/tablet)
Avandia	2 mg	60 tablets/package	$153.25 ($2.55/tablet)
(Rosiglitazone)	4 mg	30 tablets/package	$113.73 ($3.79/tablet)
	8 mg	30 tablets/package	$206.64 ($6.88/tablet)
Procrit	4,000 unit/ml	25 × 1 ml package	$1,565.00 ($62.6/4,000unit)
(Epoetin Alfa)	20,000 unit/ml	6 × 1 ml package	$1,878.00 ($62.6/4,000unit)
	40,000 unit/ml	4 × 1 ml package	$2,504.00 ($62.6/4,000unit)
Avastin	100 mg	1 vial	$687.50 ($687.50/100 mg)
(Bevacizumab)	400 mg	1 vial	$2,750.00 ($678.50/100 mg)

Source: AWP is based on the December 2006 *BlueBook*.

formulas to give them a pricing advantage over competitors. This allows for cost containment processes in the traditional drug forum that are not available in the Part B drug environment.

A common cost containment process used in the pharmacy benefit realm is dosage optimization. In this process, if the doctor titrates up in dosage rather than using two units of the same dosage strength, patients are dispensed the next dosage strength of the drug. For example, if the doctor wants to use 20 mg of Lipitor, the patient receives 20 mg rather than two of the 10 mg. This process often leads to cost savings for the payer and is more convenient for the patient. Contrast this to Avastin, where, regardless of the dosage the patient requires, the cost will be incremental and no savings can be derived from optimizing the dosage of the drug.

PAYER AND REIMBURSEMENT SYSTEMS

The dominance of CMS and its reimbursement protocols to reduce costs has caused private payers to rethink how they are managing this portion of the drug reimbursement. Based on the previous discussion of the challenges of the J-code versus NDC reimbursement processes, many private payers are trying to shift to a more comprehensive and cost-effective adjudication process. Private payers are trying to move physician-administered drugs from the medical side of the benefit to the pharmacy benefit in an effort to contain costs.

Payers are increasingly aware of these practices. For example, in interview with a representative from a health insurer noted the following detection of "squishy J-codes" and the overuse of the J-3940 "miscellaneous" code. As noted by one regulatory expert:

> The J-code problem is familiar to us. In our state, we have mostly group practices. We include oncology, and we have been managing the medical side pharmacy since 2003. We originally created a separate fee schedule for those J-codes and have now moved to ASP pricing for the J-codes. If Medicare does not list a price as an ASP price for a drug (e.g., Synogis) we will reimburse at AWP minus 25—and that gets their attention.
>
> If the drug is administered at a pediatrician office or nurse we will in every case try to make the drug a commodity. If it can be administered in a different fashion, through office practice infusions or retail ambulatory

pharmacy, I still want to pay the same for the drug. I may pay more for services but not the drug. We put in a therapeutic MAC on the physician side and went after oncology first.

If it is a new drug and it is released by a manufacturer, it often does not get a J-code yet and there is not an ASP—a lot of those things are dumped into the J-3940 miscellaneous code. We claim stop all of these requests and give it AWP minus 25. We go after the NDC used instead. It took a few months, and then rheumatologists figured it out, because they were getting reimbursed at cost or less than cost. So we clamped down hard on the drugs on the medical side for those offices doing "buy and bill." We have tried to take the profitability of the drug out of the equation.

This individual also noted that his company has been approached by four organizations (specialty/PBMs/oncology) who have been the most abusive on J-codes and billing practices on the physician side.

The true distinction of the medical versus pharmacy benefits really took hold in the managed care arena. In the late 1980s, the managed care insurance model became a part of the healthcare insurance landscape. The managed care concept centered on a prepaid capitated premium arrangement among payer, insurance carriers, and doctors. Many of the managed care carriers servicing Medicare patients have since categorically parsed Part B drugs and services into what is now known as the medical benefit side of insurance.

As such, oncology drugs were included with the doctors' professional responsibility as a part of the medical benefit. The key distinction for being responsible for the drugs under the medical benefit is that doctors are financially responsible for the procurement and provision of Part B drugs to member–patients. Contrast this to the pharmacy benefit where physicians are not directly responsible for the procurement and provision of drugs. It is the responsibility of the insurance carrier to provide network pharmacies from which member–patients can obtain drugs.

Prior to the mid-1990s, the differentiation between medical and pharmacy benefit did not play a major role in cost containment because oncology drugs were few and relatively inexpensive. Nonmanaged care and managed care stakeholders did not feel the brunt of financial burden for oncology drugs. However, as we moved into the new millennium, biotechnology brought tremendous advances to pharmaceutical research and development where many newer, more effective, and more expensive oncology drugs came onto the market. Now, these newer and more expensive anticancer agents are lumped into the medical side of the benefit, and physicians are feeling the financial pressures of being responsible for these drugs. In managed care, drugs designated as part of the medical benefit relegate the primary care physicians (PCPs) as the entity that is given a subcapitation and financial responsibility for Part B services. Thus, the PCPs act like the payer of services similar to an insurance carrier.

Regardless of who pays for Part B drugs, physicians reimbursed for drugs dispensed in the office often endure complications and delays in obtaining proper reimbursement by payers. One such challenge is that Part B or medical claims for drug adjudication do not operate in the NDC format or in real time. Medical claims are normally invoiced through retroactive paper format with drugs being identified in J-codes. As described previously, J-codes are not as specific as NDC in terms of the drugs dispensed. For example, if a drug does not have a J-code, physicians can invoice it under J-9999 and provide the name of the drug and sometimes its strength. Another such nonspecific J-code is J-3490 and J-3590, also known as not otherwise classified (NOC). According to a statement from CMS, "If a claim is received for HCPCS J-3590 or J-3490, it will suspend for review of documentation for coverage and payment determinations."

Contrast that to the pharmacy reimbursement system where all drugs adjudicated for payment must have an NDC designating the exact name, strength, and quantity of the drug. With specific information in a real-time environment, pharmacy claims can be adjudicated and reimbursed in a timely manner, and, more importantly, payers are capturing accurate and timely data for review, documentation, and analysis.

In sum, claims invoiced through the medical benefit are less accurate, less timely, and often involve more administrative oversight as compared to the pharmacy system. This is one of the main incentives to move at least the drug component of the Part B benefit to the pharmacy benefit. However, because oncologists and physicians as a whole do not have pharmacy adjudication systems, any transition of Part B drugs from the medical benefit to the pharmacy benefit would necessitate separating how doctors procure drugs. This means that pharmacies will need to be involved as the provider of the drugs to either the doctor or the patient and invoice the payer for the provision of drugs.

Managed Care Synopsis

In managed care, payers pay a fixed capitated premium to managed care organizations (MCOs) to take care of healthcare needs of the beneficiaries.

The MCOs in turn carve out subcapitated arrangements to stakeholders for the actual provision of healthcare services. For example, hospitals have carved a negotiated capitated pool of funds to pay for hospital services and products—Part A services. Physician's professional services are carved into a separate capitated pool of funds to pay for ambulatory physician services and products—Part B services. Ambulatory pharmacy services are typically an estimated capitated pool of funds to pay for pharmacy services that is retained by the MCOs. The MCOs use the pharmacy pool to pay for medications through the service of PBM companies.

MISALIGNED INCENTIVES IN THE ONCOLOGY SUPPLY CHAIN

The net effect of these changes and relationships in this space is that there are misaligned incentives between payers and providers. This is discussed in the following sections.

Payers

The incentive for payers is to contain expenses for services under a defined benefit structure. Payers want to make sure that the dollars allocated to healthcare service benefits promised to patients in the benefit program can pay for the services rendered over a specific period of time. Simply put, payers want to make certain that the premiums they receive for a defined set of benefits for people in the pool can pay for all the services used by the patient pool. A profit is achieved if the payment for services is below the total premium, and a loss will occur if there is not enough money to pay for all the services.

As a payer, the federal government decided to contain costs by lowering drug payment to providers. It created the ASP model, which reduces cost in the short-term, but the inadvertent long-term result may be an overall increase to the market cost structure. Private health insurances are finding other ways to cut costs besides lowering drug payments. For managed care payers, the subcapitated program has run its course, since the hefty costs of newer oncology drugs have caused subcapitated providers to give back the drug portion of the capitation and caused a shift to using specialty pharmacies. This shift to specialty pharmacies will not result in lower costs because of the COT issue as well as challenges in delivery of drug such as late or lost drugs, delays in treatment, oversupply of product, or co-pay collections. This can result in increases in use and total cost to the payer.

Oncologists

Along with this change, three situations occurred in which payers found themselves playing a pivotal role in the handling of oncology drugs, which has created a difficult environment for providers. The first situation is where the pharmacy manager in the payer's organization identifies areas where they believe savings to the system exist. The second situation is where subcapitated PCPs are returning oncology or Part B drug risks to the health plan. The third scenario is where the health plan decides to branch its pharmacy program into the specialty drug space. By doing this, health plans create their own specialty pharmacy to handle these drugs internally. Therefore, health plans have been prompted to get involved in the supply chain of medication provision, and oncologists are now facing numerous new challenges:

- **Oncologists have to manage different inventories.** Since not all payers require the use of a specialty pharmacy and oncologists have contracts for services with numerous health plans, the doctors have to maintain an inventory of oncology drugs for their patients in the specialty pharmacy program as well as those not in the specialty pharmacy program.
- **Oncologists need to have a backup system to deal with delays in getting drugs from the specialty pharmacy.** Any delays have and will continue to occur, since specialty pharmacy is in essence a mail-order pharmacy. As such, doctors almost have to carry extra inventory to prepare for such glitches in the system. Since these situations are resolved with replacement inventory, doctors are not compensated for all the administrative resources necessary in dealing with this type of occurrence. A replacement system is where physicians use their own inventory of drug and a specialty pharmacy contracted to the payer replaces the drug. Now consider if 30% of the doctor's contracted payers use the services of specialty pharmacies.

The aforementioned administrative glitches can potentially turn into a total administrative nightmare for doctors.

- **Oncologists incur additional administrative burden due to numerous calls and interruptions caused when the specialty pharmacy requires information for its prior authorization (PA) process.** Specialty pharmacies typically promise management control to the health plans and potential savings to the program. One way to "manage" drugs is to place expensive drugs under a PA program with established guidelines and various other requirements (e.g., lab test) for PA approval. The PA process typically requires the pharmacy to contact the doctor for information. This causes additional burden for doctors because they have to do double PA work for the same patient. They have to submit a PA to the payer for the medical part of the service and another PA to the specialty pharmacy for the medication. This two-PA submission process used to be a one-PA process in the past for both medical and drug requests from one entity, namely the payer. This is not the end of the PA process, however, as the specialty pharmacy will contact the doctor periodically to coordinate continuation of pharmacy treatment. Specialty pharmacies perform periodic updates to make sure the patient is still with the same payer or the patient is still on the treatment protocol. This further adds to the doctor's ongoing administrative burden.

One solution to the delays in shipping drugs to the doctor by the specialty pharmacy is the drug replacement program. Under the drug replacement program, oncologists use the drugs they have in stock and then order a replacement from the specialty pharmacy. This process eliminates any delays in treatment, and the doctor's business is kept whole.

The replacement process demands that the doctor has a large panel of patients that require similar drugs. In this case, the doctor will use drug A for patient A and get a replacement for drug A and can then be used for patient B and so forth. The theory behind drug replacement may appear to be sound on the surface. However, for the oncologist, it is both a financial and inventory burden. This is because cancer regimens and the patients treated by oncologists are not similar or have high turn ratios. For example, a doctor has two patients who need Herceptin, but one patient is on a replacement program and the other is with a payer where the doctor bills for the drug. In this case, the doctor will be reserving inventory for one dose of Herceptin for the patient who is on a replacement program. Due to the high cost of this drug, the doctor is in essence paying for and holding the Herceptin in inventory, which leads to an added financial burden of incurred holding costs. If the doctor returns the Herceptin to his wholesaler for refund, then this will add to his administrative burden. The impact to oncology practices from reimbursement changes implemented in 2007 could have detrimental effects on patient care. The net result of the lower drug payments under the ASP model and the CPT code-driven professional fee scheme will depend on the mix of drugs and services provided by each oncologist. However, one thing is certain: change will be the norm in the way an oncology practice operates and is reimbursed. Oncologists must be able to be flexible and diligent in conducting business both clinically and financially to profitably navigate through the next few years of uncertainty.

Specialty Pharmacies

The primary incentives for oncologists are similar to those of specialty pharmacies. They have focused their attention on the drug reimbursement component of the equation and have allowed the professional part of the reimbursement equation to lag. Having driven profits from drug reimbursement for so long, they are now in a situation where they are not being properly reimbursed for their services. For specialty pharmacies, the dispensing fees for pharmacists are so far behind that they are willing to accept no professional fee just to capture the drug business.

Both specialty pharmacies and oncologists are designated as providers in this process. In the specialty pharmacy case, as with any pharmacy, this stakeholder lives in an FFS environment. Although it is offering a lower per-unit drug cost to payers, its profitability resides in increased use and less barrier to access. Additionally, due to the class of trade (COT) in drug pricing, increasing volume in drug purchases does not yield the same result as it does in the merchandising world where volume drives price elasticity. As an example, Walmart or Costco has tremendous leverage in product pricing due to purchasing power and exclusivity in product selection. However, in the COT environment, more purchases do not necessarily translate into lower cost structure. For a major retail chain drug store such as Walgreens, its drug purchase volume is second to none. But because of COT, its cost of goods is higher across the board than for a closed-door pharmacy. As previously noted, all three major PBMs in the United States predicted that use would be the main driving force behind increases in spending for specialty drugs for the next few years.

As stakeholders, incentives for specialty pharmacies and oncologists are very different from those for payers. The way these providers expand their revenue stream is to provide more drugs more frequently (higher use) and to use those drugs with the highest margins or cost. Contrast that to payers, who seek to manage drug costs by making sure the most cost-effective agents are prioritized for use with patients.

Home Infusion Companies

The more significant obstacles to blending and aligning of purchasers from different classes of trade are rooted in tradition.[7] Pharmaceutical manufacturers' infrastructures are set up according to their market COT as defined by each manufacturer. A company with oral and self-injectable products may lump specialty pharmacies into the same COT as mail-order pharmacies or PBMs and view home infusion companies as a different COT. A different manufacturer may lump specialty pharmacy, specialty infusion, and home infusion companies into the same COT, effectively blocking these companies from limited distribution contracts that are typically awarded to national companies.

Although home infusion companies may not be able to purchase the products at the most favorable rates, they are still competing with other infusion providers in terms of billing. This infusion market is effectively an alternative site specialty infusion provider and includes physician offices, ambulatory infusion suites, hospital outpatient clinics, and even inpatient settings. As a COT, hospitals and physician offices enjoy much better pricing on infusible products than do home infusion companies.

Hospitals

In the middle of this, hospitals are also playing a role. My research reveals that hospitals are being caught in the middle. One of the specialty pharmacies at a major hospital in Minneapolis revealed the following:

> Infusible drugs with the CAP program have caused major problems and are pushing the medical benefit to a pharmacy benefit, based on localization

of the decision with physicians. I can't afford to infuse drugs to a patient for $300, which is what Medicaid pays me. Now we have situations where patients are coming in with their own meds and want to be in control, and I can't make a margin on the services covered by Medicaid alone. And oncology clinics are driving patients to the hospitals, and we can't refuse to treat them.

Hospital executives are very upset that physician offices are benefiting from class of trade while they cannot:

Class of trade was originally developed as a differential cost in the marketplace: if there was a different cost to deliver a product to a customer, then you charged them a different price. This has morphed into a situation where the rebate is now going to the decision maker, which in this case is increasingly one of the big wholesalers.

Manufacturers

Manufacturers of specialty drugs typically live in a monopolistic or oligopoly environment. The biological medicines they provide have strict patent protection and offer them huge price control. As such, the only barrier to usage, and corresponding profits, relies on support by oncologists. And since oncologists have traditionally controlled their own destinies in terms of drug purchase, provision, and receiving payment from payers, drug companies cater to these profitability drivers through COT pricing schemes.

The biggest change in the market is the move toward customized cancer therapies. These therapies involve individualized medicine. These treatments link a diagnostic of a specific condition with a therapeutic. The diagnostic defines the kind of tumor and the stage of the tumor and the required treatment. One of the most successful drugs in this category is Herceptin (Genentech) for breast cancer. It was so successful that it was passed by the FDA and registered in a shortened Phase 2 cycle and did not go to trials. There are about 50 drugs like Herceptin on the market that are linked to pharmacogenetics. Companies are now seeking to replicate this model. Genentech developed drugs that are uniquely formulated for breast cancer patients who exhibit the HER gene that can be targeted by Herceptin. These fall into the category of biologics, which are peptides and cannot be given orally. Larger molecules must be infused, so noncompliance is very low.

Physicians in general do not care for the term *personalized medicine*, because they feel that they have been practicing this way their entire career (e.g., matching a series of drugs and compounds to individual patients). But they have not had the tools to define specifically how to do so until the rise of genetic science. Molecular genetic tools are able to provide a much better descriptor of how individual characteristics, disease symptoms, propensity for diseases up front, and potential tumor typology can shape the drug's ideal populaton. The biggest changes are the linkages between diagnostic and therapeutic medicine, which will affect the market and the dynamics of the drug industry.

This has important implications for physicians, who will not be allowed to deliver medicines unless they are parsed with the right set of diagnostics. Today for the most part they are not linking them properly. The biopharmaceutical industry is increasingly developing diagnostic tests that should be used with these sets of indications. Physicians take out a sample, analyze the lab results, and consult a formula-based sheet to prescribe the proper amount to infuse.

One of the challenges with this approach is that patient management is being influenced by the third-party reimbursement structure. Oncology is one of the few areas impacted by this individualized medicine of pharmacogenetics. Every one of the big life sciences companies has such programs and understands the implications for life-cycle management. Initially, pharmaceutical manufacturers did not like the approach. Only 30% of the individual patients responded in a therapeutic way to small-molecule oral drugs, but Big Pharma companies made money on it. But with pharmacogenetics physicians avoid giving drugs to patients for whom it will not have an effect or to people who may have a side effect (a much smaller population). As a result, biopharma companies have raised the cost of the drugs, and by linking the diagnostic to the therapeutic they have now raised the price for these medicines and have recaptured the cost of the medicine.

To summarize, manufacturing companies understand that if a doctor enjoys a high margin for its drug and the drug is clinically safe and effective, then the likelihood of persuading the doctor to use its drug will be enhanced. This is one of the major drivers for employing a class of trade pricing mechanism.

Patients

As for patients who are unfortunate enough to be afflicted with cancer, they are seeking "any" option that offers hope. As with their colleagues on the traditional drug manufacturing side of the fence, specialty drug companies are turning to direct-to-consumer (DTC) advertisements as a way to promote drugs. This is an effective way to get noticed because they are selling hope, and patients are often shielded from the total cost of the product since patients typically pay only a small portion for these drugs in terms of copayments. As stakeholders, the incentive for specialty drug manufacturers is very different from that of payers. The way these manufacturers expand their revenue stream is to identify new and novel drugs through the U.S. patent system, to establish higher margins to oncologists, and through DTC to promote treatment options to patients. In essence, the manufacturers are promoting more drugs, more frequent usage, and drugs with the highest margins or cost. Contrast that to payers, who would prefer to manage drug costs by making sure only cost-effective agents are used.

These misaligned incentives are likely to collide in the next three years, unless significant collaboration among physicians, manufacturers, payers, and distributors occurs.

CONCLUSION

Clearly, the incentives among stakeholders are not aligned to promote cost-efficiency. Therein lies the true opportunity for this space. If an entity can formulate a way to mutually align the incentives of the stakeholders in the oncology arena, then true cost-effective treatments will be available to cancer patients.

In assessing this market, several key forces in the market should be taken into account. By now, readers recognize that the model for distribution of oncology products is unsustainable for all players. The medical oncologist is at the center of all therapies, and payers have direct access to ASP. Specialty pharmacists can drive volume increases by shipping volumes to patients that exceed what they require, and this practice has been noted in a couple of our interviews as a growth strategy to meet manufacturer objectives.

The following critical issues summarize the challenges that must be overcome:

- Manufacturers are focused on targeting physicians and have established positions with existing distributor–GPO partnerships. They understand that physicians have the balance of power in making the treatment decision and have established in-depth programs at pharmacogenetics to combine diagnostics and treatment into a single process, administered and controlled by the physician. As such, they have established COT programs to target physicians.
- Manufacturers reward COT pricing to distributors with significant market share. Wholesalers have a strong relationship with manufacturers and have a volume-based approach that allows them to pass on preferential pricing to physicians.
- Hospitals cannot drive compliance to physician formulary preferences, making this a more difficult market to penetrate. Also, they are seeing a greater proportion of Medicare patients and are losing margins on these patients. Although these hospitals are open to growth from new entrants, it is difficult to envision how this would be a profitable channel in the long term or even in the short term.
- Getting new drugs into distribution will be a challenge for oncology. Although companies can drive existing relationships from within the hospitals, there is not a strong presence in specialty pharmacies. Both GPOs and hospitals are open to having new entrants participate more openly in the hospital. An administrator at a hospital noted that "this has morphed into a situation where the rebate is now going to the decision maker, which in this case is increasingly the wholesaler. We hope that other wholesalers will drive competition."

Insurance providers, wholesalers, hospitals, and oncology manufacturers need to begin to consider these forces as well as collaborative approaches to delivering value in the face of shrinking margins, increasing regulation, and an imminent growth in the demand for oncology treatment. Collaborative models can begin to identify joint value-added services that can benefit patients and render the cost of healthcare more amenable to productivity improvements and improved efficiencies. The need to establish a profitable model that can deliver oncology products to hospitals, clinics, and all COTs that cover costs of delivery and patient care will be a major challenge for the future.

ENDNOTES

1. Reeder, Claiborne, RPh, PhD, and Debra Gordon, "Managing Oncology Costs," the *American Journal of Managed Care, 2006 12: S3-S16.*
2. Oncology Purchasing and Distribution Groups, Knowledge Source, August 2007.
3. Oncology Purchasing and Distribution Groups, Knowledge Source, August 2007.
4. Oncology Purchasing and Distribution Groups, Knowledge Source, August 2007.
5. Major sections of this part of the paper are derived from *Oncology DrugManagement: A White Paper on Marketplace Challenges, Opportunities and Strategies.* Written by Chris Nee, Pharm.D., M.B.A., President, PharMedQuest Published by Atlantic Information Services, Inc., and PharMedQuest, March 2007.
6. Source: Payment for Medicare Part B Drugs, Herb Kuhn, Director, CMM House Subcommittee on Health of the Committee on Ways and Means, July 13, 2006.
7. *Specialty Pharmacy Resolution of Pharmacy 'Class-of-Trade' Issues Is Key for Specialty Infusion.* Reprinted from the July 2005 issue of SPECIALTY PHARMACY NEWS, a monthly newsletter designed to help health plans, PBMs, providers, and employers manage costs more aggressively and deliver biotechs and injectables more effectively.

6

The Changing Landscape of the Life Sciences Supply Chain: Recommendations for Players in the Industry

INTRODUCTION: AN INDUSTRY IN FLUX

This book was developed over an eight-year period through interviews, conference presentations, one-on-one discussions, and reviews of multiple research papers, presentations, books, and articles. I met with hundreds of biopharmaceutical executives from various stages in the value chain, including manufacturers, group purchasing organizations (GPOs), retail pharmacies, hospital pharmacies, physicians, consultants, academics, clinical researchers, third-party logistics providers, and pharmacy benefits managers (PBMs). Over the eight years, the level of anxiety in the biopharmaceutical and healthcare space has been mounting considerably, culminating with the angry response to President Barack Obama's healthcare act in 2010 and the ensuing set of debates and judicial proceedings that are taking place as this is being written in 2012.

Although there are many flaws with the Obama healthcare legislation, this book is not going to take on the task of focusing on these flaws. As stated in the first chapter of this book, the objective here is to understand the historical context of the life sciences value chain, to describe the current set of challenges facing the industry, and to establish the agenda for change that lies ahead. Moreover, my position is that "Obamacare," as many critics have named it, is really nothing more than a manifestation of what is happening globally in the healthcare ecosystem. The primary element that all players need to focus on is that current business models for the life sciences are no longer sustainable and will surely result in collapse unless something radical changes. This view is not just an opinion—a multi-agent simulation model shows it to be the case.

I develop this thesis through several convergent approaches that together form a triangulated level of support for the hypothesis that network integration is the primary element for continued growth and success of the industry. I first emphasize the unsustainable elements in the current biopharmaceutical business model, using a multi-agent simulation analysis. Next, I detail nine core disruptive ecosystem elements that have and will continue to change the way that biopharma companies engage in business not just with each other, but also with the entire value chain of stakeholders. Most importantly, I identify the need for a "patient-focused network integration" approach. I then identify the hidden opportunities that lie beneath the surface of these changes and describe how innovative companies that embrace industry changes can prosper. I describe each of these four opportunities (global market channel development, personalized medicine and compliance, pedigree and serialization, and specialized distribution capability development) in more detail, based on interviews with hundreds of industry participants. Finally, I conclude with key insights and actions going forward.

A MULTI-AGENT SIMULATION VIEW

The proposal that current models are not sustainable has been validated by simulation findings, using multi-agent-based simulation.* Using current models of biopharmaceutical development, the research suggests that the evolution of the current operating model, when carried out, results in complete collapse.

A multi-agent system (MAS) involves interplay among multiple interacting agents. Although individual agents may follow a simple strategy, it may result in complex evolution of the system. Therefore, MAS methodology is used to analyze systems that are too complex to be solved using

---

* Jetly, Guarav, Rosetti, Christian, and Handfield, Robert, "A Multi-Agent Simulation of the Pharmaceutical Supply Chain (PSC)," Proceedings of the POMS 20th Annual Conference, Orlando, FL, May 1–4, 2009.

alternative methods (traditional mathematical or statistical). Application of MAS is ideal for problems whose solution is dynamic, uncertain, and of distributed nature.

When applied to the biopharmaceutical industry, MAS analysis suggested that, in the end, bigger biopharmaceutical enterprises are not better. According to our model, when manufacturers consolidate, they cannot cover the cost of supporting their large asset base—for example, plants, equipment, research laboratories, administration. Although their research productivity increases as they grow, as measured by the number of drugs released by individual manufacturers, the productivity of the supply chain diminishes. In addition, since drug sales represent a fixed pie, only blockbusters will support the cash drain from larger assets. Because blockbusters are increasingly less likely to occur, it does not take a genius to determine where this ends up.

In the simulation, merger activity is based on the acquirer's determination that the acquisition will perform above itself as well as industry average. As appears to be the case in reality, the agents assume that past performance in drug development is a good predictor of future performance. The acquirer examines each manufacturer based on the number of drugs it has released in the past two years. Unfortunately, by this time the drug is approaching its maximum sales. Although the larger manufacturer has a greater chance at creating a drug over many games, results show that over the course of a sample of 177 games, the manufacturer is not assured that this increase in probability is greater than that of two large manufacturers.

The chart shown in Figure 6.1 is a direct illustration of how all players are losers in this competitive model, as it shows the assets of each class of firm per 20 quarter increments. All games result in lower assets for players. There appear to be several reasons for this. The first is that suppliers are allowed to bid below cost. Since there are twice as many suppliers as manufacturers, the competition among suppliers is intense. Margins quickly reduce to zero though costs remain constant at 5% of assets. Consolidation and oligopolistic competition leads to stabilization of assets, but at a much lower level than this tier of the supply chain started with. Manufacturers fare best in the simulation. Since their cost structure contains a component of fixed and variable costs, manufacturers gain the most from blockbuster drugs. They are hampered by diminished productivity relative to size. The manufacturers lose 5% of their assets, but they release drugs based on a random component that is correlated to size. The games tend to release drugs of comparable sales to those found in industry

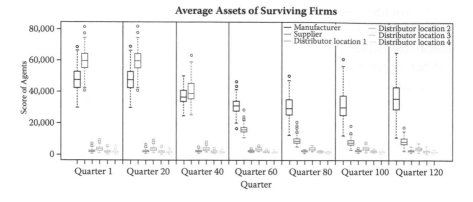

FIGURE 6.1

Average assets of surviving firms—multiagent simulation model. (From: Handfield, Rosetti, and Jetly, 2009. Working paper.)

and also in greater quantity. The revenue from these drugs cannot compensate for the loss of assets due to the manufacturer's size. To say it another way, the entropy of the manufacturer's assets cannot be compensated for by the increased probability of success given its larger assets. This result is confirmed by what is occurring in large pharmaceutical companies today. With more and more drugs falling off the patent cliff and the only source of new revenue coming from specialized drugs, these large enterprises are barely able to keep their heads above water.

Policymakers may be tempted to regulate manufacturer prices to decrease their share of supply chain profits and pass savings on to consumers. Our findings show that this form of regulation may have a limited impact. Currently, manufacturers are spending in excess of 20% of their revenues on sales and marketing activities. This activity is deemed necessary to fulfill a requirement for blockbuster drugs. Our results indicate that blockbusters are more necessary than the number of drugs released. If prices are limited, manufacturers will more likely cut back on research and development (R&D) activities and focus more energy on marketing.

In addition, the results found that distributors have a limited impact on supply chain profitability. Manufacturers and suppliers through drugs released and consolidation impact profitability greatly. Consolidation at the manufacturer level tends to decrease profitability, generally because of reduced research productivity. Consolidation at the supplier level increases supply chain profitability because rents from increased bargaining power are passed on to the consumers.

MASSIVE DISRUPTIONS IN BIOPHARMA VALUE CHAINS

As this simulation result demonstrated, not only is the old operational model broken, but the rules of the game are changing as well. The very nature of the healthcare industry is undergoing a rapid series of changes: the nine major changes that are driving these changes are described next.

Growing Adoption of Price Restrictions by Regulators and Governments

This is a trend that is not just occurring within the United States but also throughout the world. Even though pharma and biologics constitute 10% of the healthcare bill in most countries, the pharma bill is an easy target because it is so concrete and can be directly influenced as it is a fixed price. In fact, research has found that administrative costs are responsible for between 20 and 30% of U.S. healthcare spending.[*] Hospital spending accounts for nearly 33% of all expenditure and prescription products for just 10.1%. Governments focus on pharmaceuticals, often because of the public perception that the medicine bill is much higher than it really is. For example, a survey conducted by the PWC Health Research Institute found that 97% of consumers estimated that prescription medicine accounted for at least 15% of overall U.S. healthcare costs, but 63% put the figure between 40 and 79%.[†] These elements of healthcare (e.g., physician fees, overhead) are more slippery and difficult to measure and thus more difficult to control. As we have seen, in many global regions such as the European Union, India, Brazil, and China, there is only one payer: the government. This increases negotiating leverage and is one reason that prices in the United States are higher than anywhere else in the world. This is going to change. The U.S. market is now under increasing pressure for price reduction, and Obamacare is only the first of many new forms of regulation that are coming down on the industry.

---

[*] Anna Bernasek, "Health Care Problem? Check the American Psyche," *New York Times,* December 31, 2006, Business Section, p. 3.

[†] PricewaterhouseCoopers Health Research Institute, "Recapturing the vision: Restoring trust in the pharmaceutical industry by translating expectations into actions," (2006).

Declining R&D Productivity

It is no secret that the number of blockbusters has all but dried up. A core problem has been the lack of innovation in making effective new therapies for the world's unmet medical needs. A second problem has been the increasing scrutiny of new medicines. The U.S. Food and Drug Administration (FDA) has become more severe in its regulatory stance on "me-too" drugs that do not have measurably improved efficacy over existing drugs. Despite the record billions of spending on R&D, the number of new approved drugs has been paltry relative to the number of branded products going off patent. There is no doubt that pharma's R&D processes have become complex and cumbersome. However, the increased scrutiny has not helped. When they start developing a new medicine, researchers do not know whether it will be eligible for reimbursement, and they are not allowed in many countries to seek guidance from the relevant government agencies. Most of the money invested in R&D is going to line extensions and other work, as distinct from new development projects. The international laws governing intellectual property rights have compounded this problem. And to complicate the problem, the push to maximize the number of candidate molecules in Phase 3 of development, to improve analysts' valuation of the company, may incur extra costs. It may have been better to weed out some of these molecules at an earlier and cheaper stage of development. As a result, manufacturers will need to focus more on targeted therapies that will address the world's most critical disease. For instance, the number of people in India with diabetes is projected to reach 73.5 million in 2025.* Fear about flu pandemics has driven more interest in vaccines, and preventive medicine is becoming an area of increasing support by governments. But oncology is by far the most significant new therapeutic area. According to IMS, there are 90 therapeutic vaccines for cancer in the pipeline. And many of the new diseases (e.g., obesity, liver and pancreas disease, lung cancer, melanoma) will require greater focus on preventive medicine, not just pills for ills. Healthcare payers will not just be negotiating prices but will begin to stipulate best medical practices and access to extensive amounts of outcome data will provide more ammunition.

---

* PricewaterhouseCoopers Health Research Institute, "Recapturing the vision: Restoring Trust in the Pharmaceutical Industry by Translating Expectations into Actions," 2006.

Emphasis on Pay-for-Performance

As we have discussed earlier, the emphasis on pay-for-performance is a phenomenon that is here to stay. Several countries have set up agencies specifically to compare the safety and efficacy of different forms of intervention and promote the use of evidence-based medicine. These include the U.S. Agency for Healthcare Research and Quality, the UK Centre for Health Technology Evaluation, the Australian Pharmaceutical Benefits Advisory Committee, and the Finnish Office for Health Care Technology Assessment. In the United States and Europe, the call for an electronic medical records network will be established by 2020, which will form the basis for evaluating the clinical and economic performance of many therapies. In this environment, healthcare policymakers and payers will use outcomes data to determine best practice, and there is no doubt some medicines will not be passed. Second, the price any therapy can command will be based on its performance, not what the manufacturer thinks is a fair price. A value-based pricing system in which the prices of products are set by comparing their clinical value with that of other treatments for the same condition is likely.[*]

Increasing Emphasis on Personalized Medicine

The growing emphasis on personalized medicine will continue to grow. This will radically change the manner in which prescriptions for most primary care medications will be fulfilled. As boundaries blur, patients will require more information about the medicine they take, more advice, education, and monitoring. This will profoundly change delivery of medicines to patients, and companies will need to be providing a full range of products and services. Increasingly, diagnostics will be a much bigger part of the overall product offering, which is a function of personalized medicine. A foundational principle for personalized medicine is pharmacogenomics, the science that allows researchers to predict the probability of a drug response based on a person's genetic makeup. Mass-produced drugs for a "one-size-fits-all" market are a thing of the past; no longer will people take "average doses" and adjustments made if the patient experiences side effects. The terms *personalized medicine* and *targeted therapies*

---

[*] PricewaterhouseCoopers Health Research Institute, "Pharma 2020: The Vision. Which Path Will You Take?" 2007.

imply that interventions will be for a specific disease or condition, based on an understanding of the relevant genetic variation between individuals with that disease. These differences between individuals will guide the use and interpretation of diagnostics as well as choices in therapies and preventions. What this means, practically, for the industry is that therapies will now be paid based on certain biomarkers being present. A biomarker could be an enzyme, a DNA sequence, or an RNA expression profile that defines a physiological space. For example, a biomarker for breast cancer is the expression of a particular protein called HER. Females who have an expression of HER in their breast cancer are at a high risk of death, because that tumor will metastasize, grow, and be lethal. Genentech designed a drug called Herceptin that is specifically targeted at HER. Herceptin worked so well that the FDA did not conduct a Phase 3 clinical trial but approved the product after Phase 2. For these types of drugs, an indication of a certain condition will be the requirement for approval. Similarly, the presence of certain diagnostic evidence may disclose that the drug will not be effective and will therefore not be approved for certain populations. We are in the early stages of this science, but this is a phenomenon that will grow more in the future.

Fragmentation of Mass Markets

It is no surprise that global markets have become the focus of many manufacturers. The expansion of supply chains will bring many complications, including the challenges of parallel trading and counterfeiting. In addition, the number of products companies make will increase, and the nature of packaging and regulatory requirements will fractionate many product lines for presentation into these different global markets, each with its peculiar regulatory requirements. Some have suggested that this will result more in an "assemble-to-order" production and distribution environment in the future, which may entail postponement strategies for late-stage packaging and customization in the global supply chain at remote locations and distribution centers.[*] This has indeed already begun, as many third-party contract manufacturers and third-party logistics providers have entered the global life sciences landscape.

---

[*] PricewaterhouseCoopers Health Research Institute, "Pharma 2020: The Vision. Which Path Will You Take?" 2007.

Unfortunately, there is a massive need for greater collaboration in an outsourced environment—something the traditional players have not done well in the past (as documented in this book). Strategic partners, close integration at all stages in the product life cycle, and support services tailored to the specific needs of personalized medicine will need to be developed. This will require a radical rethinking of current operating models.

Emergence of Biotech and Biologics

As we have noted earlier, biologics are an important emerging area of growth. For distribution, however, unique challenges are presented. Biologics are particularly hard to manufacture and transport, because they are more fragile than small molecules and more susceptible to impurities in the manufacturing process. There may also be unique technologies for delivery, including controlled-release implants and magnetically targeted carriers. Cold chain requirements, requiring temperature-controlled distribution monitoring, is also challenging in a global environment. We will cover in greater detail some of the specific elements that may drive this in the future.

More Restrictive Regulations

Some of the changes outlined here will depend on the willingness of regulators, but there are indications that key agencies such as the EMEA in Europe and the FDA in the United States are moving in these directions. PWC believes that by 2020, all medicines that receive approval will be approved on a real-time basis with live licenses contingent on the performance of extensive in-life testing, for specific patient subpopulations and a predetermined schedule for reviewing each set of results. They also predict that the regulatory landscape will change dramatically. The public will demand independent verification of all pre- and postmarketing clinical data submitted by manufacturers. Regulatory decisions will be based on risk–benefit analyses rather than data on "comparative effectiveness" across large populations. All reviews will be accompanied by an assessment of the cost-effectiveness of new drugs as well as safety and efficacy. And finally, increasing monitoring of the treatment throughout the lifetime of a patient is more likely to occur. All of these changes will create increased complexity for the supply chain.

Increasing Use of Pervasive Monitoring

As noted earlier, healthcare policymakers and payers will increasingly use outcomes data to determine the future application of a drug and whether it will be covered. This means channel providers will need to build relationships with the agencies that perform the health technology assessments on which many healthcare payers will rely. Diagnostic monitoring of outcomes, combined with patient outcome counseling, will need to occur. This will be especially important in a world of bundled payments, where the fee for a medicine may be bundled with the physician services and hospital fees associated with a particular patient therapy, and the outcome is split between among based on the patient's actual outcome. A big part of this landscape will also focus on patient compliance to a regimen. The use of remote devices to monitor patients on a real-time basis wherever they are will also allow the industry to test new medicines outside a clinical setting. The infrastructure to be able to collect information through embedded devices could be transmitted to a hub at a medical center, electronically filtered, and doses adjusted via automated systems. Driving increased compliance will not only determine whether payment will occur but also can drive sales. Patient compliance has been a major challenge in the past. This is covered in greater detail in this chapter.

Changing Roles of Primary and Secondary Care

As noted earlier, changes in the way healthcare is delivered will require a radically different model than the one used today. The primary care sector is becoming much more regimented, as general practitioners (GPs) perform more minor surgical procedures and payers increasingly dictate the treatment protocols that must be followed.* This, of course, also includes which drugs can be taken. The secondary care sector is contracting and is moving more toward secondary care at home. More self-medication is also occurring, as more prescriptions are sold in over-the-counter (OTC) formats. The definitions of primary and secondary care are blurring, and some forms of primary care are being transferred to the patient. This will further redefine distribution models. As noted in a recent report, a better understanding of the taxonomy of disease, together with better diagnostic tools and monitoring devices, will provide the means with which to bring

---

* PricewaterhouseCoopers Health Research Institute, "Pharma 2020: The Vision. Which Path Will You Take?" 2007.

healthcare delivery even closer to the patient. Patients will one day be able to use Web-based receiving algorithms to establish whether they have a condition that will sort itself out without a recourse to the use of biopharmaceutical drugs. But as treatment protocols replace individual prescribing decisions and technology improves the ability to diagnose conditions, the decision-making authority is gradually moving from doctors to healthcare policymakers and payers. What this means is that as payers typically focus on risk and cost-effectiveness, doctors put safety and efficacy before cost.

To summarize, these changes will mean that patient outcomes must become the focal point of any conversation involving the life sciences supply chain. If it is not, supply chain participants will not be able to leap over the infrastructural challenges that have plagued them for the past 20–30 years. The discussion around fee-for-service (FFS) will increasingly move toward a need for network integration among players in the chain. Companies that do not learn to collaborate and build solutions that rely on payment for outcomes will, quite simply, disappear. Outdated financial systems and strategic planning that relies on transaction optimization, formulary negotiations, and marginal pricing will do nothing to impact whether the drug will be paid for in the channel. And without payment by the end customer, every entity in the chain will dry up, including physician services and hospitals themselves.

OPPORTUNITIES

Despite the severity of these threats, there are many hidden opportunities to be discovered here for innovators who can look beyond the current doom and gloom. Companies can initiate programs to explore value-added services in the form of outsourced reimbursement services to providers. This can be enabled through the strong relationships that exist between key channel partners in identifying how best to deal with the complexities of this situation. Medicare Part D will result in a proliferation of different insurance providers that is likely to overwhelm and confuse the average consumer, especially the senior aging population. A "one-stop shop" approach may be a potential opportunity for exploration by participants to explore new business models that add value in emerging market channels.

First, global market channel development and reimbursement models aligned with these markets will need to be developed. It seems likely that the current dominance of FFS distributing will continue in the short term in the United States but will more than likely move toward a patient-centric value delivery model in the future. It is also increasingly clear that global markets are also very much aligned with patient-centric models and have even fewer degrees of freedom when it comes to reimbursement options. There is no doubt that the U.S. FFS distributing certain has proven itself to have a number of advantages relative to the buy-and-hold model. Drug price increases have been restrained for a variety of reasons in the new environment, making "buy-and-hold" distributing less profitable. FFS distributing is more transparent in that it is easier to explain to manufacturers what they are paying wholesalers for, even though there is significant disgruntlement among small and medium-sized manufacturers that are typically charged higher rates. However, service providers will need to develop methods for reimbursement that share risk and rewards of the new healthcare landscape on a global scale and develop innovative approaches to managing patient compliance, customized therapies, and pay-for-performance challenges aligned with the specific regulatory landscape for each regional growth market globally.

Second, personalized medicine, pervasive monitoring, and patient services hold the promise of market expansion for participants in the chain. Increased application of patient compliance technologies will be important here. Large wholesalers may realize some advantages relative to their smaller rivals in mail-order and Internet-based dispensing of prescription drugs. Small, unaffiliated websites and mail-order companies do not have the resources to invest in multistate licensing qualifications, whereas wholesalers do. Currently, states protect their citizens from unscrupulous Internet healthcare entities through licensing requirements for pharmacists, doctors, and wholesalers. In several other industries, state licensing laws have been struck down as being unconstitutional barriers to interstate commerce and a similar fate could occur for pharmaceutical drugs if it becomes clear that state authorities are engaging in economic protectionism of in-state healthcare businesses.

Third, the need for ascertaining pedigree and serialization can provide greater visibility into the channel, meet regulatory requirements, and provide additional value-added capability in the supply chain. It seems likely that wholesalers are going to be expected to do more in the future as the regulatory challenges of compliance become more daunting. The pharmaceutical supply chain requires sophisticated wholesaling to combat the challenges posed by counterfeiting. One of the most significant services an FFS wholesaler can offer a manufacturer is a licensed, environmentally controlled, PDMA compliant, secure facility. Tracking technology is rapidly evolving from a paper-based system to more high-tech methods, particularly serialization. It seems likely that wholesalers that are first to adopt sophisticated tracking technology will realize cost advantages relative to paper-based methods for establishing pedigree and that FDA regulations will accommodate and encourage high-tech (electronic) track-and-trace methods of establishing pedigree.

Fourth, the value of specialized distribution will become more critical, as the emergence of biologics, cold chain, and global distribution becomes more pervasive. In one possible scenario, direct sales between large manufacturers and retailers could become the norm, relegating wholesalers to servicing the currently less profitable business of small manufacturers. A more proactive approach would be for these entities to begin to collaborate to create new market channels that bring together wholesalers, physicians, and pharmacists enabled by electronic integration, with a focus on delivering value to the patient. Compounded by improvements in track-and-trace technology, transparency and linkage to patient compliance, replenishment, and inventory positioning in the global supply chain could provide a radical advantage over less nimble competitors.

I review each of these four opportunities here in more detail.

GLOBAL MARKET CHANNEL DEVELOPMENT AND ALTERNATIVE REIMBURSEMENT MODELS

It could be said that when wholesalers are merely middlemen they are vulnerable to price squeezes between large manufacturers and customers. On the other hand, when wholesalers are doing more than middlemen arbitraging, their raison d'être is on much more solid ground. The FFS wholesaling model emphasizes that the wholesaler does more than just buying and selling pharmaceutical products. In the near future technologically adept firms that use sophisticated track-and-trace technology linked to serialization will have significant legal and efficiency advantages over firms that rely on paper to establish pedigree.

Growth of Global Markets

FFS has been welcomed by regulators as Medicare and Medicaid reforms are enacted. Although the reimbursement formulas being developed in Washington, DC around Medicaid are likely to negatively impact wholesaler margins, ultimately the formulas should increase cost transparency in the supply chain. This will, in turn, increase visibility of the FFS model and reduce the opportunity for buy-and-sell margins. Interviewees believe that Medicare legislation will also change the landscape for retail, hospitals, oncologists, and other physicians. My research indicates that radical changes will be required in the manner that channel participants manage and administer the new requirements of these programs. There will be additional pressure put on pricing at the retail and physician level and that the pressures of pay-for-performance and targeted therapies will also require manufacturers to approach their markets in a very different manner. This is particularly true, since many of these markets are in emerging countries such as India, China, and Brazil that provide a unique set of circumstances for operating in.

Global market expansion presents an opportunity for all participants in the life sciences value chain, particularly wholesalers. Value-added services in the form of outsourced reimbursement services to providers may contribute to better relationships among wholesalers, government regulators, and payers–administrators. In the United States, changes to Medicare Part D may increase the number of insurance providers causing increased confusion to the average consumer, especially the aging senior population. This may create a potential for a member of the supply chain to provide a "one-stop shop" approach to drugs.

We believe that pharmacy benefits managers (PBMs) and payers will continue to have a great influence in the channel and will dictate what levels of service will be appropriately reimbursed in the future. With the move toward personalized medicine, it will be incumbent for wholesalers and manufacturers to work together to define these new spaces, innovate to leverage technology where it makes sense, and consider entering and codeveloping a greater number of different potential value-added services that adapt to the changing marketplace.

The new competitive environment will be characterized by a higher share of market by generics, increasing customization of channels, therapeutic services, e-prescribing, and other innovations that will cause channel conflict. Out of this conflict, a number of interesting value-added services for global markets will emerge by those who partner and innovate in an open-source mentality.

Opportunity: Emerging Markets

Pharmaceutical firms' relationships with emerging markets have been a hot issue within the past few years. The rising costs and associated prices of drugs are putting medicines out of reach of many people around the world, especially those residing in less-developed nations. Many critics of the biopharmaceutical market, and much of the media coverage as well, have argued that drug companies are charging far more than the marginal cost of the drugs and in such a manner are failing to address the specific health needs of the less-developed countries.

The biopharma industry recognizes the fact that the affordability of healthcare and treatment is a problem in most developing countries. Most firms have reacted by selling drugs at discounted prices to nations that could not otherwise afford them or are actually giving them away as donations. While discounted pricing is one way to get drugs to those nations, it is available only to nations that can afford the drugs even at the discounted price and guarantees that nation only a fixed amount of drugs. If a pharmaceutical firm were to negotiate with the Brazilian government for $300 million worth of discounted drugs, the Brazilian people would have access only to a fixed amount of medication. If the Brazilian government were to run out of that drug earlier than expected, they would not have access to more of the drug until they came up with more money or unless the pharmaceutical firm decided to donate more drugs. It should be noted, however, that the decisions to sell drugs at discounted prices reflect individual company decisions, not industry agreements that would contravene with antitrust laws.

While it is true that the prices for drugs have indeed been rising in recent years, biopharma firms are fast to point out that price is not the only factor that influences drugs sales in the developing world. Even when drugs are sold to developing countries at discounted prices, there is no guarantee that the drugs will reach the poorest people that need it the most. Despite inadequate budgetary resources, many other factors play a key role to the distribution of drugs in those areas, for example, a lack of medical personnel, health facilities being located far from rural populations, inadequate infrastructure, information gaps, and political barriers.* Social barriers also play a critical role in the distribution of drugs to remote areas of the world. Threats also exist that the drugs might fall into the wrong hands and may not be distributed to the people at all.

Due to rising international pressures and for a concern of the general welfare of the world, the European pharmaceutical industry has been working hand in hand with committed governments, international organizations, and nongovernmental organizations to broaden access to healthcare and treatment in developing countries. Partnerships with local organizations are necessary to ensure that the discounted drugs are reaching those in need.

Despite the efforts of the biopharmaceutical industry around the world, critics still point out flaws in the industry's practices. Critics argue that biopharmaceutical firms have shifted their focus away from the development and discovery of innovative drugs to marketing the products that provide the most profit. Some believe that the redistribution of surplus medication is one possible solution to the problem. These activists are attempting to collect any leftover prescription drugs used by U.S. patients that have not yet reached their expiration but would have otherwise been thrown away and send them to regions of the world where they can't afford those drugs. Activists see this as one important solution to the problem of getting drugs to less-developed nations, but industry insiders are quick to point that this is still considered illegal.† Even if the drugs actually reach the nation in need, there is no guarantee that the drugs will actually reach the people who need them.

Patent Protection Issues

Patent protection issues are another problem that pharmaceutical firms face when they operate on a global scale. Many developing nations have been known to infringe upon the patent rights of biopharmaceutical firms, which increases the risk for counterfeit sales and reduces any potential profits a biopharmaceutical firm might realize in that country. Because most of these issues are present in the developing world where patent rights are not protected, pharmaceutical firms have less incentive to sell

---

* "PhRMA: Healthcare in the Developing World," *The Issue of Discounted Pricing in Developing Countries*, http://www.world.phrma.org/discounted.pricing.html
† Torassa, Ulysses, "Activists get AIDS drugs to poor lands: Surplus medications are otherwise wasted," *San Francisco Examiner*, June 25, 2000.

their drugs there. The respect of intellectual property rights in developing countries as well as advanced industrialized countries is of utmost importance to ensure that patented products do not "reappear" in markets where the products are sold at another price. Patent protection is another reason that biopharmaceutical firms have a difficult relationship with the developing world.

The World Trade Organization (WTO) has dedicated a portion of its activities solely to trade-related aspects of intellectual property rights (TRIPS) to help pharmaceutical firms and other high-technology firms in their relationships with developing countries. This organization helps alleviate the reservations companies have of entering into third-world countries because of intellectual property rights issues. Through TRIPS, many developing countries have entered into international agreements that will ensure the protection of patents and will thus help the less-developed nations access the drugs they so desperately need.

Traditional secondary markets, such as China, are becoming more attractive. Customers in developing markets are achieving higher incomes and higher standards of living, allowing for more disposable income to be spent on life-sustaining medicines as well as less urgent treatments and "lifestyle" drugs, such as Pfizer's Viagra.* Gaining a foothold in such markets as India and China, which currently represent only small portions of global pharmaceutical sales, will become increasingly important as these markets grow.

Political changes also increase the attractiveness of secondary markets. China recently enacted several changes, making it easier for pharmaceutical companies to compete in and profit by participating in the market of the world's most populous country. China has enacted regulations, aimed at delivering new and innovative medicines to market, by guaranteeing exclusive manufacturing rights for 12 years. The new laws also allow pricing freedom and priority considerations for reimbursement for the introduction of certain products.† India has proposed changes to its patent laws as well, providing improved patent protections to extend the profitable life of compounds.‡ This extended protection is an improvement over current laws, which offer little protection from copycat manufacturers. It will protect not only protect the market in India from counterfeits but also the

---

* Javalgi et al., 2003.
† Javalgi et al., 2003.
‡ Rai, Saritha, "Generic Drugs From India Prompting Turf Battles," *New York Times* (Late Edition East Coast), December 26, 2003, p. C.

many other unprotected countries where importation of Indian-produced copycat drugs is allowed.*

There are also moves under way to simplify the process of marketing pharmaceuticals on a global scale. One of these movements is the International Conference on Harmonisation (ICH). This conference started in 1991 to establish international manufacturing standards for pharmaceutical products. The agreement progress for standards and implementation has been arduous and slow but is some movement toward standardization of regulations. Agreements on even basic standards would greatly simplify the launch of a global product by reducing the number of barriers that must be faced in each independent country a pharmaceutical company enters.[†] David Phillips, a quality manager at a contract pharmaceutical manufacturing company, stated that, while in his daily work, standards instituted by the ICH are now seen as standards across the industry for many of the functions that must be carried out in the pharmaceutical manufacturing. Furthermore, inspections under the ICH rules are done by third-party independent inspectors who submit reports to all of the countries to which the company exports, greatly simplifying the regulatory process by reducing the number of inspectors from one from each country to one overall.[‡]

In the same manner, China has recently established the SCA, an organization much like the FDA in the United States. This new agency replaces a web of interrelated agencies, each with limited authority over a small segment of the pharmaceutical industry. The new umbrella agency makes the regulatory requirements in the world's fastest-growing market simpler and easier to enter.[§]

Despite these changes, it is still extremely complicated legally, logistically, and culturally to market pharmaceuticals on a global scale. There are many challenges to overcome in the international markets before a product can truly be launched globally.

Each country in which a product is marketed, and, in the case of China, each province may have its own formulary, set of price controls, or both. Approval of manufacturing facilities and processes is still a complicated process. The United States, the world's largest pharmaceutical market,

---

* Ibid.

† Javalgi et al., 2003.

‡ Phillips, David. Presentation in BUS 590X, Issues in and Pharmaceutical and Biotechnology Management at North Carolina State University, Raleigh, North Carolina, April 20, 2004.

§ Javalgi et al., 2003.

has only 300 inspectors to evaluate international plants for importation into the country. This results in potentially long waiting periods for manufacturing approval. Other problems include dealing with local politicians who insist on a manufacturing facility in the country before product can be sold.* Another issue involves the complexities of currency exchange. The drastic changes in some unstable currencies make the difference between profit and loss in some situations. Logistics is another concern. While the United States, Europe, and Japan have well-established infrastructures for the distribution of medical products, many developing countries do not have reliable systems in place. This includes everything from well-organized healthcare systems, security, reliable transportation, and information technology systems. Although the large developing markets of India and China are making great strides in these areas, logistics will continue to be a challenge.

Solutions to overcome some of these problems include more than simply the import and export of products. The establishment of subsidiaries in a country to market, transport, or manufacture a product may be most effective or even necessary to participate in that market. Other measures include acquiring a local company, forming a joint venture with or forming a licensing agreement with a company already established in the desired market.† These later options involve giving up control over part of the operations but stand to provide valuable local knowledge to an organization in a timely and economic manner.

Another large challenge for the marketing on an international scale is cultural differences. There are numerous examples of a product that was successful in one market failing when transferred to a new market. One example is the introduction of an asthma treatment by GlaxoSmithKline (GSK) in China. Predictions that the product would sell well in the market of over 60 million asthma patients were incorrect. The product sold poorly because elderly consumers were loyal to traditional treatments such as pills and injections, and younger consumers, who were willing to try the inhalers, could not bear the taste when using the product frequently. Only after two years and an extensive media campaign did GlaxoSmithKline begin to see its sales increase.‡

---

* Cooper, John, president, Global Manufacturing, Valeant Pharmaceuticals. Lecture in Issues in Pharmaceutical and Biotech Management, Aril 6, 2004, North Carolina State University, Raleigh.
† Javalgi et al., 2003.
‡ Javalgi et al., 2003.

Rather than developing a totally separate message for each market, the pharmaceutical industry should follow the examples of companies like Coca-Cola and McDonalds.* These companies are and have been truly global companies that market through one consistent message that may be tailored for the local needs. For example, McDonalds consistently delivers the same-tasting food quickly at an economical price. In markets such as India, it serves a non-beef menu to accommodate local dietary needs.

According to Andrew Kay, vice president of marketing at Novartis, the pharmaceutical industry needs to focus on the delivery of solutions to unmet medical needs. The health needs of a great number of people throughout the world are similar and should require only one solution.[†] The solution may require local tailoring as in the taste of the GSK inhaler product in China, but the same solution and the same message would still apply. This trend is even more apparent today as patient groups and medical professionals have also become more global. The availability of information technologies allows for better-informed patients in traditionally underserved markets and promotes communication between medical professionals on a global scale.[‡]

Pharmaceutical companies face many challenges in the global market. Simplifications and removals of political barriers will play a key role in the expansion into new markets. Significant challenges will remain in logistics, language, culture, and understanding of the local markets.

The AIDS Epidemic

The issue of AIDS in Africa is one that spans all three serious regional issues discussed: difficulties with the developing world, counterfeit sales, and patent protection issues. AIDS is running rampant in Sub-Saharan Africa and is threatening much of the population. In December 2002, there were 29.4 million cases of AIDS reported in Sub-Saharan Africa out of a total worldwide AIDS incidence of 42 million. This means that approximately 70% of all AIDS cases are present in this area. So far, over 17 million have died from the incurable disease in this region alone, and

---

* Thomaselli, Rich, "Kay seeks common language for global marketing effort," *Advertising Age* (Midwest region edition), May 19, 2003, Vol. 74(20), p. 130.
† Ibid.
‡ Ibid.

25 million are expected to follow if immediate action is not taken. It is estimated that a child is orphaned by AIDS every 14 seconds.[*]

The international community and pharmaceutical firms alike have realized that one of the only ways to ensure the survival of millions of suffering people is to distribute AIDS medication at highly discounted prices to the governments of nations that need those drugs. However, due to many complicating circumstances previously discussed, the distribution of AIDS medication to Africans is not as simple as one might think. In many countries in Africa, the people are so poor that they can barely feed themselves. For the governments of such nations, exterminating AIDS is not exactly on the top of their list of things to do. In many cases, merely feeding oneself is a greater concern. To top this off, AIDS medication must be taken with food three times a day at very specific times. If the medication is not taken properly, it can actually make the patient sicker since the AIDS virus develops immunity to the drug.

Another obstacle to the distribution of AIDS drugs is that there is merely not enough infrastructure. A lack of roads and qualified medical personnel, coupled with the wars going on in the area, poses serious physical limitations to the distribution of AIDS drugs. African nations are also highly prone to corrupt governments, and there is a high risk of AIDS medications ending up on the black market. As a matter of fact, many medications distributed to African nations actually end up back in the United States, rather than helping the people who need them the most. Due to counterfeit issues or improper storage and handling, FDA studies have found between 20 and 90% of AIDS medications in Africa to be ineffective.

Another serious issue to the distribution of drugs in Africa, and other developing countries as well, is local customs. One key element of the AIDS issue is preventing further infection. Educational programs are in place to inform those at risk of protectionist measures, including abstinence and the usage of condoms. These programs, however, often clash with local customs. For example, the issue of AIDS in Argentina is becoming a serious problem, but because it is a strong Catholic country, educational programs centered on the usage of condoms are unheard of.

So far, it is estimated that only 50,000 Africans out of the several million who would benefit from AIDS medications have access to the drugs. Out

---

[*] World Health Organization, "AIDS Epidemic Update," December 2002, http://www.who.int/hiv/pub/epidemiology/epi2002/en/

of those, studies show that 29% of the patients acquired the drugs through their doctor or pharmacy, 30% bought the drugs in the local market, and 21% had them sent from relatives abroad. Nearly two-thirds of those have also reported that they often interrupt their treatment because of a lack of regular supply, a major trigger for resistance.[*] Clearly, serious steps must be taken to increase the efficiency of drug distribution and dosage implementation for AIDS patients around the world.

"Acting Locally"

Operating on a global scale poses many threats and obstacles to pharmaceutical firms. On a "think globally" scale, firms face the difficulties of establishing a global brand, dealing with acquisitions and mergers, regulatory bodies, developing a pricing strategy, and responding to political pressures. On an "act locally" level, pharmaceutical firms face issues surrounding the developing world, counterfeit and black market sales, and patent protection. Local customs also play an important role in the sales of drugs in many regions around the world. Combining all the elements, the international pharmaceutical market can be broken into several different regions: (1) the US, the most important region; (2) Europe, an area of growing importance; (3) Asia—Japan, which is a current viable market, and China, a great future potential; and (4) the rest of the world—Central and South America and Australia represent the greatest opportunities.[†]

The United States

The United States has the highest pharmaceutical prices in the world, which poses the threat of importation of counterfeit drugs from other countries, especially Canada. The U.S. prices are the highest because the market, rather than the government, dictates how much drugs sell for. The United States thus represents the most important region of the world because it is one of the most profitable markets in the world. The FDA is working to secure the safety of the U.S. supply chain against counterfeit drugs.

---

[*] Ingram, Richard, "Black Market, Drug Resistance Are Risks for Africa's AIDS Push," Agence France-Presse, September 23, 2003.

[†] Information in this section was acquired in a personal interview with Mr. Cesar Selema, former Latin American regional director for Gilead Sciences, March 17, 2003.

Europe

Pharmaceutical firms must negotiate with each nation in the European Union separately, despite the fact that the drugs can be freely traded within the boundaries of the European Union. Pharmaceutical firms must negotiate with different governments and deal with pressures from many different healthcare systems. Counterfeit issues due to reimportation are a minimal threat in this region, since prices are already low due to government implemented price controls. With the addition of Eastern European nations to the European Union, however, some of these trends might change as pharmaceutical firms may be challenged with similar problems of developing nations.

Asia

China

Patent protection issues are serious here. To sell medicine in China, the Chinese government requires the drugs to be produced locally. The Chinese communist government seeks to gain access to proprietary Internet protocol (IP) to initiate production of local substitutes although manufacturing quality may not meet FDA requirements in the process. Although China is notorious for patent infringement, the huge population present in China poses a great opportunity for pharmaceutical firms.

Japan

There is a very viable market here that does respect patent protection. Many American pharmaceutical companies are striking deals with Japanese companies so that they can learn more about their current drug technology and to take advantage of partnering advantages. The Japanese market is very profitable, but only to a certain extent because it is very small. However, product packaging quality is exceptionally high and far more rigorous than what one would find in Western countries.

The Rest of the World

South America

For the most part, this region of the world is not able to afford drugs, with the exception of Mexico, Brazil, Argentina, Chile, and sometimes Colombia. Brazil represents the largest market for pharmaceuticals in

South America. Despite recent efforts to implement patent protection in this region, pharmaceutical companies still have many worries over this region. Black market and counterfeit sales are a huge problem, particularly in Argentina.

Australia

The government of Australia implements price controls, so pharmaceutical firms receive little profit here. Besides price controls, the sale of pharmaceuticals here faces few threats—patent protection and counterfeit issues are not very serious threats. However, since Australia represents a very small market, this region often does not receive a lot of attention.

India

This region has not really played much of a role in the pharmaceutical market in the past but is gaining momentum. The huge population here poses a great potential for the sale of drugs. In the past, they have not enforced patent rights but they are beginning to do so. Many counterfeit drugs are produced here, so that is a major issue that must be tackled before more investment in this area is made.

Africa and Other Developing Nations

These regions of the world are highly susceptible to the problems previously discussed. Most of these countries cannot afford drugs and rely on the distribution of free or very inexpensive drugs. Counterfeit and black market sales are a huge threat, and corrupt governments only exacerbate the problem. Many of these countries do not respect patent rights. AIDS is a huge issue, and a solution has yet to be found. Pharmaceutical firms often avoid these regions.

Partnering with Governments as Part of the Solution

To succeed globally, pharmaceutical firms must overcome many different regional obstacles. All governments must take an active hand in reducing the amount of counterfeit sales. Such activity infringes upon the rights of pharmaceutical firms and poses a great health risk as well. The implementation of new technologies can help reduce counterfeit threats, but the most important step to be taken is to increase the penalties on offenders.

Manufacturers must begin working with governments to better understand reimbursement and pricing formulas and establish relevant biomarkers and diagnostics for subpopulations that may be specific and unique to that region of the world.

The WTO must also increase their involvement with international compliance agreements to assure patent protection rights. Pack management firms must also consider how to drive compliance and regulatory risk issues that may impact logisics tracking, such as 2-D bar codes and track-and-trace technologies (covered later). Although there are many obstacles in the global market faced by biopharmaceuticals, doing business on a global scale is becoming a necessity, and firms must find ways to overcome those obstacles.

OPPORTUNITY: PERSONALIZED MEDICINE AND CUSTOMIZED THERAPEUTIC DISTRIBUTION

The same features that will ensure expansion of the global market for biopharmaceuticals have also exposed the limitations of the current approaches to funding this growth: namely, that most of the world's pharmaceutical spending is for the treatment of disease rather than its prevention. But as the global population ages and demand for healthcare increases, the emphasis on prevention will be an outcome that is manifest destiny for the industry. The emphasis on prevention will be much more important, especially as the dietary changes and more sedentary lifestyles of the West are spreading to other regions of the globe. Nevertheless, the markets of the developing world possess very different clinical and economic attributes, vary in their use of traditional medicines, have different laws governing IPs, and have varying reimbursement and healthcare infrastructures. What is common among them is that many governments in both developed and emerging countries are trying to shift the focus from the treatment of disease to its prevention. For example, 18 countries have introduced nationwide bans on smoking, and many have established programs to drive down obesity support services and lifestyle planning.

Therapeutic management services tied to track-and-trace technologies are an emerging trend in the BPS. Therapeutics are "boutique" drugs customized to patient requirements. Manufacturers would begin by segmenting patients based on success of clinical trials in the sub population. The segments would correspond to therapies best suited for specific individuals, based on predefined biomarkers or diagnostics. A patient seeking treatment would be tested and segmented into a category of treatment, and the physician would then recommend the therapy best suited to the individual's particular condition, including their recommended dosage. The BPS then plays an important role in creating specific "boutique" customized therapies to align with individual requirements and genetic characteristics. In this manner, a truly customized set of therapies that is most effective would evolve. Follow-on technologies would then be used to patients followed through with prescribed therapies.

Personalized Medicine

We have already noted that personalized medicine is a theme that continues to move forward as the development of biomarkers for specific disease identification and conditions evolves. More and more drug candidates that were once written off are being reconstituted for patient-specific subcategories. For example, several drug candidates in areas ranging from cancer to schizophrenia that fell short of becoming blockbuster drugs are being applied in niche areas because of the emergence of novel genetic tests. For example, methotrexate, a chemotherapy drug developed in the 1940s that is now limited to treating leukemia, was recently found to destroy cells that contain a mutant MSH2 gene, which is responsible for about 5% of bowel cancer cases.[*] There is also a longer-term payback for healthcare costs here. Typically, many people incur an overwhelming portion of lifetime healthcare expenditures at the end of life. Targeted therapies can shift the economics from excessive, end-of-life spending to investing in prevention, earlier diagnosis, and early treatment of chronic conditions identified through biomarkers and early testing. Using earlier diagnosis technologies, techniques such as advanced screening for disease, improvements in the drug discovery and approval process, avoidance of drug reactions, safer drugs and vaccines, and more accurate methods of determining appropriate drug dosages can translate into major cost savings for the U.S. economy.

---

[*] Borrell, Brendan, "Pharma CPR," *Scientist*, Volume 23(12), p. 61, December 1, 2009, accessed October 4, 2011, from http://classic.the-scientist.com/article/display/56179/;jsessionid=03221DC 283B43370A72A15E743C52899

To achieve this, the industry will need to move beyond the traditional mind-set of "one drug for all patients." A recent study by Deloitte[*] identifies four potential models of targeted therapies that are likely to emerge:

- One drug for one phenotype: This is today's economic model, in which a physical manifestation of a disease is described in a standardized way and one particular drug is taken by a large group of patients. In such cases, the drug may be effective for 60–70% of the population but is used uniformly in any case. This is generally the basis for comparative effectiveness payer policies that are used in many cost–benefit analyses.
- One drug fits a small group: A subset of patients within a given disease population have a common genotype. Examples include HER-positive breast cancer patients prescribed Herceptin, or CM leukemia patients who receive Gleevec. The problem here is that many diagnostics are not covered by health plans, and these are typically not profitable business services, so few companies are willing to go into this line of business.
- One regimen for one patient: This model is similar to HIV regiments, in which safety, dosing, and toxicity at the individual patient level occur when deciding which therapeutics should be combined into an effective treatment. This model points to the need for continuing development of electronic medical records (EMRs).
- One pill for one patient: This model will probably not materialize soon but may occur in the future. There are major challenges associated with manufacturing and distribution of this program based on specific diagnostics. Interestingly enough, this is how many early forms of pharmacy occurred in the early 20th century, when pharmacists would produce pills in their shops for specific customers.

The key stakeholders in this business model will include the following parties who all have a significant return on investment associated with this model:[†]

---

[*] Deloitte Center for Health Solutions and Deloitte Consulting LLP, "Targeted Therapies," Navigating the Business Challenges of Personalized Medicine, December 3, 2007, accessed October 4, 2011, from http://www.deloitte.com/assets/.../us_chs_targetedTherapies_012307(1).pdf

[†] Deloitte Center for Health Solutions and Deloitte Consulting, LLP, "The ROI for Targeted Therapies: A Strategic Perspective," Accessed October 4, 2011, from http://medicalcenter.osu.edu/pdfs/.../Deloitte_White_Paper_ROI_PHC.pdf

- Consumers: people of all ages in all stages of health and disease, including but not limited to patients interacting with the healthcare system. Individuals who are currently healthy will receive diagnostics that could lead to early treatments of preventive diseases. There is also the potential for counseling and lifestyle programs for fitness, dietary planning, and other elements that may prevent problems later in life. Consumers have a strong return on investment (ROI) due to the decrease and avoidance of unnecessary treatments and prevention of costly life-changing diseases, resulting in an increased quality of life.
- Diagnostic companies: businesses that research, develop, manufacture, distribute, sell, or conduct molecular diagnostic tests. There are relatively few dedicated diagnostic companies in existence today, but these companies would be focused on executing tests to be used for early and continuing disease detection, diagnosis, and treatment response monitoring. The Deloitte study projects that there will be a relatively high price point for many such diagnostics and that there is a relatively flat revenue line that is a direct function of consumers who present symptoms of a particular disease.
- Biotech/pharmaceutical industry: companies that research, discover, develop, manufacture, market, and sell biotechnology and drug products used in preventing and treating both disease and symptoms of disease. As noted earlier, many of these companies will face higher complexity of manufacturing, distribution, and greater uncertainty for payment based on benefits of the treatment. There will surely be fewer individuals who receive a given therapy, as diagnostics may rule out a substantial portion of the patient population.
- Personalized medicine therapeutics companies: a subset of the pharmaceutical industry—businesses that manufacture, market, and sell molecular-based therapies. However, companies that are better able to link treatment and response through identification of biomarkers will be able to bring a targeted therapy to market more quickly, as the case of Herceptin showed. Those that are slow to adapt to the new paradigm will not only lose market share to newer therapies but will experience pushback from payers unwilling to fund a treatment that does not have an evidence-based outcome associated with it.
- Payers: funders of healthcare. Includes public programs such as CMS, Veterans Affairs, and commercial funders such as private

insurers. Payers will be most interested in requiring substantial evidence-based results of personalized medicine, whether this is in a comparative effectiveness format or through bundled payments. Payers have a longer ROI for this model, particularly if there is turnover in customers during the life of their investment in the patient. This may make it difficult for payers to recoup their early reimbursement of a companion targeted therapy. For the federal government agencies, however, there is a long-term business case to be made. As noted earlier, the Obama healthcare legislation is a step in this direction, with the creation of electronic health records as well as moving toward bundled payments and pay-for-performance.

The implications of such a model evolving are significant. To begin with, this would significantly change the look and feel of the channel, based on the set of relationships and transactions. As shown in Figure 6.2, channel design will need to be significantly changed, and a much more "hands-on" approach to cross-functional channel design will be required to integrate product and demand realization strategies. Supply chains are no longer just tasked with shipping products in this environment but must also provide services that accompany these products. Cash incentives may also be required to ensure the right type of patient behavior is encouraged, especially as it relates to compliance. Different players in the channel now find that they need to collaborate more than ever.

Another one of the key changes here is shown in Figure 6.3. As customer channels are redefined, cross-functional channel design will be required to align the product–service bundle to customer-specific requirements. In this case, patient intimacy will be a cornerstone for development of these channels. Customer intimacy would begin with understanding customer needs, interaction with prescribers, patients, and payers. More than ever, the patient will be a focal point of all activity in the chain, with all actions designed to meet specific targets in terms of patient compliance, delivery, service, convenience, and most importantly outcomes.

Partnering through network integration will become a core competency for success. Manufacturers can no longer claim success in this managed care environment simply by having the best product for all customers and charge exorbitant fees, handing over management of delivery to third parties. Instead, customized therapies indicate having to define patient subsectors much more closely. Finally, partnerships between manufacturers

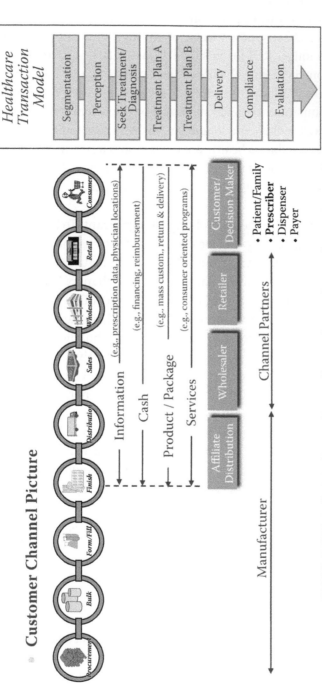

FIGURE 6.2
Life sciences network integration.

Redefining Customer Channels

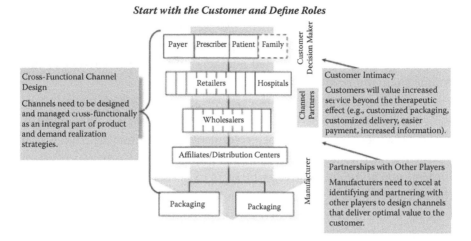

FIGURE 6.3
Redefining customer channels.

and channel partners will be needed to design channels that deliver optimal value to the customer through customized delivery.

A manufacturer of biological products has already begun exploring technologies to promote compliance and track usage of its home-delivered products for improved therapeutic services:

> We recently looked at an interesting technology. For one in-home medicine we are considering a little palm pilot device with a bar code scanner for our patients who are self-infusers. The PDA has a disease management module and fits in the cradle. When you take the product out of the fridge you scan it on the PDA and check the reason you need to use it. Did we need to treat on demand, or prophylactically and why? Maybe they enter that "I got hurt and cut my elbow," and we can send the information to their physician. The PDAs can track lot numbers, so in a recall we can notify them instantaneously: "that one in your fridge is on recall." Right now we don't have that ability. We need to look at track from container to patient infusion. We also need to track compliance. Today we just found out through advisory committees when we moved from a manual compliance system to a new electronic device that we piloted, we moved from 16 to 43% compliance. It gives us so much information on whether patients are taking the dose when they were supposed to.

Opportunity: Compliance

One of the critical areas here that will drive patient outcomes involves patient compliance to a treatment. As we noted earlier, better patient monitoring and outcomes data will provide improved opportunities for prescribing medicine in a targeted manner, but the other outcome of this is that it will improve compliance.

Compliance is a metric that assesses the degree to which patients take their medicines as prescribed optimally by the physician. We generally assume that people adhere to their treatment regimes, but the truth is that a large number do not. In fact, the FDA and National Council on Patient information and Education report that 14 to 21% of U.S. patients never fill their original prescriptions, 60% cannot identify their own medications, and, most alarmingly, 12 to 20% use other people's therapies.[*] This trend spans a variety of diseases, including life-threatening conditions such as breast cancer, renal transplants, and antibiotics for the common virus. In developed countries, the rates are even lower than in the United States. The cost of noncompliance has been estimated at between $77 billion and $300 billion a year, involving costs such as wasted medications, retesting and acute or emergency care, and lost productivity.[†]

Herein lies an opportunity for supply chain providers to offer *services* that promote compliance to prescribed therapeutics. Compliance in studies suggest that most people stop taking medicines that are proven to be therapeutically effective. Thus, a significant value proposition not satisfied is how to promote compliance to ensure that patients are taking their medicine. This would also provide a valuable service to manufacturers, in the form of increased revenues and increased channel loyalty. Datamonitor estimates that better compliance could generate more than $30 billion a year in additional sales.[‡] It is also true that compliance should be enforced for certain sectors of the population more than others. Analysis of healthcare expenditure[§] in the United States shows that 5% of the population account for 49% of the total bill, whereas 50% account for just 3%. People

---

[*] Albert I. Wetheimer and Thomas M. Santella, "Medication Compliance Research: Still So Far to Go," *Journal of Applied Research*, 3 (2003), pp. 254–261.

[†] Cutting Edge Information, "Pharmaceutical Patient Compliance and Disease Management," November, 8, 2007, http://www.informedix.com/noncompliance/Diabetes1.pdf

[‡] Datamonitor, "Addressing Patient Compliance: Targeted Marketing Driving a Shift in Focus from Acquisition to Retention," August 23, 2004.

[§] PricewaterhouseCoopers, 2008.

with the most costly diseases that make up 37% of the total healthcare bill have diseases including heart disease, cancer, trauma, mental disorders, and pulmonary conditions. Clearly, these individuals are good candidates for compliance efforts.

Recent changes to Medicare and Medicaid, as well as decreasing state and federal budgets, point toward decreasing dispensing fees for retailers. Compliance management and pharmacy services may become a substitute form of revenue. However, this will require collaboration among manufacturers, wholesalers, and pharmacies. Manufacturers are unlikely to be able to drive this. The problems begin when the patient first receives the scrip from the physician. One retailer interviewed noted that 15–25% of prescriptions are never filled. Even if they are filled, the falloff on compliance is substantial. A patient who takes the medication 80% of the time on a daily dose med is at the high end of compliance. Electronic alternatives such as reminders sent to a cell phone, email, or calls to a patient's house may be a valuable aftermarket service. Such services may increase fill rates as well as increase revenue for the BPS.

One retailer and expert in the area of compliance noted the following:

> In the e-prescribing area, no one has explored whether a scrip is filled in the first place. For example, if a patient's cholesterol is at 450, the physician will write a prescription for Lipitor. The patient then comes back in 30 days, and his cholesterol is still at 450. So the physician will automatically assume, "I picked the wrong drug or dose." But the patient may not have had it filled in the first place. With e-prescribing, the physician would be able to quickly perform a trace revealing that the scrip was sent to CVS and the patient never picked it up, or that the patient received a 90-day supply on March 1 and hasn't had a refill and it is August.
>
> Today what happens is the doctor assumes she has prescribed a nonoptimal therapeutic and that the drug was taken the way it was ordered. In the field, that is often not the case. Pharmacies today have the information, but they are not mining it. Scripts are not collected electronically, and manufacturers certainly do not have that information. There is major room in the pharmaceutical sector to get around the current safe harbor regulations to encourage e-prescribing. This would entail getting the doctor wired, the pharmacy wired, and the patient more involved and tied together. The single biggest key is to get doctors wired—they are hesitant, and it interferes with their current workflow—but there is change. Younger doctors understand technology and are willing to do different things.

A PBM also noted that the area of therapeutics and compliance was an area for improvement of services:

> Clinical intervention programs are one of the first buckets where patients can be directed to switch products. We are interested in partnering with pharmacies to see where it is appropriate. Some people will chase it. Clinical intervention programs are in the best interest of consumers, and we wish to work with pharma to that. We are initiating a pilot with a manufacturer where the pharmacy will enter the claim, and we approve and send it back. We would then adjudicate the claim—do you plan to counsel the patient? Depending on the answer, we will pay them for that intervention. Our rationale is that we believe if we prompt the pharmacist to counsel and interact with the consumer, they will be persistent in therapy. That means they will come back and get it refilled, and with more tablets filled, everybody wins. The patient gets better and the pharmacy gets more revenue. The point of sale interaction is the next frontier. If you can work with this system and ask the pharmacy to do something at that point of sale, it is the best opportunity to drive compliance. In the end this will also increase sales to manufacturers and wholesalers.

Many believe that compliance services will become a standard feature of packages that biopharmaceutical companies provide. To do so, increased application of technology such as serialization will be instrumental in supporting these efforts.

Aligning Capabilities to Drive Solutions

Although the pharmaceutical industry is unique in some ways, principally the amount of government regulation, it also possesses many common features that have been analyzed by economists in other industries. At the beginning of the supply chain are a number of large and small manufacturers of pharmaceutical products that require a wide range of care in distribution. Similarly, at the retail level, there are a number of large and small retail outlets, ranging from chain pharmacies such as Walmart to unaffiliated pharmacies, healthcare providers, and websites that prescribe or fulfill orders for pharmaceutical products directly from patients.

Distributors and manufacturers are increasingly being required to align their capabilities to meet the changing dynamics of the medicine. One of the major upcoming necessary changes is to address the emerging need for new forms of distribution.

To adapt to the changing landscape of personalized medicine, participants in the value chain will need to work together to build an information network linked to patient outcomes and begin building databases supported by appropriate middleware and aligned performance metrics that will encourage the sharing of information in the supply chain. This should begin with a series of small pilots on test programs that start on a small scale and begin to establish aligned objectives including not only inclusion of patient outcome data but also compliance measurement, customized distribution channels, and education and support networks for patient counseling and communication. All parties in the chain need to develop a patient-centric perspective, which is focused on delivering value to patients and driving improved health outcomes.

Manufacturers must begin working with governments to better understand reimbursement and pricing formulas for customized therapies and establish relevant biomarkers and diagnostics for subpopulations that may be specific and unique to the medicines in their pipeline.

Finally, organizations should explore the development of partnerships or new firms focused on diagnostic testing and should begin building a foundation to grow on that will address the need for personalized medicine.

E-PEDIGREE AND SERIALIZATION: THE WAR ON COUNTERFEIT DRUGS AND BLACK MARKET SALES

Counterfeit Drug Challenges

One of the major challenges at the top of many biopharma companies in many regions of the world involves counterfeit and black market sales. The International Federation of Pharmaceutical Manufacturers Association (IFPMA) estimates that 2% of drugs sold worldwide are counterfeit, while the World Health Organization (WHO) estimates that 5–8% of drugs worldwide are counterfeit. The impact of this activity on sales, brand name, and patient safety is significant. Based on these estimates, the international market for counterfeit drugs could represent between $7 billion and $26 billion of the $327 billion global drug market.* In addition, the FDA has experienced a fourfold increase in the number of counterfeit drug cases being investigated during 2001–2002.[†]

While the FDA asserts that the U.S. drug supply is safe, it has developed rising concerns over the reimportation of drugs from other nations since the origins of such drugs are often of a questionable nature. The root of the problem lies in the fact that many U.S. patients believe they are paying too much for their medications and therefore are increasingly tempted to buy their drugs at online "pharmacies," bypassing the traditional pharmacist without the consent of a physician. Most consumers believe they are buying drugs from Canada, but research shows many of those drugs are indeed counterfeit drugs coming from unreliable sources, such as India and Pakistan. In fact, an FDA task force that undertook a spot check of more than 1,100 packages of mail-order drugs from foreign suppliers found that 9 of every 10 of those packages showed evidence of tampering or counterfeiting.[‡]

Most consumers who buy drugs off the Internet believe they are getting a great deal on the drugs, but just because the drugs are cheaper does not mean they are more effective.

While the issue of counterfeit drugs is present in nearly every country around the world, even advanced industrialized countries like the United States, it is an even greater issue in developing countries. The WHO discovered that counterfeit and substandard medications are frequently detected in Cambodia, China, Myanmar, Thailand, and Vietnam, and the problem seems to be increasing. The market for counterfeit drugs is said to be 8.5% of the market in Thailand, 8% in Vietnam, and 16% in Myanmar. Likewise, research in Africa has revealed that up to 90% of the AIDS products tested failed quality testing, either the result of counterfeit drugs or improper storage and handling that contaminated the supply.[§]

Counterfeit and black-market drug sales in developing countries are extremely serious, because of not only the sheer size of the problem but also the nature of the problem itself. Often, the counterfeit drugs in ques-

---

[*] NACDS Leadership Council Counterfeit Prescription Drug Initiative, December 8, 2003. http://www.nacds.org/user-assets/PDF_files/final_accenture_report_counterfeiting_executive_summary.pdf

[†] Ibid.

[‡] Drug Store News, "FDA Takes Aim at Counterfeit Drugs," October 20, 2003.

[§] Manufacturing Chemist, "WHO Acts against Counterfeit Substandard Medicines," December 6, 2003.

tion often come from within the nation, which makes the problem harder to tackle. Sometimes the government is actually at the root of the problem. It is not unheard of in developing nations around the world for the government to seize drugs that were purchased at a discounted price and sell them for profit on the black market. Governments also sometimes sell the drugs back into the United States, again collecting profit, and then produce counterfeit drugs to sell to its people. In both cases, those less advantaged peoples in the developing countries suffer. Their choices are to either pay exorbitant prices for drugs on the black market or to buy counterfeit drugs that may not work or that may cause them harm.

Many steps are being taken to reduce the threat of counterfeit drugs. One initiative being taken is by the pharmaceutical firms, where they work directly with the wholesalers to crack down on the distribution of counterfeit drugs. In these arrangements, the wholesaler is bound by contract only to purchase drugs that come directly from the pharmaceutical firm manufacturing that drug. This will help reduce the sales of counterfeit drugs since the drug wholesalers are obligated to ensure that the drugs come directly from the firm that produced the drug. If a pharmaceutical firm realizes that the wholesaler is distributing drugs that came from a third party, then business between the two parties will be severed. While the FDA has no involvement in the enforcement of the arrangement, the contracts between the pharmaceutical firm and the wholesaler should reduce the amount of counterfeit drugs being sold.

The Rise of E-Pedigree Regulation

Serialization was originally driven by the need for creating an e-pedigree for all pharmaceuticals. Much of this was a direct result of the book *Dangerous Doses* (2004), which documented the practice of unethical wholesalers who were selling counterfeit or expired products such as Avastin to cancer patients and profiting from illegal distribution of expired product, relabeled doses of medication, and counterfeit medicine. Many of the wholesalers engaged in this activity were located in Florida where the requirements for becoming a pharmaceutical wholesaler were simplified and became a vehicle for organized crime syndicates to profit from counterfeiting activity. In addition to counterfeiting, the rise of parallel trade among different countries in the European Union, the Heparin scare for biologics, and other incidents have driven political agendas for e-pedigree in the pharmaceutical and biologics distribution business.

Commissioner of Food and Drugs Mark McClellan formed a Counterfeit Drug Task Force in July 2003, which received extensive comment from security experts, federal and state law enforcement officials, technology developers, manufacturers, wholesalers, retailers, consumer groups, and the general public. The taskforce considered alternatives and criticisms at its public meetings to develop a comprehensive framework for a pharmaceutical supply chain that will be secure against modern counterfeit threats. The specific approach to assuring that Americans are protected from counterfeit drugs included the following elements:

- **Implementation of new technologies to better protect drug supply.** Because the capabilities of counterfeiters continue to evolve rapidly, there is no single "magic bullet" technology that provides any long-term assurance of drug security. However, a combination of rapidly improving track-and-trace technologies and product authentication technologies should provide a much greater level of security for drug products in the years ahead. The primary element would consist of the adoption and common use of reliable track-and-trace technologies that would help secure the integrity of the drug supply chain by providing an accurate drug "pedigree," which is a secure record documenting the drug was manufactured and distributed under safe and secure conditions. Authentication technologies for pharmaceuticals were viewed as a critical component of any strategy to protect products against counterfeiting. Potential actions at the time included addition of radio frequency identification (RFID) tags, packaging, labeling for detecting counterfeit trucks as well as evaluation of forensic technologies (e.g., use of product fingerprinting, addition of markers), and other analytical methods for rapid authentication of drug products.
- **Adoption of electronic track-and-trace technology** to accomplish and surpass the goals of the Prescription Drug Marketing Act. RFID was initially defined as a de facto electronic pedigree that could surpass the intent of PDMA and do so at a lower cost. The FDA continued to stay its regulations regarding certain existing pedigree requirements, allowing suppliers to focus on implementing modern effective pedigrees as quickly as possible.

- **Adoption and enforcement of strong, proven anticounterfeiting laws and regulations by the states.** The FDA began working with the National Association of Boards of Pharmacy on its effort to develop and implement revised state model rules for licensure of wholesale drug distributors.

Other elements of the FDA recommendations included:

- Increased criminal penalties to deter counterfeiting and more adequately punish those convicted.
- Adoption of secure business practices by all participants in the drug supply chain. The FDA will continue to work with wholesalers and other major participants of the drug supply chain to develop, implement and disseminate improved secure business practices.
- Development of a system that ensures effective reporting of counterfeit drugs to the agency and strengthens the FDA's rapid response to such reports.
- Education of consumers and health professionals about the risks of counterfeit drugs and how to protect against these risks.
- Collaboration with foreign stakeholders to develop global detection and deterrence strategies for counterfeit drugs.

Tom McGinnis, director of pharmaceutical affairs for the FDA, also admitted during this period that there were many challenges ahead for RFID technology:

> We are at this crossroads and have to look at the cost. Chips haven't come down in cost, which means there is no good business model for RFID. Industry is looking at matrixed bar codes for serial numbers. Pfizer wants to put a chip on Viagra and back up the distribution tracking system with serial numbers on a matrixed bar code. So we may see mass serialization in matrixed bar codes and use that as the basis for building the infrastructure as chip prices come down. The biggest possibility for RFID is for the most vulnerable products, the top 100 in sales, which is where the counterfeiters will focus. No one will counterfeit a generic drug, and it may not be necessary to have protections at that tier. Six states have passed laws implementing a pedigree. The movement by the states (Florida, California, and Nevada) may be the next driver in this issue, and wholesalers and pharmacies will have to develop pedigree. Florida is allowing wholesalers to develop an electronic pedigree. When oncologists buy a lot they will

give an inspector the PIN number. This number goes to wholesalers, which would be responsible for checking the pedigree so the doctor's office will not be burdened. The wholesaler will have the PIN number, thereby establishing an electronic pedigree without too much burden on small businesses such as pharmacies and doctors' offices. So I think that will be the next driver. The global [Electronic Product Code] EPC will have a standard by the end of year to have a universal serial number that will be the same as bar codes, and there will finally be a standard.

In June 2006, Florida enacted legislation that required a pedigree (either electronic or on paper) to be provided for the sale of all prescription medications sold to customers in that state. California later followed with a similar law that all drugs have an electronic pedigree by 2012, a requirement that was later postponed to 2015. Numerous other states as well as countries such as Turkey and India have also introduced legislation that will eventually culminate in the requirement of an e-pedigree.

Although e-pedigrees were first viewed as a "flash in the pan" in the global life sciences industry and isolated to Florida and California, the reality is that pedigrees have rapidly spread as a requirement for doing business in an increasing number of countries and will soon become a requirement for biopharmaceutical distribution globally. Several regions in particular have experienced rapid changes in serialization regulation.

Several requirements for ascertaining pedigrees have emerged from this landscape. First, pedigrees are not required for OTC medications. An e-pedigree must contain product information (e.g., NDC, lot, expiration) as well as the chain of custody for the product from the manufacturer to the customer. Furthermore, the burden of initiating pedigrees currently falls on distributors. Manufacturers are not required to provide pedigrees upon sale.

Complications also arise in the supply chain as a result of this effort. For example, product received from an alternate source (another distributor) must have a pedigree provided to receive the product. The pedigree can be provided electronically or on paper. Most are still provided on paper, but regardless of the development process pedigrees must include all changes of ownership, including returns.

The Early Promise of RFID Technology

One of the early technologies believed as the key to item data synchronization was RFID tags. The U.S. government also proposed new legislation to further the involvement of law enforcement in cracking down on counterfeit sales, and it is also investigating technical measures to do so. The early focus in 2004 was primarily on RFID tags as the technology solution to assure the safety of the drug supply. RFID involves authentication and track-and-trace technologies being applied to drug packages to stop counterfeit drugs from reaching consumers. The initial proposition was that biopharmaceutical companies would be able to track where their drugs are anywhere in the world, which would thus help identify drugs that may have been sold and seized on the black market. This new technology, in its early phases, was projected to become increasingly sophisticated, reliable, and inexpensive.*

Early proponents of this technology espoused the position that RFID could be applied not only as an authentication technology for pedigree but also as a track-and-trace technology that would enable improved materials and inventory management in the supply chain.

RFID tags are tiny microchip and antenna units that store and transmit information. *Passive tags* have no power source of their own and can transmit data only when they are activated by an external electromagnetic field. Passive tags are cheaper and quite well suited to applications for product and asset identification. They have a read range of only a few feet. *Active tags* have their own tiny battery, which allows them to periodically transmit data. This gives them a longer read range of 35 to 85 meters. The more sophisticated circuitry makes them more expensive.

The promise of RFID was that individual cases and pallets would never have to be checked when a truck comes into a warehouse to unload them, as the RFID system would track each incoming one. The truck driver would simply drive under a gateway equipped with RFID readers. RFID technology was also projected to improve picking activity in the warehouse and distribution center. An accurate up-to-the-moment inventory record would be available at any time. Stockouts could be minimized through automatic replenishment and theft curtailed thanks to inbuilt tracking ability. Inventory and demand would be visible across the network; stockouts, safety stock, theft, and counterfeiting would be reduced; and many time-consuming tasks such as scanning, cycle counting, and searching for misplaced inventory would be eliminated.

---

* Wehr, John, "Zebra Supports FDA Report on Counterfeit Pharmaceuticals," *RFID News*, October 20, 2003.

Today, this kind of data sharing upstream and downstream is not common practice. The problem relates specifically to serialization, synchronization, and complex integration of data that needs to be shared among many supply chain participants and partners. Recent RFID mandates in the retail industry and the global EPC global standards for RFID in the supply chain are acting as powerful catalysts to move in this direction and encourage enterprises to rethink their business models and deploy new processes and applications that extend the benefits to all of their trading partners. However, the high cost of tagging, combined with the low read rates that occurred in a warehouse and distribution environment, rendered the technology incapable of delivering on the early promises envisioned by the FDA and others.

One executive we interviewed noted:

> Everybody ended up backing off RFID because there were a lot of physics problems—read rates were low in liquid, foil packages. And a lot of people spent a lot of money trying to make it work, but at the moment people are backing off and going cold on it. But in the end government mandates may require it to happen. RFID will give you chain of custody to reduce counterfeiting and importation that will meet all of the state and federal government mandates.

Item-level tagging is arguably the final frontier for RFID deployment. This concept permeates almost every type of supply chain application. From a practical standpoint, there are many challenges to item-level tagging. On the consumer side, a number of security and privacy issues create concerns and will impact its pace of adoption. Regarding cost-effectiveness, tags costing under 5 cents each will be the milestone before the potential of item-level tagging will be realized. Today, several pilots are under development in specialty retail and drug store outlets. The pace of adoption varies widely among analysts, but as of 2011 the pack of RFID deployment had slowed considerably and has moved toward development of serialization through 2-D bar code technology that is less cost prohibitive.

Very little is known about the actual commercial benefit that could be accrued by implementing tagging systems, and as of now, a few pilot studies are all that are available to judge costs and savings opportunities. There is, however, little doubt that tagging will have a major impact on supply chain operations over the next few years.

Meetings with major retailers suggest that the major benefits of the technology will be in the "last 100 yards"—between the pharmaceutical back room and the customer—but that suppliers that are slow to adopt the technology will suffer in terms of a steep learning curve to meet customers' requirements.

The weakest link from a supply chain perspective exists between the wholesaler or retailer and the consumer. Consumers do not necessarily have a desire to link their identity and purchases to the rest of the supply chain. This practice is already applied in drugstore chains and grocery store chains consumer reward cards and programs. In light of consumers' knowledge or understanding of what tagging is, its applications, and the fear of identity theft and privacy infringement, consumers are wary of tagging.

A trend in the future is for continued, intensified debate around tagging privacy from consumer advocacy groups, vendors, and lobbyists. Governments will be pressed to impose new privacy legislation to calm consumer concerns. The challenge of government is to strike a balance between the public and business interests.

Many executives we interviewed were highly dubious of the supposed "returns" on investing in tagging. In particular, the feeling among manufacturers is that the only winners will be the retailers and that few tangible benefits can be derived from tagging for manufacturers. Some of the more cogent quotes include the following:

> We need to compare notes about what we are hearing and then take it down through the supply chain. It is tougher to capture the return on investment on original packaging as you push back down the supply chain....

> We will find out one day how to do RFID less expensively, and we will be able to do business with less inventory, with lower order quantities, smaller deliveries, and costs adjusted for inflation will continue to go down. Net–net costs will go down, and services will go up.

> I don't know where RFID is going, as retailers stumble along with pallet and case test processes. What is the true benefit of RFID? I am getting frustrated, as I don't see a business case or a big play on the consumer side. The trade infrastructure is a long way away from a solution for the industry.

> Our position is that we will not lead the RFID process; we don't want to make an error in investment and have to throw it away and start all over again later....

> There are lots of ways to drive pedigree and visibility without going the RFID route.

Counterfeiting and Pedigree Technology Solutions

As noted, RFID or serialization tagging was the technology most frequently mentioned as the main bulwark to be used against counterfeiters, but other technologies involving shifting inks, holograms, and fingerprints are also part of the high-tech battle to maintain integrity in the U.S. pharmaceutical industry. There are a number of unresolved issues related to full adoption of various track-and-trace technologies, particularly RFID, including whether these technologies will be proprietary (or interoperable), the amount of data sharing, and whether such data sharing contravenes FFS contracts and IP restrictions. Large wholesalers that adopt the most efficient track-and-trace technology may be able to realize a significant competitive advantage. The FDA continues to be very cautious in implementing pedigree regulations but has not been reluctant to prosecute firms that it believes have violated relevant antifraud statutes.

This hypothesis was explored through discussions with *regulatory experts* as well as *legal experts*. There is no question that pedigree and security are at the top of many manufacturers' list of trends that will drive distribution strategies in the next three to five years. For example, one manufacturer we interviewed noted:

> Pedigree and securing the supply chain will be the biggest issue in the next three to five years. We made a statement that required all of our direct distributors that purchase from us to buy only from us and nobody else. We have been auditing our customers for the last six months to see if they are holding to that agreement and complying. We have established in the last three months a supply chain security taskforce exploring five or six components. We have established a legislative component exploring where pedigree is going to go and what other areas the pharmacies are looking at. We have also established a technology component, exploring RFID, overt, covert, and partnering to look at front and reverse logistics to ensure a secure supply chain to ensure customers get their products every time.
>
> We have a big project to take control of our distribution channel. We deal with a lot of controlled substances—pain medication. We keep tight control over everything we have. How do counterfeit drugs get to the patient? It doesn't take a lot. All you need is people who know how to make tablets.

A hospital pharmacist also agreed that pedigree continues to be an important issue. This individual emphasized that hospital pharmacists are under the greatest pressure to keep drugs in stock, especially as hospitals are often the last resort for patients who are ill and are turned away by physicians' offices. Hospitals typically do not refuse patients yet are often constrained by distributors due to the lower margins typically associated with Medicare and Medicaid payments through these channels. Theft and pilferage are also much more common in hospitals. As such, hospital pharmacists are in some cases tempted to resort to secondary wholesalers and unreliable sources of drugs advertised on fax machines, Internet websites, and email. This has driven increased scrutiny and has become a major issue for hospital pharmacists:

> I think pedigree is a big issue. Incentive for counterfeiting is higher on high ticket items. I wouldn't anticipate that pedigree would be an issue for the 80% of drugs that are high volume and low cost. But there is already a trend in some cases for some of the high ticket items having specialized distribution systems, because there is a supply scarcity issue or an FDA-directed issue to be high potential targets for counterfeiting. It is very likely that a target for counterfeiters is high unit-cost items going through an alternative distribution system to be targeted for pedigree requirements. I could see that happening. It will be a while before we get to a spot where the low-cost generic drugs will be tagged and transferred using RFID. But in the next several years, the high unit-cost items will go to some control access distribution chain.

There is no doubt that pedigree will continue to be an escalating issue in the years ahead. We interviewed an FDA regulator who was an expert in this field, and he shared his views on the importance of pedigree from the FDA's perspective:

> Pedigree is something that would be very useful in the cold chain and other channels to track product and provide assurance that it is an authentic product. We don't believe that paper is the way to go but believe that technology is on the horizon that will eliminate paper. Instead of applying the 1987 law, we decided to stay that law and allow this technology to come online and do the same thing. Instead of putting paper into the cold chain system, which would be unbearable, we did an update to that report, which in turn opened a lot more cases of counterfeit product being put into the chain. We are not sure yet why this occurred, as it could be a Hawthorn effect. We will know more as we do an update and see how the system is reacting to new pedigree requirements.
>
> One good outcome is that a lot of manufacturers have moved to protect their product. Pharmacists would then scan that unique serial number

(either RFID or bar code), and that number would be authenticated against the company's database to validate pedigree.

I have a hard time understanding how wholesalers will not get counterfeit product as long as they buy from the secondary market. There is always that chance that a diverted product will get into the distribution system. So there is a need for authentication in the system, until major wholesalers and smaller ones buy directly from manufacturer. It makes sense.

From a regulatory perspective, the FDA initially viewed RFID as the "silver bullet" that would address counterfeiting and pedigree concerns. The long adoption of the bar code (which did not establish a global standard until January 2005) suggests that a technological standard for pedigree may be long time coming.

Several companies have begun to establish pilots for storing and transmitting e-pedigrees. For example, in June 2006, Harvard Pharmaceuticals launched one of the first live implementations using an e-pedigree solution developed by Axway. The product was integrated with Harvard's Warehouse Management System (WMS) and website to provide an end-to-end solution. This required significant modifications of the WMS to track information about inventory and to generate pedigree data for submission to the system.

GS1 and the Serialization Alphabet Soup

To integrate consumers, retailers, distributors, and manufacturers, a single flow of commonly accessible data is required. The global EPC was one of the early standards developed to enable this capability. Data for a product consist of both static and dynamic information, as shown in Figure 6.4. Static information contains high-level core data about commercial entities and product and service groups. It conveys core data of a certain object class (i.e., information applicable to all widgets and ensures the quality of static information). Dynamic information consists of heterogeneous data that is specific to, and variable for, individual items, whether the item is a pallet, case, book, or vial. It conveys data specific to an individual instance of an object (i.e., information about this particular widget). There are two types of dynamic information, instance data and history data (see Figure 6.5).

Embedded products with data are a core element associated with improving data integration. The core question involves how to generate

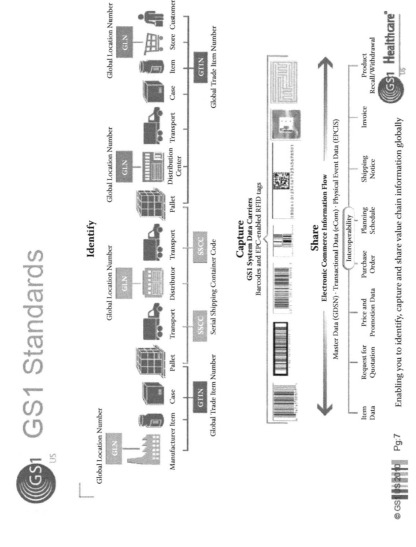

FIGURE 6.4
GSI standards.

Distinguishing Between Types of Information

Static Information: High level, <u>core data</u> about commercial entities and product/service groups. Conveys core data of a certain object class (i.e., information applicable to all widgets.) Ensures the quality of static information.	
Commercial Entities	▪ Party role (e.g., store; warehouse; etc.) ▪ Address ▪ Telephone number
Product/Service Groups	▪ Target market ▪ Product classification ▪ Product description

Dynamic Information: Heterogeneous data that are specific to and variable for individual items, whether the item is a pallet, case, book, or vial. Conveys data specific to an individual instance of an object (i.e., information about <u>this particular</u> widget.) There are two types of dynamic information, Instance Data and History Data.	
Instance Data	▪ Data regarding specific information on an individual item ▪ Serial number ▪ Examples include date of manufacture, date of expiration, etc.
History Data	▪ Data regarding the movement of an individual item throughout the product life cycle ▪ *Events & states* data ▪ Examples include arrival times, departure times, destinations, current temperature, etc.

FIGURE 6.5
Types of data.

an identification that is associated with a functional subset of products. Ideally, the identification is linked to a universal coding system, such as the United Nations Standard Products and Services Code (UNSPSC). If such a system were in place, imagine now what would happen when a product arrives in a warehouse and the system must have a way of generating a unique ID. If a particular item has a unique ID, it would allow for trading from supply chain partner to partner to occur without having to relabel and would cut down receiving and repackaging of items. Today, items are often broken down and relabeled at every node in the supply chain. From an order picking point of view, instead of having an entire pallet shrink wrapped, the system could recognize subpacks on a pallet. It would be possible to raise visibility on the item—starting at the item level and continuing to the subpack to the case to the pallet—and to dynamically identify where it is in the supply chain and when it will arrive at the desired location. Product grouping would be possible, with the pallet at the "parent" level and the case its "child." If a user wanted to track at case level, it would be possible since each case and item would be embedded with a unique ID. This capability rests on the ability to create millions of serial numbers on the fly.

Such a system was initially promised using the global EPC network, which was initially developed to promote this capability. In the future, we may witness a situation where organizations have the ability to generate their own code from their EPC. The first few numbers in the EPC would be unique to a company, and then from there they could customize the numbers as they choose. The code could indicate the specific SKU as well as its date of manufacture, date of expiration, whether it is destined for a particular manufacturer, a particular promotion. The coding structure is limitless. The key to the EPC was that it provides access to dynamic information as product moves through the chain. The primary vehicle for achieving this was envisioned to be the application of RFID tags, which could be scanned and linked to middleware that would show the movement of materials throughout the supply chain. This would leverage the Internet to access large amounts of associated information that could be shared among authorized users.

The second system envisioned to promote this capability was the Global Data Synchronization Network (GDSN). This network was designed to ensure the quality of static information about commercial entities and product and service groups among partners for collaborative trading.

Early adopters hoped to integrate global EPC into item tags (this capability is not possible today as tags cannot capture all of the information yet). Many early mandates by large retailers and pharmacies required key suppliers to begin RFID item tagging, which was implemented in a "slap-and-ship" mode in the early days of tagging. However, these initiatives were first pushed back and later withdrawn as the lack of return on investment (ROI) on the cost of item tagging became clear.

One of the strongest purveyors of data standardization to emerge in the last 15 years has been the GS1 organization.[*] GS1 is a not-for-profit organization dedicated to the design and implementation of global standards to improve the efficiency and visibility of supply chains globally and across standards. It is composed of 109 member service organizations over the

---

[*] In a recent presentation at the Nexus Tracelink Conference 2011 (September, New Brunswick, NJ), Bob Celeste, director of the Healthcare group from GS1 in the United States, provided insights into the key elements surrounding the landscape for traceability, pedigree, and visibility.

last 35 years, serving as a neutral platform for supply chain stakeholders. Over a million companies use the GS1 standards, that collectively process over 6 billion transactions a day. Healthcare companies are a large portion of this network. The most important role of global standards established by GS1 is to ensure that there is a common language to span the different machine-readable bar codes and data matrices, multiple languages, and language texts used to conduct commerce globally. GS1 represents a unifying set of platform standards enabling systems to converse with one another when conducting transactions globally in the extended supply chain.

Several components of the GS1 system of standards create information visibility and traceability across multiple tiers of the life sciences supply chain. The various codes, data capture, elements, and systems are shown in Figure 6.4. Only the basic infrastructural elements are discussed here. The GS1 system has a number of different identification keys that provide standard information on products. Companies joining the GS1 voluntary organization for the first time can go to their website to construct bar codes that carry all of the relevant information that can then be used for a bar code that goes on their product, which provides the relevant information. The first objective is to *identify* items, using a variety of different codes including a Global Location Number (GLN) that identifies *where* the product is originating from and a Global Trade Item Number (GTIN) that shows *what* the product is at the case level. That GTIN may then go onto a pallet of other cases that have different GTIN numbers (more on this later). It is then transported and, during transport, is assigned a Serial Shipping Container Code (SSCC) that shows *how* it is being moved, until it reaches its next location, and so on down the line. Eventually, the case is delivered to its location, and the individual items in the case are sold on the shelf. The last piece of information in the chain is the GTIN for the item sold at the GLN store location. Again, all of this information is created, assigned, and stored in the GS1 system.

To enable capture of this information, a number of different GS1 system data carrier technologies are used. These may include linear bar codes, 2-D bar codes, EPC-enabled RFID tags, or other technologies that may emerge. All of this information is then stored and used in an electronic commerce information flow, where data can be readily shared and accessed by parties in the supply chain. All of the data are stored in the GDSN. Various transactional dates (e.g., purchase orders, planning, ship notices) may also be used to communicate in the network using transactional data (eCom) and physical event data (EPCIS).

To ensure that products are classified correctly and uniformly in the master database, the GDSN uses the GS1 Global Product Classification (GPC), a system that gives buyers and sellers a common language for grouping products in the same way, everywhere in the world. This improves the GDSN's data accuracy and integrity, speeds up the supply chain's ability to react to consumer needs, and contributes to breaking down language barriers. It also facilitates the reporting process across product silos.

Without going into additional detail, it is important to understand that the GS1 provides a holistic set of guidelines, rules, standards, messaging, and healthcare-specific guidelines for all kinds of information required to manage the flow of product in the supply chain. The standards are open, global, proven, and simple and encourage open technology-independent standards that permit full interoperability and compatibility of systems, without locking end users into proprietary solutions. The standards were designed to provide a foundation for building traceability from product manufacture to patient treatment to enable compliance and legal requirements for product traceability around the world. In cases of cross-border trade, the GTIN can be used to identify that product in any country without any restrictions or errors, providing a pathway to attack counterfeiters. (Additional information can be obtained at http://www.gs1.org.)

Distinguishing Attributes

There are several distinguishing attributes associated with understanding the difference in terminology when referring to the concepts of pedigree, visibility, and traceability. These are shown in the GS1 document in Figure 6.6.

First, as shown, *visibility* is a term that encompasses the entire space including subsets defined as track-and-trace or traceability. This term can also include the status of items that have expired or have been disposed of, which is an important element for counterfeit. (Many counterfeiters sell expired product on the open market by accessing product that has been disposed of.) Visibility is a term that may also comprise other attributes of the product. For example, the status of the product's temperature stability is critical for biological products (a topic that we cover next when we discuss cold chain distribution). It may also include information about whether the item is damaged, fit for use, has been delivered on time to the right location, and can provide information on the status of the item (e.g., whether it is in transit, in inventory). Visibility is, in a sense, the

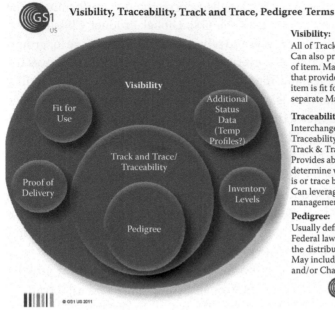

Visibility, Traceability, Track and Trace, Pedigree Terms

Visibility:
All of Track & Trace/Traceability. Can also provide status or disposition of item. May include other attributes that provide insight as to whether the item is fit for use. Leverages separate Master Data management.

Traceability/Track and Trace:
Interchangeable terms. GS1 uses Traceability while others (FDA) use Track & Trace). Provides ability to track forward to determine where the item currently is or trace back where it had been. Can leverage separate Master Data management.

Pedigree:
Usually defined by U.S. State or Federal law. Information to "trace" the distribution history of an item. May include Chain of Custody and/or Chain of Ownership.

FIGURE 6.6
GS1 capabilities.

"holy grail" of supply chain systems, where users can see what is happening to a product in real time and understand its status in the supply chain.

The terms *traceability* and *track-and-trace* are interchangeable. GS1 typically refers to an item's traceability, whereas the FDA uses the track-and-trace terminology in the context of anticounterfeiting requirements. Traceability and track-and-trace refer to systems' capability of tracking forward not only to where the item is currently but also back to where it came from and where it has been in its journey to the current state. This capability is more complex than simply identifying where an item is today; it requires a master data system that is essentially a log of an item's original birth to cradle to grave in the life cycle.

Finally, *pedigree* is a subset of the track-and-trace capability. It is a specific requirement defined by a U.S. state, by the federal government, or other countries and refers to the specific information that provides data on the distribution history of an item. The information may also include details on the chain of custody (i.e., who touched the product in its journey or had it in their possession) or the chain of ownership (i.e., who owned it but did not touch it during distribution). As we shall see, the definition around the level of information required by different governments globally varies significantly as well as the form in which it is required. Projections are that by 2016 all pharmaceuticals will be identified by the GTIN, will have a unique serial number, and will have dispositions associated with each item required and tracked through the entire end-to-end supply chain. This will be a major change in the way that business is done today. Much of this activity is being driven by the California legislation around pedigree, which states that by 2015 manufacturers must have 50% of their medicines serialized, with the remaining in 2016. By 2017, in California wholesalers and pharmacies will also be required to have full serialization of products in their pipeline.

The sheer underlying complexity required to comply with these requirements is overwhelming. It is one thing for a set of politicians to enact legislation and quite another to deal with the technical details, IT infrastructure, and logistical details that go into compliance with the legislation. There are multiple issues to confront in this environment, and large global companies have a lot of complexity in the requirements to distribute globally. First, many parties will be impacted in the supply chain, some of which we have discussed in this book: pharmaceutical manufacturers, contract manufacturers, biologics manufacturers, repackagers, hospitals, 3PLs, return processers. In short, anyone who touches the product will have some form of requirement on them and will rely on biopharmaceutical manufacturers to provide information to fulfill their legal compliance requirements.

Key Issues Surrounding Traceability

A recent conference on supply chain visibility was attended by multiple biopharma companies, CMOs, and third-party logistics providers.[*] The conference presenters and attendees identified a number of issues regarding serialization readiness and exchange requirements with supply chain partners, as shown in Figure 6.7. These issues were all discussed at length, with some of the key challenges shared in the following sections.

The Global Serialization Landscape

First, several countries have established serialization and item tracking legislation, but these vary significantly in their form and content. As

---

[*] This section is based on a panel presentation chaired by Lucy Deus, vice president of product development at Tracelink, shown at the Nexus Tracelink Conference 2011 (September, New Brunswick, NJ), The panel included speakers from Pfizer (Peggy Staver, Barry Somerville) and Merck (Steve Hudzik, Brian Lee).

	Contract Manufacturers & Contract Packagers	Pharma/Bio Companies	3rd Party Logistics	Kitters & Repackagers	Wholesale Distributors	Pharmacies (Retail, Hospital)	3rd Party Returns & 3rd Party Destruction
Do I have everything in place for assigning serial numbers (e.g., GS1 company prefix, assigned product hierarchies, selected data carrier for each level of packaging, range versus randomization plan)?	X	X		X			
Do I know how I will work with my contract manufacturers and packagers to provision and exchange serial numbers?		X					
Do I understand the serialization requirements and what is expected of me to serialize product across my customers? Do I have a plan for how I will manage differences in customer requirements?	X						
Have I determined how I will aggregate and disaggregate product serial numbers?	X	X	X	X	X		
Do I need GLNs for my locations? By when? Do I need to keep track of the GLNs for my customers, suppliers and partners?	X	X	X	X	X	X	X
Do I understand how my suppliers will be serializing their product (e.g., serial number format, hierarchies, encoding schemes)? Am I capable of working with them?			X	X	X	X	
Am I prepared to work with serial number aggregations as a recipient of product?			X	X	X	X	X

FIGURE 6.7
Global serialization landscape.

	Contract Manufacturers & Contract Packagers	Pharma/Bio Companies	3rd Party Logistics	Kitters & Repackagers	Wholesale Distributors	Pharmacies (Retail, Hospital)	3rd Party Returns & 3rd Party Destruction
Are my IT and business teams up-to-date with the GS1 standards that need to be adopted and how my company will leverage them?	X	X	X	X	X	X	X
Does my IT team understand which baseline standards we need to support and which ones we need to keep an eye on as they evolve?	X	X	X	X	X	X	X
Are my IT and business teams up-to-date with government reporting requirements and formats required in different countries?	X	X	X	X	X	X	X
Have my IT and business teams identified how we will use EPCIS events and Core Business Vocabulary for internal events and supply chain events?	X	X	X	X	X	X	X
Have my IT teams identified and selected the architectural and infrastructure components that my company needs?	X	X	X	X	X	X	X
Have my IT teams installed/upgraded equipment (e.g., packaging line equipment, visual scanners, RFID readers)?	X	X	X	X	X	X	X
Have my IT teams performed internal testing of serialization integration with my internal systems and processes?	X	X	X	X	X	X	X
Have I defined the strategy for how I will secure and manage partner access to my serialization event data?	X	X	X	X	X	X	X

FIGURE 6.7 (continued)

	Contract Manufacturers & Contract Packagers	Pharma/Bio Companies	3rd Party Logistics	Kitters & Repackagers	Wholesale Distributors	Pharmacies (Retail, Hospital)	3rd Party Returns & 3rd Party Destruction
Have I determined what serialization data and events I need to capture in my serialization management system?	X	X	X	X	X	X	X
Have I determined who I need to share and exchange data with?	X	X	X	X	X	X	X
Do I understand the business requirements of my customers, suppliers and partners for serialization data exchange?	X	X	X	X	X	X	X
Have I discussed the use of inference with customers and suppliers?		X	X	X	X	X	
Have I discussed with them how we will manage exceptions?	X	X	X	X	X	X	X
Have I decided what data I need to share with customers, suppliers, partners and how (e.g., serialized ASN, EPCIS, flat files)?	X	X	X	X	X	X	X
Have I determined what data I want to receive and how? Have I communicated to my customers, suppliers and partners? Will they be able to meet my needs?	X	X	X	X	X	X	X
Have I discussed with partners how we can harmonize requirements and leverage standards in a common way to achieve interoperability without additional complexity?	X	X	X	X	X	X	X
Do I have plans for piloting with supply chain partners to test exchange of supply chain serialization and event data?	X	X	X	X	X	X	X

FIGURE 6.7 (continued)

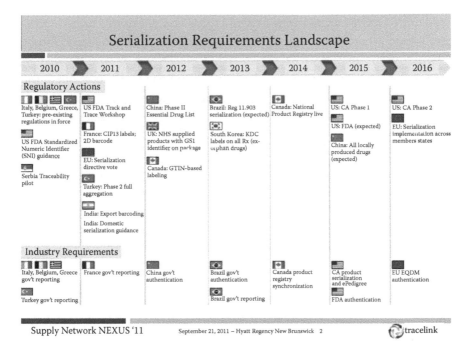

FIGURE 6.8
Serialization landscape.

shown in Figure 6.8, the timing and requirements for serialization vary not only across different countries but indeed across different states in the United States. This level of variability has made it increasingly challenging to determine how to focus efforts.

For example, Turkey, Argentina, and India all have serialization requirements focusing on government reporting on the part of manufacturers, wholesale distributors, and other participants for different transactions in which they participate. In these regions, each country's government captures information into a government managed database. Adoption of serialization standards and GLNs is being deployed to identify specific company locations for all logistics movements. In the European Union and Brazil there is also a requirement for centralized data consolidation by the government, but the burden for serialized product authentication is being placed on different parties in the supply chain. In China, the proposal is to have centralized government-issued serial numbers and a government-managed, centralized track-and-trace system.

In the United States there is no mandate to exchange information, but supply chain partners are required to serialize information to make it available to other parties in the network. This could lead to a fully distributed model where direct and indirect partners create a change of custody.

Some of the mandates have been particularly bizarre and sudden in nature. For example, India established a serialization requirement out of the blue and announced in August 2011 that serialization was required for all products sold in India by October 2011 (just three months later). One participant at the conference noted that this could have been a political show. A single incident of a counterfeit product occurred at just one site, and immediately legislation was passed that all companies should turn in serialization data to the government in three months' time. In effect, this executive noted, "We are going to dump all of our data and turn it over to them. I don't know what they plan to do with it, but we will have met the requirement."

The point here is that a bewildering array of different serialization requirements exists. In the end, however, panelists agreed that serialization is an element on the roadmap that will become a requirement for doing business anywhere in the world and that these requirements will eventually convene on an end-to-end supply chain serialization requirement.

Executives from two companies shared what their experience has been and what their plans are for dealing with these issues in the future.

These are discussed next.

Pfizer: Setting Priorities and Learning from Experience

As one of the largest suppliers to retail pharmacies, Pfizer has been on the forefront of early pilot work focused on RFID, item tagging, and serialization. It was one of the early adopters to RFID in 2005–2006 on its Viagra product in the United States. This pilot involved a lot of trials and lessons learned, and although Pfizer maintains that RFID works it is cost-prohibitive and will not work for the industry. As a result, Pfizer will soon be removing RFID tags from its items and transitioning to a 2-D bar code instead but will keep the RFID tags at the case and pallet level.

One of the challenges identified by the presenter is the aggregation of items from pallets to cases to items and trying to control the cost and complexity of material handling requirements while simultaneously addressing customers' needs. The 2005 RFID pilot was a direct response to a request by the FDA to explore RFID as a solution. In the process, Pfizer learned a lot about RFID and came to realize that the technology does indeed work but that it was challenging from a cost perspective to get widespread acceptance across the supply chain. On a global scale, 2-D bar codes were more prevalent in Europe, and Pfizer executives saw that the industry was leaning that way for item-level serialization.

The early pilots did, however, provide a great deal of experience about requirements to drive standards with Pfizer's trading partners. Pfizer is piloting the application of serial numbers through life sciences information providers such as Tracelink for others to be able to read serial numbers and authenticate transactions. However, it should be noted that the capabilities established for aggregation of cases to pallets was for only one product in the United States (albeit a significant one—Viagra), but this did not guarantee that it would be widely adopted across the industry. To ensure operability, Pfizer had a few large distributors, some regional distributors, and a few large pharmacies adopt the system but has never moved to a commercial implementation. Pfizer is continuing to run pilot projects with its large distributors and hoping to get retail customers involved in using 2-D bar codes to determine the impact on processes and customers.

Early pilots have highlighted several key issues. Serialization requires lots of decision making and process change internally, but when deployment is attempted across supply chain partners there are exponentially many difficulties and challenges.

As noted by one executive, "Pfizer is continuing to work with the FDA to adopt a drug pedigree messaging standard and through GS1 has developed something that begins to meet the spirit of what the regulators might be looking for." Pfizer is beginning pilot work with larger distributors to exchange event data but requires more input from its pharmacy segment. Several months ago the company conducted a survey of third parties currently in Pfizer's supply chain, seeking to gauge the readiness of these parties to meet the California requirements. The responses ranged from "We have plans in place" to "I'm not aware of any serialization requirements." This reveals the level of diversity in the supply chain to be able to adopt the California standards.

Merck: Learning to Manage the Process

Merck was involved in three RFID pilot studies in 2005–2006 that included the introduction of serialization in a GMP environment and the associated impacts. The organization piloted case and pallet aggregation using RFID and bar codes, and a major lesson learned was that the interaction with operations is critical. The concept of aggregation proved to be a big challenge. For example, if a case is on a pallet and the quality control inspector decides to take a case off the pallet to conduct in-process testing, he or she will simply put the case on the next open pallet when the inspector is finished. This creates errors in the case–pallet serialization matching code. As such, it is critical to explain serialization and case–pallet aggregation methods to operators in any serialization effort, as the opportunity for errors is tremendous.

Another lesson was the automation regarding operating a serialization pilot. There was a high degree of variance in operator capabilities when it came to operating computer equipment for serialization on the line. Some operators welcome the opportunity to engage, but in many cases operators are reluctant to change. Training and explaining why change is necessary are critical elements for success.

Merck's next pilot was to address the 2009–2011 California regulation. Early on, the pilot managers realized that they were not going to meet the requirements for serialization on all packaging lines. An interim solution was proposed to serialize at the distribution center and to explore where the process could be located to minimize operational disruption. The solution involved segregating every order for shipment to California, opening up the case, reading existing label information, detecting what was in the case, the quantity, and so forth, and developing a serial number that was used to individually label each carton. At that point, each pallet had to be rebuilt with the newly labeled and serialized cases and aggregated and entered into the system. The shipment was pushed into an event repository to develop the pedigree number.

This type of "home-grown" solution is very expensive as opposed to automation, and there is clearly a need for a scalable process as an alternative to this approach. The team has been working to understand what standard, event data, and other information need to be captured and entered into the information system to create the pedigree. Lessons learned from the pilot are being applied to other efforts in Turkey, Brazil, and India. It is important to note that the requirements in all of these global regions are different and vary in scope and scale, and it is becoming increasingly difficult to come up with a single solution that meets all of their situations. For example, India has its own export regulations, and the drugs being produced on a line are being shipped to multiple global locations. Flexibility, solutions, and reporting requirements as well as the infrastructure for shipping vary for each region, which is causing a great deal of logistical challenges in the production area.

Another difficulty is that regulations in global regions are changing rapidly, and in many cases the entire EPC infrastructure required to establish the serialization is not established. So organizations need to put together something quickly to meet a local requirement that is external to the long-term, high-volume infrastructure. For example, many projects in China are outside of an EPC infrastructure, and a temporary infrastructure is being used to meet local requirements.

To summarize this experience, it is critical to look at what is going on globally and to have a single infrastructure that is capable of covering all global requirements. This is, unfortunately, not the case in the current environment.

Industry executives are emphasizing that there needs to be some form of federal or global government preemptive action that can drive the 50 different regulations into a single standard around GS1. Even the U.S. requirements in California and Florida are simple compared with the complexity of other global regional requirements, and many countries are not focused on what has already been established in terms of standardized infrastructural requirements. In the European Union, serialization varies by country.

What Does It Take to Be Able to Implement Serialization?

When a company takes on serialization it has to be framed in a context that all known things are not in your control. A company's overall architecture must consider what is in development. For example, is a single repository going to be used? A distributed one? This is an unknown and may vary based on different country requirements.

A first issue to consider is whether a centralized or decentralized approach is being adopted. A centralized IT strategy often dictates that all processes must go through a central ERP solution. The IT strategy will most certainly impact the approach to serialization. The solution must also span trading partners. There is no way to control partners' supply chain systems, yet all the systems must mesh, so the approach must be targeted toward an interoperable environment.

Second, it is important to try to standardize wherever possible, and interoperability is again important here. Standards are designed to support interoperability and develop a core solution that is a repeatable solution. A realistic vision is one where there is a distributed environment versus a standardized manufacturing system with a single ERP that governs it. So organizations must identify certain components that are within their own environment and ensure they are compatible with other systems that may present themselves.

Data management is a third area. There is a common belief that the data generated through serialization will be of a massive size and volume, so consideration must be given to requirements for accessibility, response time, and capacity to maintain this massive data set.

Fourth, serialization involves exchange of data not just between different functional areas in a company but with the trading community. So consideration must be given to security issues. Who will be allowed to access the data? Who will be responsible for keeping the data secure? What are the conditions imposed on the security provider? Who will pay for the cost of this security?

As the serialization effort moves forward, it is imperative that the key companies in the supply chain create a cross-functional committee responsible for monitoring the environment. The team should be led by an intelligence leader, who is going to conferences, speaking to subject matter experts, and constantly monitoring the environment and communicating regular updates to a cross-functional IT team. The team should be formally tasked with activating and enhancing the solution as it evolves and with formally influencing decision makers and managing what the solution looks like. Ideally, such a team should include individuals in regional locations around the world who are dedicated full-time people. Then when regional requirements arise in places like the Middle East, Latin America, or Europe, there is someone there to take action and engage with the decision makers to influence and manage what the solution will look like. If the key players in the industry neglect the visibility and influence dimension, it is likely that a large number of solutions will arise independently, which will drive up costs and complexity. For example, serialization is restricted to pharmaceutical products but may indeed migrate into the area of medical devices, implants, and other medical products. Another example is the government mandate for data retention. There has been no specific timeline for maintaining data, only "until such time as it is required and made available." This is very vague, but the team should use this information to establish some standard requirements around data retention on a global basis. The team may not have an immediate ROI, but the value of this work is that it can contribute to a long-term solution to pedigree, track-and-trace, and visibility, that will benefit partners as well as will comply with the regulatory environment.

The notion of managing and monitoring the environment is a core capability for managing the entire network. Biopharmaceutical companies have customers that have different ways they want to collaborate. The industry as a whole needs to establish a single method to drive collaboration and standard exchange of information, including serialization and information sharing in the supply chain landscape.

Critical Requirements for Successful Collaboration

Several key elements must be in place for collaboration and serialization to be successful.

The first element is around *talent*. Serialization touches packaging, distribution, and IT systems, but when the initiative started out, the only functions involved included packaging and IT. Collaboration is a holistic approach to get everyone consistently involved and to create and enhance the knowledge base. One of the first steps is getting a core group of individuals together, to cross-pollinate team members, and to get packaging, distribution, and IT talking to one another.

Next, the technology must be explored in sufficient detail to develop standards and integration with existing systems. Although RFID was very big initially, many other components of technology are involved, including the service providers for cameras, scanner, and the middleware required for the network interfaces, the manufacturing execution systems, and procure-to-pay systems. The team must be able to understand requirements for each element in detail, what the technology is capable of providing, and who can provide it, and must engage the right suppliers to come in and propose solutions through pilot activity.

From there, the team needs to move to awareness creation, most importantly by educating senior management on why it is important as a company. From that awareness, the team can obtain corporate sponsorship and buy-in. Executive support is required throughout the piloting process with the core team so no momentum is lost, and frequent updates to the corporate sponsor are required.

Rx-360: Industry Collaboration Initiative for Global Track-and-Trace

Globalization has stretched the supply chain. Sourcing of product comes from every corner of the globe and frequently from China, India, Brazil, and Russia (known as the BRIC countries). On the Web, every company—big or small—looks the same so the need to understand and manage the supply chain is even greater in this expanded world, and the need to understand the supplier is more critical than ever before. Approximately 80% of all active ingredients sourced today for biopharmaceutical companies are from non-U.S. sources, which means that there is an increasing percentage coming from India, China, and other parts of Asia.

To compound the situation, the recent (current) global recession has added more stress to the already stressed market. With reduced spending and tighter credit requirements some suppliers are closing their doors—adding more strain to the supply chain as approved suppliers cease to exist—causing companies to scramble to find, test, and purchase replacement products.

Companies are working to minimize their supply chain risk by identifying the weakest link (as well as all links) in the chain. They are developing secondary sources for their manufacturing materials and securing this by purchasing from both the primary and secondary sources to maintain a business relationship with all suppliers. Pharmas are taking a deep dive into their primary supplier to fully understand any risks that the supplier may have internally or with their suppliers, and they are working to develop a disaster survival plan to anticipate major problems.

Identifying the original source provides for a level of risk avoidance that is an important foundation for progress. First, it increases the assurance of quality and reduces the risk that a hidden supplier could have a problem that compromises the quality of a supplied material, which could become be a source of problems in a finished product. Second, it provides for better traceability and avoids issues with repackaged, relabeled, or rebranded materials. It provides access to needed documentation, allows for life cycle monitoring, and provides some level of security on the product during transit through the use of tamper-evident seals, track-and-trace, and proper import issues.

As the supply chain is stretched, the view from the supplier to the manufacturer gets stretched as well and can become out of focus. It is difficult to see the end of a long supply chain, so many companies use audits as a form of quality control in their supply chains. Audits are a way of reducing risk, but audits are costly in terms of funds and time—for both the supplier and the manufacturer. Both spend time and money before, during, and after the audit. And since audits tend to "expire," this is an ongoing process. This has driven enterprises to reduce the number of suppliers (and thus the audits) and has spurred the concept of *audit sharing* as proposed by an initiative called Rx-360. This audit sharing has raised its own issues such as establishing a set of universal standards to include in the audit that is acceptable to all members, and the need to secure confidential information that is usually part of an audit from both the manufacturer and supplier sides.

In March 2009, a nonprofit organization Rx-360 was founded that includes many of the major biopharmaceutical companies. Its mission is to "Create and monitor a global quality system that meets the expectations of industry and regulators, that assures patient safety by enhancing product quality and authenticity throughout the supply chain."* Its mission will be accomplished by working as partners to share information, technology, audits, and standards for managing supply risk. To that end, the organization has created a newsletter that provides updated information on sources of risk. It has also developed standards for excipients, API, and basic chemicals.

One of the most innovative approaches being adopted by the group involves sharing suppliers' audits to improve information sharing about the supply network and its relative risk. This is being accomplished first by sharing existing audit information from one member with many members as well as sponsoring audits initiated by a single pharmaceutical firm that is shared with others in the network. Another method involves audits led by Rx-360 initiated by the consortium based on input from all members as well as collecting audits that are redacted and placed into a secure database for member access through a subscription. This approach has been highly salient to the industry, with over 45 major pharmaceutical companies, suppliers, and third-party services coming on board and agreeing to collaborate in this space. As a nonprofit organization, a "one-member-one-vote" policy has been adopted to ensure equal representation of outcomes and direction.

OPPORTUNITY: SPECIALIZED DISTRIBUTION CHANNELS

In Chapter 2, I explored the hypothesis that alternative third-party distribution channels may evolve and that manufacturers might one day sell direct to patients, thereby bypassing the Big Three wholesalers. As summarized in this discussion, my research led me to believe that the standard

---

* http://www.RX360.org

third-party logistics providers are unlikely to be able to provide logistics services on par with wholesalers. They excel at point-to-point distribution, but current service levels require holding inventory, something 3PLs are reluctant to do. This was validated in our interviews with two major 3PL providers that are actively engaged in pursuing market share and developing capabilities in the pharmaceutical wholesaler space.

One of the major reasons behind this thinking is that the high service levels required by retailers and hospitals will not dislodge current distributors. It is unlikely that hospitals and pharmacies will take lower delivery service and higher cost, both of which are inevitable with an alternative source vendor. As noted by a large generics manufacturer:

> We deal directly with big chains and big wholesalers. Big chains don't carry a lot of inventory—we have to ship to them more frequently than the wholesalers. Wholesalers may carry a lot of inventory; chains don't. So they have to replenish at least once a week.

Other retailers we interviewed agreed that a reduction in service levels was not likely to be acceptable through alternative channels than wholesalers:

> The majority of retailers receive two or three orders per week. That is a very good level of service. At our pharmacy chains, the difference between 3 and 5 a week was not that significant, but it was often the kind of thing we would look at as a tiebreaker. We first looked to see if they had to have the best bottom-line price. If they had three deliveries a week and were better on price, that would be better. The majority of retailers have a secondary supplier where they can pick up shorts, in cases when the primary has an out of stock or demand that is out of stock.

Although alternative channels are unlikely to develop for pharmaceutical products, another opportunity is opening up in biologics: specialized distribution channels. As noted in previous chapters, these opportunities are occurring because of increasingly diverse patient needs as well as the particular characteristics associated with the move toward greater application of biological and targeted remedies. As more blockbusters become generic, pharmaceutical drug channels for generics will continue to follow traditional distribution channel evolution, focused on greater efficiencies and standardized replenishment services. The real innovators in this space will focus their attention on the needs for specialized distribution that are beginning to evolve.

Direct-to-Consumer Customized Distribution for Oncology and Injected Biotherapies

As we noted earlier, an increased focus on patient compliance to prescribed medical treatments is critical not only to patient outcomes but also to commercial outcomes for manufacturers. One way that companies have sought to improve compliance is to begin exploiting web-based technologies that can monitor patient compliance levels, combined with direct-to-patient deliveries. As a result of Medicare Part B legislation, there is an increased exposure of average sales price (ASP) for patient reimbursements. As noted in Chapter 5, this is likely to be rejected by most major oncologists, who are unwilling to provide administration of oncology product dispensation when margins disappear. For many years, this product has been a stable part of the oncologists' business model. An alternative model that is being explored by manufacturers of oncology medicines is the direct-to-patient model. One company, Talecris, was a pioneer in this space and has created the benchmark for direct-to-patient monitoring and distribution. Talecris initiated the Talecris Direct program in the mid-1990s in response to a significant problem in the channel for its patients. One of the senior executives from Talecris was interviewed and explained how the model evolved. The underlying theme is that for manufacturers to effectively drive patient outcomes they must begin to become more accountable in "owning" the channel to the patient. This also means being able to provide value-added services to patients and providers in the form of real-time data regarding administration of product, compliance, and ongoing monitoring of patient health. The following interview excerpts revealed the thinking behind this innovation:

> We realized several years ago that going direct was the only way we could serve patients in the manner they needed to be served. Years ago manufacturers produced the product, shipped it to a distributor, then said, "We're done." More and more, we have a greater appreciation for the service provided by distribution. We have to own the final container to patient infusion and own that channel and that responsibility, which spans everything from serialization to electronic pedigree and establishment of a more defined channel of distribution where you have data. We are blinded to patient names—but need some unique identifier with a vial ID on it to be able to manage it.
>
> We were the pioneers of this model with Talecris Direct program— launched in the late '90s. People in the patient community have told us

that this is an innovation that we need to communicate to the community and urge others to adopt it. Talecris Direct was ahead of its time—we ship when and where you [the patient] need it. That model has now been copied by others. In effect, Talecris owned the channel of distribution as a sole source manufacturer. We recognized the model was broken when patients began to reach out to us and told us that the channel wasn't serving their needs. The birth of the program came out of the patient need. Literally overnight, we took a traditional customer base of 700–800 customers and informed the PBMs that Prolastin is a channel partner that will go direct to the patient.

The model is still alive today. Our product literally comes off the line and is shipped to a service provider. [The provider] doesn't take title to it but acts as an agent to Talecris. We ship product in bulk to a central warehouse (a service provider) and have enrolled patients that provide scripts, preauthorization, and reimbursement data. The agent then ships to patients' choice location on our behalf. It is usually a home setting, but if they change their location [such as when they go on vacation], we can accommodate that. It has been a great model.

We have also developed a customer service function through a unique entity called Alphanet [that] focuses on the emphysema marketplace. Many of the patients who suffer from this problem are not able to work. So we have hired them to work with other Alphanet patients. They help them navigate the insurance issues and understand the disease and how the medication works. In effect, this is a sales network of patients selling to other patients.

Temperature-Controlled Specialized Distribution

Control of storage and transportation temperatures is a major factor in maintaining the quality of medicinal products in the supply chain. Increasing international trade in medicines (e.g., parallel import/export of insulin) together with the growth of the biotechnology industry has resulted in an increasing reliance on the distribution chain for many companies with international operations as well as major biopharmaceutical companies. For example, some products such as vaccines are rendered ineffective or can even be potentially harmful if they are not stored and transported at the correct temperature. The threat of bioterrorism has highlighted the need for safe transportation of vaccines using secure, tamper-proof systems. The U.K. and U.S. military have both recently demonstrated an interest in secure shippers and are currently carrying out their own validation tests. With the increase in cross-border movements of pharmaceuticals, theft is a significant potential problem, and packaging specialists are now using computer technology "event loggers" and reinforced outer casing to make containers resistant to unauthorized access.

In developing temperature profiles used to design a shipping container or system, a complete analysis of the distribution process flow is required. Distributors should "walk through" their system to the extent possible to gain a better understanding of what happens to the freight. Each step should be analyzed to provide the shipper with a very clear expectation of the time–temperature relationship throughout the distribution process. This understanding will allow for the development of a temperature profile to design a package or system through the qualification process. It will provide the shipper with a high degree of assurance that the merchandise can be shipped to its final destination while minimizing the risk associated with loss of product as a result of deviations in temperature or humidity during transit. It is impossible to develop a temperature profile that will represent every shipment made, but it is important to develop a profile that is a representative model of the distribution process to minimize the risk of temperature deviations.

Why Is Cold Chain a Current Issue?

Industrial regulation and clinical trial protocols are increasing the significance of cold chain management. In a society where people want to ask questions and get answers they can understand, the importance of proof, documentation, and the audit trail is paramount.

The following sections discuss the major drives behind the increased need to manage temperature control during distribution.

Industry Changes

There has been a massive increase in the transportation of pharmaceuticals, biological test samples, vaccines, and tissues both nationally and globally. This has highlighted the breakdown in the quality control chain. "High-risk" products include vaccines, insulin, and blood products where exposure to temperatures below freezing can damage protein, leading to loss of efficacy. During transportation, maintenance of the temperature parameters can rarely be verified. This results in an estimated wastage of at least 7% of products in transit. Likewise, clinical trials may suffer delays or even the cancellation of further trials where adverse results are noted, which may have been caused by inappropriate temperature variances during distribution.

New Technologies

New cold chain systems must maintain the degree of integrity necessary to enable the industry to demonstrate audit trails and proof of compliance. Without this, public confidence in both the products and the industry will suffer. In response, a new generation of products designed to help companies and their logistics providers comply with regulations are arriving on the market.

Within the mediscience industry, niche markets are emerging with the advent of genomics and the increase in clinical trials samples and tissue engineering products. These are the result of many months' research, and as such they are being treated as high value or irreplaceable shipments. While the "chilled" sector of the cold chain (typically products that need to be maintained at +2 to +8°C in transit) remains the biggest market with the broadest range of applications, service providers are now being asked to find solutions for the transportation of frozen samples (e.g., recombinant DNA at –20 to –50°C) and a "hotbox" capable of keeping blood products at a constant temperature of +37°C. Along with conventional gel packs, eutectics, and dry ice, new *phase change materials* are currently in development to control temperature without freezing the product. Besides safeguarding against potential hazards like shock, heat, cold, vibration, or humidity, the new packaging technologies are enabling distributors to measure what actually happens to products in transit and help pinpoint inefficiencies in the supply chain.

Data Logger Technology

Data logging integrated within the container can provide invaluable information: by measuring both the external and internal temperature it is possible to trace exactly what is happening to a container throughout transportation, and controlled and recorded access makes it one of the safest ways to ship goods. The temperature history data generated by an integrated logger means both shippers and manufacturers can more easily identify any temperature discrepancies during shipping and manage corrective actions. The advent of integrated data loggers, as opposed to standalone data loggers, means that each container has a unique identity.

A complete audit trail can thus be created matching the individual product with the temperature record of the transportation.

Cooling Technology

Current packaging technology typically relies on variations of containers that use polystyrene foam as a means of insulation. Innovations in this field are now seeing the first generation of closed packaging, which has the ability to replenish the amount of CO_2, gel packs, and other means of refrigerant without accessing the contents of the package. Current processes require refrigerants to be packed around the product inside the container, so replenishing them is not possible within the shipping process. This has obvious benefits in terms of getting product to market in the best possible condition and significant synergies in terms of new and evolving industry regulations. Such new technologies and increasing enforcement activities by regulators herald the move away from disposable packaging to reusable containers to meet the increasingly global shipping and distribution requirements of the life sciences industry.

Many logistics providers now offer specialized solutions to clients in the healthcare industry, such as clinical trials supply management and quality assurance testing. Satellite and telephony tracking capabilities offer real-time information and tracking of shipments. Shipments are still prone to delays in customs, but the time is fast approaching when smart containers will alert senders via their mobile phone and signal them to take appropriate action. When that happens, distributors will find themselves in the curious position of having their own shipments track them down and request action.

A structured approach to design and execute a cold chain operation involving quality assurance, validation, and customer operations may be helpful:

1. Establish a test profile based on shipping requirements, current packaging methods, and proposed shipping systems.
2. Conduct baseline tests of current and proposed shipping systems.
3. Analyze and adjust packaging as needed, and create a test protocol for approval.
4. Approve protocol and qualify shipping systems.
5. Based on final report and approval, implement and generate SOPs and training required.

In the course of our discussions, we interviewed an industry expert representing a third-party cold chain logistics provider. The interviewee noted several important trends that were occurring in the cold chain channel space.

The FDA does not regulate the transportation industry. It does, however, regulate the management of the cold chain throughout the life cycle of each regulated substance, and this includes transportation. This is achieved by regulating the biopharmaceutical industry and holding them accountable for the transportation piece. Manufacturers are expected to be in compliance with all transport regulations today.

Transportation has historically been a "weak link" in the cold chain because it is typically outside the control of the regulated biologics industry. On timelines, these cGXP (X is a variable for Current Good Manufacturing/ Laboratory/Clinical Practices) regulations have been "on the books" for years, but enforcement activities have dramatically increased since 9/11 and the creation of the DHS. We do think cold chain management during transportation will receive increasing scrutiny.

A typical standard for temperature deviation is +/–3 degrees Celsius, but I am not sure if there is an industry average. Typically, each product will have its own stability data. All pharmaceuticals are subject to regulatory compliance, but those most critical (most affected by temperatures) are those most likely to carry a higher level of risk or be audited by the FDA for cold chain compliance and therefore subject to fines for deficiencies. This is what will drive change in the industry—the level of risk.

On capacity, you should understand that there are different ways to control quality and manage the cold chain. The decision-making process can include considerations like stability data (how wide is the tolerance and how long at an out-of-range temperature before degradation occurs), shipment value (cost to scrap or rework material), cost of other temperature control and monitoring methods. For instance, at our company [third party logistics provider], we take a consultative approach with our customers to help them select the method that will best suit their needs.

Our capacity is expected to increase significantly in cold chain. We do not anticipate any significant capacity constraints, as we recognize that this is a growing sector, and we have invested to get ahead of it. We do expect demand to increase but have plans to manage this demand on an ongoing basis.

Our vehicles are equipped with NIST traceable probes that record data during shipments. Tractor-trailers have a minimum of four probes; straight trucks have a minimum of two. These are spaced throughout the cargo hold to capture readings including "worst-case" data. The data are captured by a data logger at specific time intervals, usually dictated by the customer. A separate, redundant reading of the return air temperature is taken every 30 minutes and transmitted via satellite to our headquarters for continuous monitoring 24/7/365. This reading is also available to our customers through our website.

For the thermal-mapping (qualification) process, we use 11 probes. Our 27-hour test includes 24 hours of testing at a steady-state. We did hire a consultant to educate our folks on validation, cGXP, and qualification and help us develop an FDA and cGxP compliant service. We perform the thermal-mapping process.

I think the benefit of control over product quality and efficacy is quite significant. This quality control translates into reduced product and personal injury risk and liability as well as FDA fine avoidance. Imagine the personal injury liability associated with an ineffective vaccine that results in casualties or injuries and is found to have had poor cold chain management. Also, a major manufacturer received an FDA fine of $500 million—a record high—for cGMP violations. That means that the quality of the products in question may not have been affected, but proper procedures for manufacturing or perhaps recordkeeping were not followed.

Lastly, the FDA is unique in that it can enforce its own regulations and has the ability to prosecute individuals—in this case, the person in charge of quality control (as well as others). Individuals could face incarceration if the FDA feels that they were negligent in taking appropriate steps to ensure product integrity.

Interviews with a large biologics manufacturer identified the process used to design its cold chain with a third-party provider:

Our provider designed and deployed a cold chain transportation process, which began by working with Envirotainer to design customer temperature-controlled shipping pallets for plasma-derived therapies going to our patients. Plasma products are liable to counterfeiting, and this led to tamper-evident seals. Our products go around the globe by truck, ship, and airplane, and, for domestic sales, a range of solutions were needed for orders ranging from one or two vials to full truckload.

In the future, regulator and patient education around temperature controls will become critical. Cold chain will eventually be required for all biological shipments, but to help guide regulatory standards a number of companies got together and developed guidelines for the PDA Pharma Cold Chain Discussion Group. These guidelines were developed to "head off" potential litigation and to begin to proactively define standards. Many of these guidelines are still being debated.

Product stability is critical, because if temperature goes outside of storage requirements, there are problems. Now we know exactly what the product will do on a plane. One of the biggest problems is for shipments that go overnight by plane, because of the severe temperature variations that exist in an unheated cargo plane. FedEx Customer Critical now has temperature-controlled space on jets and a lot of validated temperature-controlled truck space as well.

To develop a temperature profile for use in designing a shipping container or system, a complete analysis of the distribution process flow is required. A walk-through of the distributor's system should be performed to gain a better understanding of what happens to each piece of freight. Every step should be analyzed to provide the shipper with a very clear expectation of the time–temperature relationship throughout the distribution process. Development of a temperature profile is key to creating a package or system that will ensure merchandise arrives at the final destination with minimal loss due to deviations in temperature or humidity during transit.

LOOKING FORWARD: WHAT'S NEXT?

If you were not convinced before reading this book, you will probably agree by now that the biopharmaceutical supply chain is a dynamic and evolving field. Indeed, by the time this book is published, there may well be many new developments in the field that have radically altered the environment. However, it is my hope that captured here are some of the major trends that have shaped the biological and pharmaceutical channel and that this has pointed to the evolving elements that will shape the future.

We began by tracing the evolution of the wholesale distribution model and the emergence of the Big Three wholesalers, Cardinal Health, McKesson, and AmerisourceBergen. These parties have developed sophisticated biopharmaceutical distribution models, have grown and shrunk their networks over the past decade, and continue to explore and innovate in new markets.

We noted the increasingly complex regulatory environment and the tightening of price controls in the marketplace as well as the stricter controls on operational elements such as cold chain, distribution, and transparency. We also described the extension of distribution services into hospitals in the form of direct to bedside dispensation, automated dispensing technology, and the evolution toward unit-dose bar codes as a way of driving down patient error. The impact of pay-for-performance in hospitals will also continue to drive the nature of biopharmaceutical prescribing, monitoring, and compliance.

The growth of biologics and the complexities in the oncology space has also led to the blurring of boundaries that has driven a new set of emerging channels. The merging of manufacturing and service providers has created a new space that is not only threatening the livelihood of traditional oncologists but also providing a new bundled product–service offering unlike any other seen in medicine before.

And finally, this chapter identified how the challenges in the industry have led to emerging opportunities in the areas of global market penetration, personalized medicine, pedigree and serialization offerings, and specialized and alternative distribution models. These trends represent an interesting set of opportunities for biological and pharmaceutical manufacturers, distributors, and providers to consider as they shape business strategy and navigate these difficult waters.

Several key themes emerge from the discussions of these trends to provide important insights of the state of things to come. These themes represent areas where future managers can innovate and exploit, as those who are first to adopt these principles will build a competitive advantage.

First, data integration will be key to success. Organizations that are able to exploit new and existing Web-based technologies, including shared databases, product serialization, collaborative planning methods, and cloud computing, and can leverage them to address the major challenges with lack of transparency and islands of decision making will no doubt triumph. The industry is in the stone ages compared with many other industries that have adopted ways of sharing information with partners to enable aligned planning, inventory positioning, advance forecasting, and risk mitigation and continuity planning. GS1 provides a sound basis on which to promote data integration, but the work done to date is in its infancy compared with the gaps in understanding that exist across the extended chain.

Second, managers in the biopharmaceutical supply chain needs to begin to adopt cost models that identify "should-cost" and "total cost" insights into the bundled products and services. This will become even more important in the face of accountable care, bundled payments, and pay-for-performance legislation that is threatening traditional FFS reimbursement models. To meet the requirements being imposed by federal and state agencies demanding to know where their health dollars are being spent and the associated effectiveness of these payments, biopharma companies must be in the lead of partnering with providers and payers to ensure that targeted outcomes are aligned with manufacturing and distribution costs. The CAVA group is a pioneer innovator on this front.

Third, it is apparent that a whole new set of value-added services is emerging in the supply chain to meet the needs of this new era. Examples include diagnostic services to test patient side effects or adoptability to drug treatments, direct-to-patient distribution, patient-compliance services, specialized material handling and transportation services, inventory replenishment and automation in hospitals and retail outlets, as well as infusion, cloud-based collaborative planning systems, track-and-trace serialization services, and real-time patient response to medications for tracking outcomes. Currently there are no well-developed business models for providing these services, but it is clear from our diagnostics that the need for these services is increasingly poignant.

Different models for business engagement and strategic partnering are also required to succeed. Current engagement models are not only arm's-length in nature but also have no precedent in alignment of requirements that are patient facing and prepared to share risks and rewards. Again, other industrial partnerships provide excellent models for benchmarking in this area. Such partnerships involve cost-savings sharing incentives, collaborative forecasting, open exchange of information, relational contracting, supplier integration into new product–process–service development, and long-term agreements focused on change management and risk mitigation. Partnerships in healthcare need to be more patient focused and less focused on optimizing transactions between immediate supply chain participants to ensure all parties up and down the chain are profitable and driving patient-focused value.

Another element is the role of regulatory parties in the supply chain. For too long the FDA, Department of Health and Social Services, and other boards have been viewed as the "enemy" and not as a stakeholder in the supply chain. A different mode of thinking would be to engage these regulatory bodies early in the development not only of new drugs but also of operating models focused on patient safety and compliance. By working with these groups, industrial partners can help set the bar for patient safety and efficacy, instead of being constantly on the defensive.

And finally, the emergence of global markets means that all parties need to be more focused on the geographical, sociological, cultural, and regulatory differences that exist across this global landscape. Different modes of thinking are required for contracting, partnering, patient dispensation convenience, the role of physicians, role of technology, and other elements that dramatically shape the healthcare landscape.

These and other challenges remain as open issues, which I personally believe will be addressed through innovation, collaboration, and network integration. But that is a subject for a different book…

References

American Urological Association, Coding and Reimbursement, n.d., available at: http://www.auanet.org/content/health-policy/practice-management/coding-tips/resources.cfm#services

ASHP Guidelines on the Safe Use of Automated Medication Storage and Distribution Devices, *Am J Health-Syst Pharm*, 1998 55:1403–1407.

Bernasek, Anna, "Health care problem? Check the American psyche", *The New York Times*, December 31, 2006, business section, p. 3.

Bio-IT World, Accessed October 2011, http://www.bio-itworld.com/archive/011204/strategic_pdma.html.

Borrell, Brendan, "Pharma CPR", The Scientist, Volume 23, Issue 12, p. 61, December 1, 2009, Accessed October 4, 2011, http://classic.the-scientist.com/article/display/56179/;jsessionid=03221DC283B43370A72A15E743C52899.

"Can Personalized Medicine and Comparative Effectiveness Coexist? The Experts Weigh In," *The RPM Report*. Saturday, October 31 2009.

Clark, Donald, S., Secretary, Federal Trade Commission, speech before The Ambit Group Retail Channel Conference for the Computer Industry, June 7, 1995, available at: http://www.ftc.gov/speeches/other.patman.htm.

Cooper, John, Global Manufacturing, Valeant Pharmaceuticals. Lecture in Issues in Pharmaceutical and Biotech Management, North Carolina State University, Raleigh, North Carolina, April 6, 2004.

Copacino, WC. "Connecting Supply and Demand." *Logistics Management*. April 2003. Vol 42. Issue 4. p56.

Correia, Randell J., "Oral oncology therapies: Specialty pharmacy's newest challenge" *Pharmacy Times* Published Online: Wednesday, May 18, 2011.

Cote, Bryan, "Evolution of the oncology GPO", *Oncology Business Review*, November 2007.

Cutting Edge Information, "Pharmaceutical Patient Compliance and Disease Management", November, 8, 2007. http://www.informedix.com/noncompliance/Diabetes1.pdf.

Datamonitor, "Addressing patient compliance: Targeted marketing driving a shift in focus from acquisition to retention", August 23, 2004.

Deloitte Center for Health Solutions and Deloitte Consulting, LLP, "The ROI for Targeted Therapies: A Strategic Perspective", *medicalcenter.osu.edu/pdfs/.../Deloitte_White_Paper_ROI_PHC.pdf* Accessed October 4, 2011.

Deloitte Center for Health Solutions and Deloitte Consulting LLP, "Targeted Therapies, Navigating the Business Challenges of Personalized Medicine," December 3, 2007, www.deloitte.com/assets/.../us_chs_targetedTherapies_012307(1).pd, Accessed October 4, 2011.

Duke, Elizabeth M., "Medicare Part D Creates Challenges for Safety-Net Providers and Law Enforcement," *American Journal of Health-System Pharmacy*, July 11, 2005, available at: http://www.ajhp.org/cgi/content/full/62/16/1646.

"Ensuring product availability", Healthcare Distribution Management Association, 2003. Available at www.nwda.org/issues_in_dist/pdf_product/hdma_datf_whitepaper.pdf.

Evans, Melanie. "Moody's report shows margins slid in 2008." *Modern Healthcare*.

"FDA takes aim at counterfeit drugs". *Drug Store News,* October 20, 2003.

Fein, Adam J. "Getting what you pay for from fee-for-service," February 2005. Retrieved from www.eyeforpharma.com/print.asp?news=45205.

Fein, Adam, "Understanding evolutionary processes in non-manufacturing industries: Empirical insights form shakeout in pharmaceutical wholesaling", *Journal of Evolutionary Economics*, 1998, pp. 262–265.

"Glaxo seeks guidance from health systems," *Wall St. Journal*, July 7, 2008.

Great Atlantic & Pacific Tea Co. v. FTC, 440 U.S. 69, 76 (1979). 15 U.S.C. Section 13(a)—(f).

Herper, Matthew, "Why pharma wants ObamaCare", *Forbes*, August 20, 2009. http://www.forbes.com/2009/08/19/pharmaceuticals-obamacare-reform-business-healthcare-washington.html.

http://www.healthcenter.caltech.edu/pharmacy.html.

http://www.natbiocorp.com/mc-biologics-cost-prohibitive.htm.

http://www.ncbi.nlm.nih.gov/pubmed/20740607.

http://pharma.about.com/od/Government_IP/a/How-Are-Pharma-Companies-Preparing-For-Proposed-Changes-To-U-S-Health-Care.htm.

IbisWorld, 32541a—Brand Name Pharmaceutical Manufacturing in the US, 2011.

IMS Health. http://www.imshealth.com/portal/site/imshealth/menuitem.a46c6d4df3db4b3d88f611019418c22a/?vgnextoid=4b8c410b6c718210VgnVCM100000ed152ca2RCRD&vgnextchannel=b5e57900b55a5110VgnVCM10000071812ca2RCRD&vgnextfmt=default.

"In American healthcare, drug shortages are chronic," *The New York Times*, November 1, 2004, B1.

Ingram, Richard. "Black market, drug resistance are risks for Africa's AIDS push," *Agence France-Presse*. September 23, 2003.

"The Issue of Discounted Pricing in Developing Countries", *PhRMA: Healthcare in the Developing World*. http://www.world.phrma.org/discounted.pricing.html.

Iver, Rjaram, "Changing Market Access Strategies in Pharmaceutical Industry", Ananth Consulting Group, White Paper, August 2010.

Javalgi, R., and Wright, R., "An International Market Entry Model for Pharmaceutical Companies: A Conceptual Framework for Strategic Decisions", *Journal of Medical Marketing*, September 2003, vol. 3 no. 4, 274–286.

Jetly, Guarav, Rosetti, Christian, and Handfield, Robert, "A multi-agent simulation of the pharmaceutical supply chain (PSC)", Proceedings of the POMS 20th Annual Conference, Orlando, FL, May1–4, 2009.

The Johns Hopkins Arthritis Center: "Rheumatoid arthritis treatment," *Arthritis Today*: "Drug Guide: Biologics."

Jones, Paul, and Jan Malek, "Prospering in a Pay-for-Performance World. White paper, Cisco.

Kaiser Health News: "Checking in with Patricia Danzon on the hot topic of 'biologic" Medicare.gov: "5 Ways to Lower Your Costs During the Coverage Gap," "Help with Medical and Drug Costs." Adapted from http://www.dlapiper.com/implementing-the-biologics-price-competition-and-innovation-act/.

Kuhn, Herb, "Payment for Medicare Part B Drugs", CMM House Subcommittee on Health of the Committee on Ways and Means, July 13, 2006.

Landro, Laura, "Hospitals combat errors at the 'hand-off'" *Wall Street Journal*, June 28, 2006, p. D1.

Lewis, Russell, "Dockside to bedside: A new paradigm for health system medication management", www.hctmProject.com.

Medicaid Drug Price Comparisons: Average Manufacturer Price to Published Prices, OIG, June 2005, OEI-05-05-00240, Washington, DC.

Medicaid Drug Price Comparison: Average Sales Price to Average Wholesale Price, OEI-03-05-00200, June, 2005, Washington DC, Office of Inspector General.

Medicaid Pharmacy—Actual Acquisition Cost of Brand Name Prescription Drug Products (A-06-00-00023).

Medicaid Pharmacy—Actual Acquisition Cost of Generic Prescription Drug Products (A-06-01-00053).

NACDS Leadership Council Counterfeit Prescription Drug Initiative, December 8, 2003. http://www.nacds.org/user-assets/PDF_files/final_accenture_report_counterfeiting _executive_summary.pdf.

Naik, Gautam, "To reduce errors, hospitals prescribe innovative designs", *Wall Street Journal, May 8, 2006, p. A1.*

National Center for Health Statistics: Preliminary Estimates of Electronic Medical Record Use by Office-Based Physicians: United States, 2008, Retrieved December 2009.

Nee, Chris, "Oncology Drug Management: A White Paper on Marketplace Challenges, Opportunities and Strategies", *PharMedQuest.* Published by Atlantic Information Services, Inc., and PharMedQuest, March 2007.

NICE website, http://swww.nicemedica/pdf/MyelomaDoHSummaryREsponderScheme.pdf.

Oncology Purchasing and Distribution Groups, Knowledge Source, August 2007.

Pedersen, Craig, Schneider, Philip, and Scheckelhoff, Douglas, "ASHP national survey of pharmacy practice in hospital settings: Dispensing and administration—2005", *American J Health-Syst Phar*, vol. 63, February 15, 2006.

Phillips, David. Presentation in BUS 590X, Issues in and Pharmaceutical and Biotechnology Management at North Carolina State University, Raleigh, North Carolina, April 20th, 2004.

PricewaterhouseCoopers Health Research Institute, "Pharma 2020: The vision. Which path will you take?", 2007.

PricewaterhouseCoopers Health Research Institute, "Recapturing the vision; Restoring trust in the pharmaceutical industry by translating expectations into actions," 2006. http://www.hgsa.com/professionals/refman/chapter2.shtml.

Rai, Saritha. "Generic drugs from India prompting turf battles," *New York Times. (Late Edition–East Coast).* New York, December 26, 2003. p. C.

Rao, SK. "Pharmaceutical marketing in a new age," *Marketing Health Services.* Spring 2002. vol 22, issue 1, pp. 7–12.

"Recommended guidelines for pharmaceutical distribution system integrity," Retrieved from http://www.healthcaredistribution.org/gov_affairs/pdf_anti/Guidelines%20 for%20Rx%20Distribution%20System%20Integrity%20FINAL%20Board%20 Approved%2011-5-03.pdf.

Reeder, Claiborne, and Debra Gordon, "Managing oncology costs", *American Journal of Managed Care,* 12: S3-S16, 2006.

Roland, Michael P., "Managed care and a changing pharmaceutical industry", *Health Affairs,* 1990.

"The Role of Distribution in the U.S. Healthcare Industry", Healthcare Distribution Management Association, 2004.

Rosetti, C., Handfield, R., and Dooley, K., Forces, "Trends, and decisions in pharmaceutical supply chain management", *International Journal of Physician Distribution and Inventory Management,* 2011, 49(8).

Schacht, Wendy H. and John R. Thomas, "Patent law and its application to the pharma-ceutical industry: An examination of the drug price competition and Patent Term Restoration Act of 1984", Congressional Research Service, Report for Congress, updated January 10, 2005.

Sharpe, Don, "McKesson buys US Oncology: What does this further consolidation of the specialty pharmaceutical channel mean to manufacturers?", *Oncology Business Review*, posted November 22, 2010.

"Specialty pharmacy resolution of pharmacy 'class-of-trade' issues is key for specialty infu-sion", *Specialty Pharmacy News*, July 2005.

Standard & Poors Industry Survey for Pharmaceuticals, June 26, 2003.

Strax, Jacqueline, "Lupron kickbacks betrayed prostate cancer patient trust," Retrieved from: http://psa-rising.com/upfront/lupron-scam-mar01.htm.

TAF: Top 20 False Claims Act Cases. http://www.taf.org/top20.htm Accessed February 2012.

Terry, Nicolas P., "Prescriptions sans Frontieres (or How I Stopped Worrying About Viagra on the Web but Grew Concerned about the Future of Healthcare Delivery)," 4 *Yale J. Health Pol'y L. & Ethics* 183 (Summer 2004).

Thomaselli, Rich, "Kay seeks common language for global marketing effort. *Advertising Age. (Midwest region edition)*, Chicago. vol. 74, iss. 20, p. 130, May 19, 2003.

Torassa, Ulysses. "Activists get AIDS drugs to poor lands: Surplus medications are other-wise wasted. *The San Francisco Examiner*, June 25, 2000.

Wehr, John. "Zebra supports FDA report on counterfeit pharmaceuticals", *RFID News*: October 20, 2003.

Welch, B., *American Family Physician*, December 2008, vol 78, pp. 1406–1408.

Wetheimer, Albert I. & Thomas M. Santella, "Medication compliance research: still so far to go", *Journal of Applied Research*, vol 3 (2003), pp. 254–261.

Whalen, Jeanne, "Hurdles multiply for latest drugs", *Wall St. Journal*, August 1, 2011, p. B1.

"Which healthcare companies could benefit from Obama's government healthcare plan?" *iStockAnalyst*, March 2, 2009.

"WHO acts against counterfeit substandard medicines", *Manufacturing Chemist*, December 6, 2003.

World Health Organization: AIDS Epidemic Update, December 2002. http://www.who.int/hiv/pub/epidemiology/epi2002/en/.

ADDITIONAL READING

Associated Press, "Major Insurer Pushes Pill-Splitting Savings: UnitedHealthCare Encourages Patients to Cut Drugs in Half," June 10, 2005, available at: http://www.msnbc.com/id/8172095/page/2/print/1/displaymode/1098/.

Baird, Brian (Webpage) "Legislative initiatives affecting the health sector," accessed August of 2005: http://www.house.gov/baird/issues/health.shtml.

Blank, Dennis, "State Pedigree Laws Running into Some Barriers," *Contemporary OB/GYN Newsline*, July 2005, available at: http://www.drugtopics.com/drugtopics/article/articleDetail.jsp?id=169480.

Center for Medicare & Medicaid Services, "Medicare Announces New Preventive Benefits and Physician Payment Increases in Final Physician Payment Rule for 2005," available at: http://www.cms.hhs.gov/media/press/release.asp?Counter=1248.

DePompa, Barbara, PDMA. "Compliance in 12 Steps: Prescription Drug Marketing Act violations can cost millions. To save that money, follow this program", available at: http://www.bio-itworld.com/archive/011204/strategic_pdma.html.

Fein, Adam, (Online interview). *Pharmaceutical Business Strategies*, Spring 2004, available at: http://www.pbsmag.com/Article.cfm?ID=73.

Food and Drug Administration, "Combating Counterfeit Drugs," February 2004, available at: http://www.fda.gov/oc/initiatives/counterfeit/report02_04.html.

Food and Drug Administration, "Profile of the Prescription Drug Wholesaling Industry: Examination of Entities Defining Supply and Demand in the Drug Distribution," 2001, available at: http://www.fda.gov/oc/pdma/report2001/attachmentg/4.html.

Food and Drug Administration, "The Prescription Drug Marketing Act: Report to Congress," June 2001, available at: http://www.fda.gov/oc/pdma/report2001.

Frederick, James, "Wholesalers Turning to Fee-For-Service Model," *Drug Store News*, August 23, 2004, available at: http://www.findarticles.com/p/articles/mi_m3374/is_10_26/ai_n6194372.

Gale, Thomas P., "Fallout from Pharmaceutical Inventory Management Agreements Study Suggests IMAs Produce Opposite Effect on Healthcare System," 2005 available at: http://www.mdm.com/stories/imas3506.html.

Healthcare Distribution Management Association, Recommended Guidelines for Pharmaceutical Distribution System Integrity, November 5, 2003, available at: http://www.healthcaredistribution.org/gov_affairs/pdf_anti/Guidelines%20for%20Rx%20Distribution%20System%20Integrity%20FINAL%20Board%20Approved%2011-5-03.pdf.

Hook, Matthew B. Van and Wheeler, George Y., III, "Drug Diversion and Counterfeiting: Can RFID "Track and Trace" Technology Protect Consumers," July 2004, available at: http://www.hklaw.com/Publications/Newsletters.asp?ID=500&Article=2717.

Leb, Nickolas J., and Marty Baum, (Offline interview) Executives of Teammpharma.com on August 16, 2005. Teammpharma is a small manufacturer of several pharmaceutical products (see: http://www.accentia.net).

Miller, Jim, "New supply-chain dynamics: Create a distribution services sector," *Pharmaceutical Technology*, Jan. 2004, available at: http://www.pharmtech.com/pharmtech/data/articlestandard/pharmtech/032004/81448/article.pdf

National Opinion Research Center at the University of Chicago, "Drugs in the Development Pipeline: Impact on Part B Medicare Spending," available at: http://www.medpac.gov/documents/Aug03_DrugsDev(cont)Rpt.pdf

Robinson-Patman Act, 15 U.S.C. Section 13(a)—(f).

Schanz, Stephen, Esq., (Offline interview) Health attorney and adjunct professor of law, the North Carolina State University, Department of Business Management, August 22, 2005.

Simonwitz, Lee H., and Ronald F. Wick. (Memorandum to Mike Kaufmann, re: Robinson-Patman Act (its applicability to FFS)). Baker and Hostetler, LLP, February 12, 2004.

Yost, R. David, "New Economics of the Pharmaceutical Supply Chain," 62 *Am. J Health-Syst Pharm*. 525-6 (2005). Available at: http://www.ajhp.org/cgi/content/full/62/5/525

Index